(The Psychosocial Aspects of the Family)

The New Pediatrics

Edited by

Morris Green, M.D.
Indiana University School of Medicine

Lexington Books
D.C. Heath and Company/Lexington, Massachusetts/Toronto

Library of Congress Cataloging in Publication Data
Main entry under title:

The Psychosocial aspects of the family.

   Based on a symposium held May 11–13, 1984, under the co-sponsorship of the Institute for
Pediatric Service of the Johnson and Johnson Baby Products Co. and the Dept. of Pediatrics of
the Indiana University School of Medicine.
   Includes bibliographies and index.
   1. Pediatrics—Psychological aspects—Congresses. 2. Child development—Congresses. 3.
Family—Health and hygiene—Congresses. 4. Parent and child—Congresses. I. Green, Morris.
II. Johnson and Johnson, inc. Institute for Pediatric Service. III. Indiana University. Dept. of
Pediatrics.
[DNLM: 1. Child Development—congresses. 2. Child Psychology—congresses. 3. Family—
congresses. 4. Pediatrics—congresses. 5. Psychology, Social—congresses. WS 100 P974 1984]
RJ47.5.P787   1985   618.92   84-48800
ISBN 0-669-09768-3 (alk. paper)

Published simultaneously in Canada
Printed in the United States of America on acid-free paper
International Standard Book Number: 0-669-09768-3
Library of Congress Catalog Card Number: 84-48800

The Psychosocial Aspects
of the Family

A Publication of the
Institute for Pediatric Service
of the

Johnson & Johnson
BABY PRODUCTS COMPANY

To All Who Care for
Children and Their Families

Contents

Figures and Tables

Figures

Tables

Preface and Acknowledgments

Pediatricians and other child health professionals are increasingly expected to be concerned and competent in relation to the prevention, early detection, and management of psychosocial problems. The psychotherapeutic contribution of child health professionals is used in the following clinical situations: (1) the continuing care of well infants, children, and adolescents; (2) the management of family crises such as divorce, death, the birth of an infant with a handicap, and child abuse; (3) the preparation of children for hospitalization and surgery and the child's mastery of those experiences; (4) the care of those disorders for which pediatric diagnostic and management are appropriate, for example, hyperactivity, school avoidance, anorexia nervosa, psychogenic somatic complaints, and the psychological aspects of long-term illness and handicap; and (5) the management of those disorders for which diagnostic and referral skills are needed, for example, autism, chronic depression, and parental emotional illness.

This book is based on a symposium, Psychosocial Aspects of the Family: The New Pediatrics, held at the Drake Hotel on May 11–13, 1984, under the cosponsorship of the Institute for Pediatric Service of the Johnson and Johnson Baby Products Company and the Department of Pediatrics of the Indiana University School of Medicine. The authors of the chapters in this volume are experts in their field and their contributions seek to help prepare child health care professionals to practice state-of-the-art clinical care in relation to this rapidly evolving area of pediatrics—the psychosocial aspects of child and family health. Selection of topics and contributors were made to present material of practical interest to physicians, nurses, social workers, psychologists, child life workers, nutritionists, occupational therapists, physical therapists, educators, and parents.

This book is intended as a review of current knowledge relative to the developmental issues and tasks in the various age groups from infancy through adolescence along with guidelines to the new morbidity and the new prevention in pediatrics. The chapters emphasize the prevention, early detection, and management of psychosocial problems pertinent to optimal child and family health and development. Psychosocial and developmental problems which adversely affect the health of many children and adolescents are comprehensively discussed; normal and disturbed emotional development in infants, young children, adolescents, and their families are presented; and appropriate preventive intervention measures are suggested.

I am indebted to Dr. Steven Sawchuk, director of the Institute for Pediatric Service of the Johnson and Johnson Baby Products Company, for the opportunity to convene this symposium. Special appreciation is owed to the contributors to this book who gave so generously of their time, expertise, and wisdom. My special thanks go to my secretary, Mrs. Glenna Clark, who shepherded this enterprise from its first conceptualization through preparing the manuscript for publication. I appreciate deeply her dedication and skill.

1

The Adaptation of Children and Families: The New Pediatric Agenda

Morris Green

The perspective of child health professionals is biologic and psychosocial, cross-sectional and longitudinal, preventive and therapeutic, group and individual, and centers on the growth and development of the child, the family, and the community. Today *adaptation* must be added to this traditional pediatric agenda, highlighting the special opportunities that pediatricians and their child health colleagues have to help children and families adapt to crucial life events and psychosocial stressors. It is the daily business of the pediatrician to promote the child's capacity to adapt to a variety of biologic stressors: the administration of antibiotics to an infant with bacteremia helps the baby successfully adapt to a potent life threat; measles immunization offers a prospective adaptation to a potentially deleterious stressor; and insulin contributes to the child's adaptation to the physiologic derangements caused by juvenile diabetes. These biomedical interventions are now highly valued functions of pediatrics.

One of the purposes of the symposium on which this book is based was to address the role of the child health clinician in helping children and parents adapt constructively to the numerous psychosocial stressors they so frequently confront. Whether pediatrics in the next decade will become more identified with this aspect of adaptation depends, in part, on advances in pediatric psychoendocrinology, psychoimmunology, developmental neuroanatomy, psychopharmacology, psychology (developmental, behavioral and social), sociology, epidemiology, and cultural anthropology (Cohen and Lazarus, 1983; Prugh, 1983).

Recent advances in psychobiology have contributed greatly to an understanding of how psychological stimuli initiated by life experiences are translated in the brain to produce physiologic changes and how alterations in the body may be transduced through endocrine and neurotransmitter channels in the brain to cause psychological effects (Reiser, 1980). That biologic and psychosocial factors are inseparably intertwined in child health and illness and that diseases have multiple causes is becoming generally recognized. As Alan Gregg remarked over thirty years ago: "No part can be changed without changing in some way and in some measure all the others. . . . It is intellectual weakness that prompts us to ascribe a given result to only one sufficient cause. We ignore the value of suspecting that a result may be due to a convergence of several causes" (Gregg, 1951).

Pediatric Psychobiologic Disorders

Although our present knowledge base does not permit a psychobiologic nosology of child health or illness on specific psychosocial and physiologic factors, numerous pediatric disorders have joint psychological and physiologic components. These psychosomatic or somatopsychic syndromes include anorexia nervosa, bulimia, obesity, conversion reactions, depression, substance abuse, failure to thrive, psychogenic pain, and rumination. Psychosocial (psychoendocrine) dwarfism, a dramatic experiment of nature, which occurs in some emotionally deprived young children, is characterized by abnormal eating habits, understature, and deficiencies in adrenocorticotropin and growth hormone secretion. These biologic and behavioral findings are rapidly reversed when the child is transferred from an emotionally disturbed to a nurturing enviroment (Powell et al., 1967).

Psychosocial sequelae occur in some children and adolescents with such chronic disorders as asthma, blindness, burns, cerebral palsy, craniofacial anomalies, cystic fibrosis, deafness, diabetes, end-stage renal disease, epilepsy, hemophilia, inflammatory bowel disease, iron deficiency anemia, malignancies, migraine headaches, myelodysplasia, obesity, rheumatoid arthritis, and Tourette's syndrome.

Developmental syndromes and disorders with both biologic and psychosocial determinants include attention deficit disorder, delayed speech, environmental deprivation, failure to thrive, infantile autism, learning disabilities, mental retardation, pervasive developmental disorder, and sleep disorders.

Prenatal maternal substance abuse may adversely affect the infant's development and behavior. Cranial radiation and chemotherapy administered in the treatment of leukemia may later cause learning problems in some children. Psychobiologic nutritional problems include failure to thrive, anorexia, obesity, insatiable appetite in the Prader-Willi syndrome, and pica.

Biologic health disorders due to psychosocial factors overrepresented in children from families of low socioeconomic status include congenital anomalies, infectious diseases, intrauterine growth retardation, iron deficiency anemia, lead poisoning, mental illness, prematurity, and infant mortality.

Stressors Affecting Children

Numerous studies, including the Institute of Medicine report, *Stress and Human Health,* have concluded that persons who experience emotionally disruptive situations are at increased risk of developing a physical or mental disorder (Elliott and Eisdorfer, 1982; Holmes and Rahe, 1967; Syme, 1979). Stressful events of sudden onset that demand a rapid change in attitude or behavior are often accompanied by physiologic changes. Dissimilar events, if perceived psychologically in the same way by two different individuals, may cause similar neuroendocrine and clinical responses in each.

Although most studies on vulnerability to stress have been conducted on adult rather than pediatric populations, many childhood and adolescent life changes and vicissitudes appear to be causally associated with somatic complaints. Clusters of stressors especially seem to increase vulnerability. Emotionally charged events do not always lead to symptoms and disease, but they are frequently noted in the history of children with pain and other psychosomatic syndromes. A list of several such stressors includes the following:

accidents; trauma

entrance to a new school

family arguments; violence

hospitalization, especially if the child is unprepared

acute or chronic illness

natural disasters (floods, fires, tornados, hurricanes)

parental emotional illness (depression, anxiety, alcoholism, affective disorder, schizophrenia)

parental unemployment

physical abuse

remarriage of parent

actual or potential separation experiences (death or anticipated death of a significant person; divorce, desertion, or separation; family move; older sibling leaving home)

parental life-threatening illness (cancer, coronary artery disease)

sexual abuse

surgery

Lewis has documented other stressful experiences in school-age children, including not spending enough time with parents, fighting with parents over rules, pressure for high grades, not good at sports, not enough money, not able to dress the right way, being smaller, being bigger/overweight, not getting along with a teacher, being left out of groups, body changes, and pressure by peers to try something new (Lewis, 1985).

Some emotionally charged experiences appear to have long-term sequelae. Children who are expected by their parents to die prematurely because of a serious illness from which the child is not expected to recover may demonstrate the vulnerable child syndrome. Such children may display continuing anxiety along with separation problems, infantilization, bodily overconcern, and school underachievement (Green and Solnit, 1964). Children are at special risk for the development of antisocial behavior following the separation or divorce of their parents (Rutter, 1974). Those who are below eleven years of age at the death of one or both parents have an increased susceptibility to depression (Brown and Harris, 1978).

The nature of the clinical disorder associated with stressful life events differs depending upon the child's developmental stage (Green, 1975). Rumination and failure to thrive, for example, occur in infants; sleep disorders and anorexia appear in the toddler; hyperactivity and psychosocial dwarfism are seen in the preschool child; and somatic complaints, conversion symptoms, and depression are noted in the school-age child and the adolescent. These developmental stage differences are unexplained, but they may be related to individual biologic variability, changes in the degree of the child's dependency on his or her parents, biologic rhythms, maturation of the brain and endocrine system, gender, the stage of cognitive reasoning, and experience.

Children whose parents are experiencing deleterious stressors are also at special risk if, as a result, the quality of their parenting is compromised. In addition to many other personal or environmental stressors, some adverse parental life events may be causally related to the child and, therefore, may come to the attention of the child health professional. For example, in the perinatal period stressful events may include the birth of an infant with a congenital anomaly, a critical neonatal illness, stillbirth, neonatal death, maternal guilt about returning to work, illness in other family members that creates a burden on the parents, an infant's difficult temperament, multiple births, prematurity, and maternal depression. In the older child, serious illness, injury, or need for surgery cause parental stress.

The Psychobiology of Health and Disease

The daily clinical experiences of the pediatric clinician can be of great heuristic value in identifying specific research hypotheses relevant to four questions (modified from Weiner, 1982): (1) Why do some children become ill while others with similar life experiences do not? (2) Why does a specific child respond to adversity with one manifestation or disorder rather than another? (3) Why do certain stressors or psychosocial experiences produce such a broad variety of symptoms, diseases, or developmental aberrations? (4) Why does a small percentage of children have such a high percentage of the total illness of a population of children? Because it is not feasible to summarize here the extensive psychobiologic research literature that addresses these complex questions, the following discussion touches upon selected work of interest to child health professionals.

Psychoimmunology

Studies of the neuroendocrine mechanisms through which the immune system is regulated and modulated by the brain are of special pediatric interest. (Ader and Cohen, 1975; Ader, 1980, 1981). Acute and chronic family stresses have been shown to be significant determinants of whether individual members of a family became ill with streptococcal infections. The risk of such infection increases threefold to fourfold after a stressful event (Meyer and Haggerty, 1962; Haggerty, 1980). In animal studies, a number of experimental conditions including physical restraint, unavoidable electric shock, loud noises, and isolation and crowding increase susceptibility to infectious agents. Both humoral and cell-mediated immunity may be affected by psychosocial stressors. In animal studies, disruption of the mother-infant relationship increases vulnerability to infection (Ader, 1980). Clinical evidence suggests that psychosocial stress in adults may increase their vulnerability to immunologic disorders such as infections, autoimmune diseases, and malignancies.

Mother-Infant Interactions

In addition to demonstration of possible repression of immunity and augmentation of vulnerability to infectious illness, psychobiologic studies of mother-infant interactions and attachment are of great pediatric relevance. There is already a vast psychological literature about these relationships, and a growing number of biologic studies are being pursued. For example, the enzymes tyrosine hydroxylase and phenylethanolamine N-methyltransferase have been reported to be altered in mice who are socially isolated in early life (Henry et al., 1971).

Hofer has been especially interested in the "hidden regulatory processes which usually govern the interaction between mother and infant." In a series of elegant animal studies, he found that separation of the infant from the mother led to changes in a number of variables, including rocking behavior, sleep patterns, heart and respiratory rate, growth hormone secretion, vocalization, motor activity, and enzyme concentrations. He further demonstrated that the mother's milk regulated the sleep of her infant and that sleep patterns were disrupted by maternal-infant separation (Hofer, 1976). Maternal separation also led to a fall in cardiac and respiratory rates (Hofer and Weiner, 1972). Based on this work, Hofer concluded that a variety of components appear to be involved in the interaction between a mother and infant, each mediated by a separate input channel and brain circuit leading to physiologic responses and behavioral changes in the infant. The mother, in effect, externally regulates her offspring's behavior through multiple sensory input pathways, physiologic responses, and brain chemistry (Hofer, 1981, 1982). These regulatory actions are interrupted by separation of the mother from the infant.

Circadian Rhythms

The biologic systems that govern patterns of sleep, cortisol levels, growth hormone, aldosterone, estrogen, insulin, thyroid hormones, neurotransmitter release, eating, and body temperature have a rhythmic nature (Anders, 1982). Circadian rhythms have an effect in both children and adults on the appropriate timing of diagnostic procedures such as blood and urine levels and on therapeutic interventions such as administration of drugs, surgery, and radiation. Resistance to disease has also been thought to vary with time of day (Moore-Ede, Czeisler, and Richardson, 1983). Emotional stress may disrupt an individual's circadian rhythms (Stoebel, 1971). Disturbances of the circadian timing system occur in infancy in sleep disorders and in adolescence in anorexia nervosa. In the latter, the circadian patterns of luteinizing and follicle-stimulating hormone are inappropriate for the patient's age (Boyar et al., 1974).

Endocrine Effects

Hormonal influences on behavioral patterns and cognitive function in children represent another aspect of biologic investigation germane to pediatric research. The precise neural circuits and neurochemical mechanisms through which environmental stimuli lead to behavioral, endocrine, autonomic, and other bodily changes and the feedback circuits for these processes are not yet established.

A number of investigators have demonstrated the action of several peptides in the regulation of feeding behavior. Androgens are reported to affect cognitive abilities: Hier and Crowley (1982) suggested that spatial skills may be influenced by an androgen effect at or before puberty. This hypothesis, however, has not been proved (Kagen, 1982). Plasma androgen levels have been positively correlated with aggressive behavior and social rank in a number of species (Lloyd, 1975; Rose, Holaday, and Bernstein, 1971). Secondary amenorrhea attributable to changes in gonadotropin excretion secondary to stress is a well-known phenomenon.

Two of four prepubertal children with major depressive disorders of the endogenous subtype demonstrated cortisol hypersection during their illness. In a manner similar to adults, this pattern returned to normal during recovery (Puig-Antich et al., 1979). Catecholamines, corticosteroids, and growth hormone are thought to account for differences in the responses of individual children to stress, including coping patterns. The level of secretion of epinephrine has also been related to the social and emotional adjustment of children (Frankenhaeuser and Johansson, 1975). Temperament in infants and young children may also have a neurobiologic basis. Marked increases in plasma cortisol levels were demonstrated to occur after twenty minutes of crying in young infants (Anders et al., 1970). The stage of cognitive development in a specific infant, child, or adolescent will also influence whether an environmental event is perceived as threatening. In an important clinical study, Wolff, Hofer, and Mason (1964) were able to relate the level of adrenocortical excretion to the psychological defenses in parents of children with leukemia.

Vulnerability and Invulnerability

The concept of vulnerability or invulnerability to stressful circumstances is important in understanding individual responses to stress. Many persons who would appear to be at risk of developing a disease such as peptic ulcer based on the presence of an elevated level of the pepsinogen isoenzymes, a specific biologic marker, do not become ill.

Since vulnerabilities represent potential precursors of disease, their identification in individual children could provide specific opportunities for prevention. The number and nature of these vulnerabilities depends on multiple factors such as genetic inheritance, psychological background, chronological and developmental maturation, environment, socioeconomic status, family constellation, past experience, lifestyles, and the presence of disease, especially chronic illness. Environmental events appear to have their greatest negative impact when perceived as unpredictable, threatening, and outside personal control or coping ability. Social supports or an internal rather than an external locus of control may diminish susceptibility to such stressors (Rotter, 1966).

Invulnerability is analogous to what Caplin (1981) has termed *mastery*: "behavior by the individual that (1) results in reducing to tolerable limits physiological and psychological manifestations of emotional arousal during and shortly after a stressful event and (2) mobilizes the individual's internal and external resources and develops new capabilities in him that lead to his changing his environment or his relation to it so that he reduces the threat or finds alternate sources of satisfaction for what is lost." Other synonyms for invulnerability include *plasticity* and *reserve*. Among the resources contributing to what they have termed *resiliency*, Werner and Smith (1981) have identified "adaptability on the biological, psychological, social, and cultural levels: profound ties to concrete immediate others; and formal or informal ties between the indivdual and his or her community."

Genetics

The biologic and behavioral responses to stress are also conditioned by genetic differences in endocrine responsiveness, psychoneurologic mechanisms, and immunologic competence. Biologic markers may also permit the identification of persons at risk in a population. The further delineation of genetic influences on an individual's response to stressful experiences would facilitate preventive pediatric intervention.

Implications of Psychobiology for Pediatrics

Prevention

Advances in psychobiology may permit the pediatrician to use biologic and psychologic markers to identify individuals at risk. Coupled with an awareness of such high-risk situations as bereavement, the pediatric clinician may be able to help the vulnerable individual avoid or modify behavioral patterns or habits that may be damaging and to use social support networks. A major task for child health professionals in the future, perhaps in concert with educators and other disciplines, is to help children learn how to develop skills to adapt to, cope with, and, if possible, master biologic and psychosocial stressors.

Treatment

Psychoneuropharmacology has contributed to the treatment of such psychobiologic disorders as Tourette's syndrome, attention deficit syndrome with hyperactivity, depression, and anxiety. The physiologic effects of biofeedback, relaxation therapies, and hypnotherapy are also open to pediatric investigation.

Opportunities for Collaboration in Research

As child health care is being transformed and reinstitutionalized to meet the needs of a rapidly changing society, new opportunities exist for fruitful collaboration between pediatrics and the behavioral and biologic sciences.

The New Prevention and Health Promotion in Pediatrics. The scope of child health supervision visits is being broadened to include clinical application of information from child development and the behavioral sciences and more of a family orientation.

In recognition of the many changes in the family and the need to make richer use of periodic pediatric assessments, the American Academy of Pediatrics Committee on the Psychosocial Aspects of Child and Family Health has written content packages for health supervision visits from the prenatal period through late adolescence. These guidelines, to be published in 1985, include attention to biomedical, developmental, psychosocial, and family issues.

Operationally, this new prevention includes evaluation of the biomedical and psychosocial status of the child and the family; physical and developmental assessment; anticipatory guidance and containment of vulnerabilities, including accident prevention; education in and enhancement of parenting skills; promotion of positive parent-child interactions; early intervention for identified problems; and attention to health promotion through physical activity, sufficient sleep, adequate nutrition, and avoidance of smoking and substance abuse (Green, 1983).

The New Initiative on Adaptation. The traditional interest of pediatrics in growth and development is now being extended to include adaptation. Pediatrics is thus becoming the discipline concerned with growth, development, and adaptation. The child health professional will increasingly be prepared to help children and parents adapt to and cope with the stressors they experience.

Contributing to an Increase in Function, Comfort, and Realization of Potential. The child health professional has long been involved in increasing the functional capacities and the comfort of children with pain, chronic disorders, or psychological discomfort. Clinically useful methods to enhance these efforts need to be further pursued.

Pediatric Psychobiologic Research. The vitality of any discipline derives from self-renewal through continuous revitalization and extension of its knowledge base. To pursue the clinically relevant but highly complex lines of psychobiologic investigation, a new generation of pediatric investigators must be developed.

David Hamburg has termed this field "integrative biology—pulling together observations at all levels of organization from molecular to behavioral characteristics of living organisms." The pool from which such future academicians may be recruited includes pediatric endocrinology, genetics, epidemiology, pharmacology, immunology, biochemistry, molecular biology, neurology, and neonatology as well as that aspect of general pediatrics concerned with the psychosocial aspects of child health. Pediatric psychobiologic research will use animal models in which simultaneous attention may be directed to the whole organism at various stages of development and to events at the cellular, organ, and body system levels. Animal studies use pure genetic strains of animals and allow control of the timing, quality, and quantity of stressors.

Investigation of the correlations between the periodicity and rhythmic function of biologic systems will further our understanding of the temporal occurrence of psychobiologic disorders. Psychoimmunologic studies are needed to assess the relationships between stress and immunosuppression.

Genetic and epidemiologic studies may be expected to relate biologic and psychological markers to the vulnerability or invulnerability of individual children and populations to biopsychosocial disorders. Finally, epidemiologic and longitudinal clinical studies offer significant opportunities for the delineation of immediate and long-term psychobiologic causes and effects.

References

Ader, R.: Psychosomatic and psychoimmunologic research. *Psychosom. Med.* 42:307, 1980.

Ader, R. (ed.): *Psychoneuroimmunology*. New York, Academic Press, 1981.

Ader, R., and Cohen, N.: Behaviorally conditioned immunosuppression. *Psychosom. Med.* 37:333, 1975.

Anders, T.F.: Biological rhythms in development. *Psychosom. Med.* 44:61, 1982.

Anders, T.F., Sachar, E.J., Kream, J., Roffwarg, H.P., and Hellman, L.: Behavioral state and plasma cortisol response in the human newborn. *Pediatrics* 46:532, 1970.

Boyar, R.M., Katz, J.L., Finklestein, J.W., Kapen, S., Weiner, H., Weitzman, E.D., and Hellman, L.: Anorexia nervosa: immaturity of the 24-hour luteinizing hormone secretory pattern. *N. Engl. J. Med.* 291:861, 1974.

Brown, G.W., and Harris, T.: *Social Origins of Depression: A Study of Psychiatric Disorders*. New York, New York Free Press, 1978.

Caplin, G.: Mastery of stress: psychosocial aspects. *Am. J. Psychiatry* 138:4, 1981.

Cohen, F., and Lazarus, R.S.: Coping and adaptation in health and illness. In Mechanic, D. (ed.): *Handbook of Health, Health Care, and the Health Professions*. New York, The Free Press, 1983.

Elliott, G.R., and Eisdorfer, C. (ed.): *Stress and Human Health: Analysis and Implications of Research*. New York, Springer, 1982.

Frankenhaeuser, M., and Johansson, G.: Behavior and catecholamines in children. In Levi, L. (ed.): *Society, Stress and Disease*. Vol. 2. *Childhood and Adolescence*. London, Oxford University Press, 1975.

Green, M.: A developmental approach to symptoms based on age groups. *Pediat. Clin. N. Am.* 22:571, 1975.

Green, M.: Coming of age in general pediatrics. *Pediatrics* 72:275, 1983.

Green, M., and Solnit, A.J.: Reactions to the threatened loss of a child: a vulnerable child syndrome. *Pediatrics* 34:58, 1964.

Gregg, A.: Multiple causation and organismic and integrative approaches to medical education. Paper presented at the Conference on Psychiatric Education, American Psychiatric Association, Washington, D.C., 1951.

Haggerty, R.J.: Life stress, illness and social supports. *Dev. Med. Child Neurol.* 22:391, 1980.

Henry, J.P., Stephens, P.M., Axelrod, J., and Mueller, R.A.: Effect of psychosocial stimulation on the enzymes involved in the biosynthesis and metabolism of noradrenaline and adrenaline. *Psychosom. Med.* 33:227, 1971.

Hier, D.B., and Crowley, W.F., Jr.: Spatial ability in androgen-deficient men. *N. Engl. J. Med.* 306:1202, 1982.

Hofer, M.A.: The organization of sleep and wakefulness after maternal separation in young rats. *Dev. Psychobiol.* 9:189, 1976.

Hofer, M.A.: Toward a developmental basis for disease predisposition: The effects of early maternal separation on brain, behavior and cardiovascular system. In Weiner, H., Hofer, M.A., and Stunkard, A.J. (ed.): *Brain, Behavior and Bodily Disease.* New York, Raven Press, 1981.

Hofer, M.A.: Some thoughts on "the transduction of experience" from a developmental perspective. *Psychosom. Med.* 44:19, 1982.

Hofer, M., and Weiner, H.: Mechanisms for nutritional regulation of autonomic cardiac control in early development. *Psychosom. Med.* 34:472, 1972.

Holmes, T.H., and Rahe, R.H.: The social readjustment rating scale. *J. Psychosom. Res.* 11:213, 1967.

Kagen, J.: The idea of spatial ability. *N. Engl. J. Med.* 306:1225, 1982.

Lewis, C.E.: Health hazards associated with the coming of age in the 1980's. In Green, M. (ed.): *The Psychologic Aspects of the Family: The New Pediatrics.* Lexington, Mass., Lexington Books, 1985.

Lloyd, J.: Social behavior and hormones. In Eleft-Heriou, B., and Sprott, R. (eds.) *Normal Correlates of Behavior.* New York, Plenum Press, 1975.

Meyer, R.J., and Haggerty, R.J.: Streptococcal infections in families: factors altering individual susceptibility. *Pediatrics* 29:539, 1962.

Moore-Ede, M.C., Czeisler, C.A., and Richardson, G.S.: Circadian timekeeping in health and disease. *N. Engl. J. Med.* 309:469, 1983.

Powell, G.F., Brasel, J.A., Raiti, S., and Blizzard, R.M.: Emotional deprivation and growth retardation simulating idiopathic hypopituitarism. II. Endocrinologic evaluation of the syndrome. *N. Engl. J. Med.* 276:1279, 1967.

Prugh, D.C.: *The Psychosocial Aspects of Pediatrics.* Philadelphia, Lea and Febiger, 1983.

Puig-Antich, J., Chambers, W., Halpern, F., Hanlon, C., and Sachar, E.J.: Cortisol hypersecretion in prepubertal depressive illness: a preliminary report. *Psychoneuroendocrinology* 4:191, 1979.

Reiser, M.F.: Implications of a biopsychosocial model for research in psychiatry. *Psychosom. Med.* 42:141, 1980.

Rose, R., Holaday, J., and Bernstein, I.: Plasma testosterone, dominance, rank and aggressive behavior in rhesus monkeys. *Nature* 231:366, 1971.

Rotter, J.B.: Generalized expectancies for internal versus external control of reinforcement. *Psychol. Mono.* 80:1, 1966.

Rutter, M.: *The Qualities of Mothering: Maternal Deprivation Reassessed.* New York, Jason Aronson, 1974.

Stoebel, C.F.: The importance of biological clocks in mental health. In Robinson, E.A., and Coelho, C.V. (eds.) *Behavioral Sciences and Mental Health.* PHS Publ. No. 2064. Washington, D.C., Government Printing Office, 1971.

Syme, S.L.: The role of stress in hypertension. *J. Hum. Stress* 5:10, 1979.

Weiner, H.: Psychobiological markers of disease. *Psychiat. Clinics N. Am.* 2:227, 1979.

Weiner, H.: The prospects for psychosomatic medicine: selected topics. *Psychosom. Med.* 44:491, 1982.

Werner, E.E., and Smith, R.S.: *Vulnerable But Invincible: A longitudinal Study of Resilient Children and Youth.* New York, McGraw-Hill, 1981.

Wolff, C.T., Hofer, M.A., and Mason, J.W.: Relationship between psychological defenses and mean urinary 17-hydroxycorticosteroid excretion rates. II. Methodologic and theoretical considerations. *Psychosom. Med.* 26:592, 1964.

2

Diagnosis and Preventive Intervention of Developmental and Emotional Disorders in Infancy and Early Childhood: New Perspectives

Stanley I. Greenspan
Serena Wieder
Robert A. Nover

The last twenty years have brought enormous progress in understanding infancy and early childhood development. A wealth of observational and experimental studies have documented the infant's social and emotional growth in the first years of life. This information, added to the existing knowledge of neuromotor and cognitive development, permits the elaboration of more comprehensive milestones including physical, cognitive, emotional, and interactive patterns.

An integrated clinical approach to describing these milestones makes it possible to construct a developmental model for monitoring adaptive development and detecting early deviations and disturbances. Whether transient and mild or chronic and severe, applying this model to in-depth clinical work with multirisk families and their infants allows identification of characteristic familial and interactive patterns. Cumulative infant and family risk factors associated with poor developmental outcomes may prove useful for screening populations. Approaches to clinical detection of disturbances early in their course and high-risk profiles of family and infant characteristics also provide a basis for preventive intervention strategies. The state of the art regarding the efficacy of preventive intervention research is optimistic, but new research is required to improve the specificity of both diagnostic and preventive intervention approaches.

Multiple Lines of Development

The view of the infant as developing along multiple rather than single lines (that is, physical, cognitive, social-emotional, and familial) is perhaps self-evident; however, this approach is not always put into practice. It is important to have an intervention strategy that takes into account the existence of multiple lines of development in a unique pattern to approach a presenting problem in ways that will facilitate crucial development in all areas of the infant's life. For example, babies who have been nutritionally compromised improve physically and gain weight more efficaciously when nutrition is provided together with adequate social interaction. A baby born with an auditory or tactile hypersensitivity will tend to withdraw when talked to or held. A clinical approach would combine gentle exposure to the potentially noxious stimuli in low doses with soothing experiences, such as rocking and soothing sounds. At the same time, recognizing the youngster's tendency to withdraw, the clinical staff might formulate special patterns of care that would help the parents woo the baby into greater emotional relatedness.

In contrast, an approach which focused only on cognitive stimulation might attempt to enliven a withdrawn, seemingly slow baby through sensorimotor stimulation. Yet if a youngster actually has an undiagnosed sensory hypersensitivity, the child could become even more irritable and less available for human relationships as a consequence of this type of intervention.

Also, failure to consider multiple lines of development in infancy may lead to impairment at a later age. In general, a youngster who responds to human stimulation with irritability, rigidity, and gaze aversion may very well be alert and show interest in the inanimate world with inanimate stimulation. From the point of view of physical and neurologic development such a child might develop adequate cognition during the first twelve to eighteen months. However, the impairment of human relationships and capacity to organize and differentiate animate experience (coping and adapting skills) might not become clearly noticeable until the latter part of the second or early in the third year. It is during this period, when relationships with peers become important, that complaints related to unsocialized behavior or patterns of withdrawal (refusal to play with others) are heard from parents.

A Comprehensive Clinical Approach

A comprehensive clinical approach views infants in a context that includes not only multiple lines of development, but also the parents, other family members, and relevant social structures. A comprehensive approach would consider and work, for example, with the parents' predominant attitudes and feelings, family relationships, and other crucial contextual factors, such as the system of health and mental health services and relevant community structures. More isolated intervention strategies, while working to stimulate an infant's cognitive capacities, may limit other involvement with parents to help only with issues such as food and housing.

A comprehensive clinical approach must begin with the assessment of a number of conceptually consistent categories that take into account multiple lines of development in a longitudinal manner. This approach attempts to deal with the full complexity of clinical phenomena and therefore has methodological limitations when it comes to research. For example, the ideal assessment protocol would define a limited number of key outcome criteria and specify reliable and valid instruments to assess them. The variables assessed to plan interventions would differ from those employed to assess outcome in order to avoid the possibility of "teaching the test." However, a clinical orientation demands a detailed study of a minimum number of key clusters of personality variables for both clinical planning and assessment. Therefore, rather than prior selection of a few variables, the following six core areas of assessment must in one way or another be described.

1. Prenatal and Perinatal Variables. These variables all have some impact on the infant's constitutional status and development tendencies, although the extent of the impact is unknown. The prenatal variables include familial genetic patterns; mother's status during pregnancy, including nutrition, physical health and illness, personality functioning, mental health, and degree of stress; characteristics of familial and social support systems; characteristics of the pregnancy; and the delivery process including complications, time in various stages, and the infant's status after birth. The perinatal variables include maternal perceptions of her infant, maternal reports of the emerging daily routine, and observations of the infant and maternal-infant interaction.

2. Parent, Family, and Environmental Variables. These variables include evaluations of parents, other family members, and individuals who relate closely to the family along a number of dimensions. These assessments include each member's personality organization and developmental needs, child-rearing capacity, and family interaction patterns. Evaluations of the support system (extended family, friends, and community agencies) used or available to the family and of the total home environment (both animate and inanimate components) are also included.

3. Primary Caregiver and Caregiver-Infant/Child Relationship Variables. Evaluations in this area focus on the interaction between the infant and his or her important nurturing figures. Included are the quality of mutual rhythm, feedback, and capacity for joint pleasure, as well as their flexibility in tolerating tension and being able to return to a state of intimacy. Later in development, capacities to experience differentiation, form complex emotional and behavioral patterns, and construct representations are important.

4. Infant Variables: Physical, Neurologic, Physiologic. These variables include the infant's genetic background and status immediately after birth, including the infant's general physical integrity (size, weight, general health), neurologic integrity, physiologic tendencies, rhythmic patterns, and levels of alertness and activity. Special attention should be paid to the infant's physical integrity and how this factor could foster or hinder the child's capacities to experience internal

and external stimulation, regulate internal and external experience and reach a state of homeostasis, develop human relationships, interact in cause-and-effect reciprocal patterns, form complex behavioral and emotional patterns, and construct representations to guide behavior and feelings.

5. Infant Variables: Sensory, Motor, and Cognitive. The variables in this category include the development, differentiation, and integration of the infant's motor and sensory systems, and the relationship of the infant's sensorimotor development to the infant's cognitive development.

6. Infant Variables: Formation and Internalization of Human Relationships. The following variables involve the interrelationships and capacities for relationships among the infant, parents, and other family members. These early relationships help the infant develop the capacity for a range of emotions (dependency to assertiveness) in the context of a sequence of organizational stages. These stages include the capacity for purposeful interactions, complex, organized social and emotional patterns, construcing representations, and differentiating internal representations along self versus non-self and time and space dimensions.

There are also variables that focus on the mother and her capacity to reach out and foster attachment; provide physical comfort and care; perceive basic states of pleasure and discomfort in her infant; respond with balanced empathy, that is, without either overidentification or isolation of feeling; and perceive and respond flexibly and differently to the infant's cues; foster organized complex interactions; and support representational elaboration and differentiation.

Development Structuralist Approach to Milestones

Aspects of physical, sensorimotor, and impersonal cognitive development are already included in many approaches to infants and their families. Comprehensive clinical approaches to diagnosis and preventive intervention require equal attention to emotional, social, and socially relevant cognitive development.

The focus on the infant and his or her family from multiple aspects of development has allowed new concepts of developmental stages that focus on the infant's social and emotional functioning. These milestones are based on an impressive number of studies of normal and disturbed infant development. A brief overview of an approach to developmental stages with a table summarizing the stages of early development illustrate the specificity with which developmental progress can be followed.

Although there are no large-scale studies of infants and young children's affective patterns at different ages, there is extensive literature on the emotional development of presumed normal infants. Interestingly, during the past fifteen years there has been considerably greater documentation of normal emotional development in infants than probably any other age group.

It is now well documented that the infant is capable, either at birth or shortly thereafter, of organizing experience in an adaptive fashion. He or she can respond to pleasure and displeasure (Lipsitt, 1966); change behavior as a function of its consequences (Gewirtz, 1965, 1969); form intimate bonds and make visual discriminations (Klaus and Kennell, 1976; Meltzoff and Moore, 1977); organize cycles and rhythms such as sleepwake and alertness states (Sander, 1962); evidence a variety of affects or affect proclivities (Tomkins, 1962, 1963; Izard, 1978; Ekman, 1972); and demonstrate organized social responses in conjunction with increasing neurophysiologic organization (Emde, Gaensbauer, and Harmon, 1976). From the early months the infant demonstrates a unique capacity to enter into complex social and affective interactions (Stern, 1974a,b, 1977; Brazelton, 1974). This empirically documented view of the infant is, in a general sense, consistent with Freud's early hypotheses (1911) and Hartmann's postulation (1939) of an early undifferentiated organizational matrix. That the organization of experience broadens during the early months of life to reflect increases in the capacity to experience and tolerate a range of stimuli, including stable responses to social interaction and personal configurations, is also consistent with recent empirical data (Emde et al., 1976; Sroufe, Waters, and Matas, 1974; Escalona, 1968; Stern, 1974a,b; Sander, 1962; Brazelton, Koslowski, and Main, 1974; Murphy and Moriarty, 1976).

Increasingly complex patterns continue to emerge as the infant further develops, as indicated by complex emotional responses such as surprise (Charlesworth, 1969) and affiliation; wariness and fear (Ainsworth, Bell, and Stayton, 1974; Bowlby, 1969; Sroufe and Waters, 1977); exploration and refueling patterns (Mahler, Pine, and Bergman, 1975); behavior suggesting functional understanding of objects (Werner and Kaplan, 1963); and the eventual emergence of symbolic capacities (Piaget, 1962; Gouin-Decarie, 1965; Bell, 1970).

In these studies, there is a consensus (and there are no dissenting studies) that by two to four months of age at the latest, and often much earlier, healthy infants are capable of responding to their caregivers' faces, smiles, and voices with brightening or alerting and, often, with a smile and reciprocal vocalizations (suggesting positive affect) as well as other reciprocal responses. Furthermore, the infant-caregiver interaction patterns become progressively more complex as development proceeds.

In addition to the studies on normal infant emotional development, important observations on disturbed development fill out the emerging picture of new integrated milestones. Interestingly, the study of psychopathology in infancy is a new area even though the historical foundation for identifying disturbances in the early years of life is very impressive. Constitutional and maturational patterns which influenced the formation of early relationship patterns were already noted in the early 1900s with descriptions of "babies of nervous inheritance who exhaust their mothers" (Cameron, 1919) and infants with "excessive nerve activity and a functionally immature" nervous system.

Winnicott, who as a pediatrician in the 1930s began describing the environment's role in early relationship problems (1931), was followed in the 1940s by the well-known studies describing the severe developmental disturbances of infants brought up in institutions or in other situations of emotional deprivation (Lowrey, 1940; Hunt, 1941; Bakwin, 1942; Bowlby, 1951; Spitz, 1945). Spitz's films resulted in laws in the United States prohibiting care of infants in institutions.

Both the role of individual differences in the infant based on constitutional maturational and early interactional patterns and the "nervous" infants described by Cameron in 1919 and Rachford in 1905 again became a focus of inquiry, as evidenced by the observations of Burlingham and Freud (1942); Bergman and Escalona's descriptions of infants with "unusual sensitivities" (1949); Murphy and Moriarty's description of patterns of vulnerability (1976); Thomas, Chess and Birch's temperament studies (1977); Cravioto and DeLicardie's descriptions of the role of infant individual differences in malnutrition (1973); and the impressive emerging empirical literature on infants (Sander, 1962; Brazelton, Koslowski and Main, 1974; Lipsitt, 1966; Stern, 1974a,b; Emde, Gaensbauer and Harmon, 1976; Gewirtz, 1961; Rheingold, 1966, 1969). More integrated approaches to understanding disturbances in infancy have been emphasized in descriptions of selected disorders and clinical case studies (Fraiberg, 1979; Provence, 1983; Williams et al., 1984).

In order to further understand both adaptive and disturbed infant functioning, we undertook an in-depth study of normal and disturbed developmental patterns in infancy in order to develop a systematic comprehensive classification of adaptive and maladaptive infant and family patterns. Table 2–1 summarizes the observations of the adaptive and maladaptive infant and family patterns (Greenspan, 1979, 1981; Greenspan, Lourie and Nover, 1979; Greenspan and Lourie, 1981).

The capacities described by the stages are all present in some rudimentary form in very early infancy. The sequence presented suggests not when these capacities begin, but when they become relatively prominent in organizing behavior and furthering development.

The first stage is the achievement of homeostasis, that is, self-regulation and emerging interest in the world through sight, sound, smell, touch, and taste. Once the infant has achieved some capacity for regulation in the context of engaging the world, and central nervous system (CNS) maturation is increasing between two and four months of age, the infant becomes more attuned to social and interpersonal interaction. There is greater ability to respond to the external environment and to form a special relationship with significant primary caregivers.

A second closely related stage is formation of a human attachment. If an affective and relatively pleasurable attachment (an investment in the human, animate world) is formed, then with growing maturational abilities, the infant develops complex patterns of communication in the context of this primary human relationship. Parallel with development of the infant's relationship to the inanimate world where basic schemes of causality (Piaget, 1972) are being developed, the infant becomes capable of complicated human communications (Brazelton et al., 1974; Stern, 1974a; Tennes et al., 1972; Charlesworth, 1969).

When there have been distortions in the attachment process, as occurs when a mother responds in a mechanical, remote manner or projects some of her own dependent feelings onto her infant, the infant may not learn to appreciate causal relationships between people at the level of compassionate and intimate feelings. This situation can occur even though causality seems to be developing in terms of the inanimate world and the impersonal human world.

Causal relationships are established between the infant and the primary caregiver as evidenced in the infant's growing ability to discriminate primary caregivers from others. The infant also becomes able to differentiate his or her own actions from their consequences, affectively, somatically, behaviorally, and interpersonally. Usually by eight months of age or earlier, the process of differentiation begins along a number of developmental lines, including sensorimotor integration, affects, and relationships.

The third stage is somatopsychologic differentiation indicating processes occurring at the somatic (sensorimotor) and emerging psychological levels. (In this context, *psychological* refers to higher level mental processes characterized by the capacity to form internal representations or symbols as a way to organize experience.) While schemes of causality are being established in the infant's relationship to the interpersonal world, it is not at all clear whether these schemes exist at an organized representational or symbolic level. Rather, they appear to exist mainly at a somatic level (Greenspan, 1979), even though the precursors of representational capacities are observed. Some are perhaps even prenatally determined (Lourie, 1971).

With appropriate reading of cues and systematic differential responses, the infant's or toddler's behavioral repertoire becomes complicated, and communications take on more oganized, meaningful configurations. By twelve months of age the infant is connecting behavioral units into larger organizations as he or she exhibits complex emotional responses such as affiliation, wariness, and fear (Bowlby, 1969; Ainsworth, Bell, and Stayton, 1974; Sroufe and Waters, 1977). As the toddler approaches the third year of life, in the context of the practicing subphase of the development of individuation (Mahler, Pine, and Bergman, 1975), there is an increased capacity for forming original behavioral schemes (Piaget, 1972) and imitative activity and intentionality.

A type of learning through imitation evidenced in earlier development now seems to assume a more dominant role. As imitations take on a more integrated personal form, it appears the toddler is adopting or internalizing attributes of his or her caregivers.

To describe these new capacities it is useful to consider a fourth stage, that of behavioral organization, initiative, and internalization. As the toddler ap-

Table 2–1
Developmental Basis for Psychopathology and Adaptation in Infancy and Early Childhood

Stage-Specific Tasks and Capacities	Capacities		Environment (Caregiver)	
	Adaptive	Maladaptive (Pathologic)	Adaptive	Maladaptive
Homeostasis (0–3 mo) (self-regulation and interest in the world)	Internal regulation (harmony) and balanced interest in world	Unregulated (e.g., hyperexcitable). withdrawn (apathetic)	Invested, dedicated, protective, comforting, predictable, engaging and interesting	Unavailable, chaotic, dangerous, abusive; hypostimulating or hyperstimulating; dull
Attachment (2–7 mo)	Rich, deep, multisensory emotional investment in animate world (especially with primarey caregivers)	Total lack of, or nonaffective, shallow, impersonal, involvement (e.g., autistic patterns) in animate world	In love and woos infant to "fall in love"; affective multimodality pleasurable involvement	Emotionally distant, aloof, and/or impersonal (highly ambivalent)
Somatopsychologic differentiation (3–10 mo) (purposeful, cause and effect signaling or communication)	Flexible, wide-ranging affective multisystem contingent (reciprocal) interactions (especially with primary caregivers)	Behavior and affects random and or chaotic, or narrow, rigid, and stereotyped	Reads and respond contingently to infant's communications across multiple sensory and affective systems	Ignores infant's communications (e.g., overly intrusive, preoccupied, or depressed or misreads infant's communication (e.g., projection)
Behavioral organization, initiative, and internalization (9–24 mo)	Complex, organized, assertive, innovative, integrated behavioral and emotional patterns	Fragmented, stereotyped, and polarized behavior and emotions (e.g., withdrawn, compliant, hyperaggressive, or disorganized toddler)	Admiring of toddler's initiative and autonomy, yet available, tolerant and firm; follows toddler's lead and helps him organize diverse behavioral and affective elements	Overly intrusive, controlling; fragmented, fearful (especially of toddler's autonomy); abruptly and prematurely "separates"

Representational capacity, differentiation, and consolidation (1½–4 yr) (the use of ideas to guide language, pretend play, and behavior and eventually thinking and planning)	Formation and elaboration of internal representations (imagery) / Organization and differentiation of imagery pertaining to self and nonself; emergence of cognitive insight / Stabilization of mood and gradual emergence of basic personality functions	No representational (symbolic) elaboration; behavior and affect concrete, shallow, and polarized; sense of self and other fragmented and undifferentiated or narrow and rigid; reality testing, impulse regulation, mood stabilization compromised or vulnerable (e.g., borderline psychotic and severe character problems)	Emotionally available to phase-appropriate regressions and dependency needs; reads, responds to, and encourages symbolic elaboration across emotional behavioral domains (e.g., love, pleasure, assertion) while fostering gradual reality orientation and internalization of limits	Fearful of or denies phase-appropriate needs; engages child only in concrete (nonsymbolic) modes generally or in certain realms (e.g., around pleasure) and or misreads or responds noncontingently or nonrealistically to emerging communications (i.e., undermines reality orientation); overly permissive or punitive
Capacity for limited extended representational systems and multiple extended representational systems (middle childhood through adolescence)	Enhanced and eventually optimal flexibility to conserve and transform complex and organized representations of experience in the context of expanded relationship patterns and phase-expected developmental tasks	Derivative representational capacities limited or defective, as are latency and adolescent relationships and coping capacities	Supports complex, phase- and age-appropriate experiential and interpersonal development (i.e., into triangular and posttriangular patterns)	Conflicted over child's age-appropriate propensities (e.g., competitiveness, pleasure orientation, growing competence, assertiveness, and self-sufficiency); becomes aloof or maintains symbiotic tie; withdraws from or overengages in competitive or pleasurable strivings

Source: Greenspan, S.I.: Psychopathology and adaptation in infancy and early childhood: principles of clinical diagnosis and preventive intervention. *Clinical Infant Reports*, No. 1. New York, International Universities Press, 1981.

proaches the end of the second year, internal sensations and unstable images become organized in a mental representational form that can be evoked and is somewhat stable (Piaget, 1972; Bell, 1970; Gouin-Decarie, 1965). While this capacity is fragile between sixteen and twenty-four months, it soon becomes a dominant mode in organizing the child's behavior.

A fifth stage is the formation of mental representations or ideas. The capacity for "object permanence" is relative and goes through a series of stages (Gouin-Decarie, 1965); it refers to the toddler's ability to search for hidden inanimate objects. Representational capacity refers to the ability to organize and evoke internal organized multisensory experiences of the animate object. The capacities to represent animate and inanimate experiences are related and depend both on central nervous system myelination and appropriate experiences. The process of "internalization" may be thought of as an intermediary process. Internalized experiences eventually become sufficiently organized to be considered representations.

At a representational level the child again develops capacities for elaboration, integration, and differentiation. Just as causal schemes previously were developed at a somatic and behavioral level, now they are developed at a representational level. The child begins to elaborate and eventually differentiate those feelings, thoughts, and events that emanate from within and those that emanate from others. The child begins to differentiate the actions of others from his or her own. This process gradually forms the basis for the differentiation of self-representations from the external world, animate and inanimate, and also provides the basis for such crucial personality functions as knowing what is real from unreal, impulse and mood regulation, and the capacity to focus attention and concentrate in order to learn and interact.

The capacity for differentiating internal representations becomes consolidated as object constancy is established (Mahler et al., 1975). In middle childhood, representational capacity becomes reinforced with the child's ability to develop derivative representational systems tied to the original representation and to transform them in accord with adaptive and defensive goals. This permits greater flexibility in dealing with perceptions, feelings, thoughts, and emerging ideals. Substages for these capacities include representational differentiation, the consolidation of representational capacity, and the capacity for forming limited derivative representational systems and multiple derivative representational systems (structural learning) (Greenspan, 1979).

At each of these stages, pathologic as well as adaptive formations are possible. These may be considered as relative compromises in the range, depth, stability, and personal uniqueness of the experiential organization consolidated at each stage. The infant can form adaptive patterns of regulation in the earliest stages of development. Internal states are harmoniously regulated and the infant is free to invest in the animate and inanimate world, thereby setting the basis for rich emotional attachments to primary caregivers. On the other hand, if regulatory processes are not functioning properly and the infant is either hyposensitive or hypersensitive to sensations, he or she may evidence homeostatic difficulties. From relatively minor compromises such as a tendency to withdraw or become hyperexcitable under stress to a major deviation such as overwhelming avoidance of the animate world, the degrees to which the infant, even in the first months of life, achieves a less-than-optimal adaptive structural organization can be observed.

Thus, the early attachments can be warm and engaging or shallow, insecure, and limited in their affective tone. There are differences between an infant who reads the signals of the caregivers and responds in a rich, meaningful way to multiple aspects of the communications (with multiple affects and behavioral communications) and one who can respond only within a narrow range of affect (for example, protest) or who cannot respond at all in a contingent or reciprocal manner (for example, the seemingly apathetic, withdrawn, and depressed child who responds only to internal cues). As the toddler becomes behaviorally more organized and complex patterns appear which reflect originality and initiative in the context of the separation and individuation subphase of development, we can observe those toddlers who manifest this full adaptive capacity. They may be compared with others who are stereotyped in their behavioral patterns (reflect no originality or intentionality), who remain fragmented (never connect pieces of behavior into more complicated patterns), or who evidence polarities of affect, showing no capacity to integrate emotions (the chronic negativistic aggressive toddler who cannot show interest, curiosity, or love).

The child who can organize, integrate, and differentiate a rich range of affective and ideational life can be distinguished from one who remains either without representational capacity or undifferentiated (that is, one who has deficits with reality testing, impulse control, and focused concentration) or who may form and differentiate self and object representations only at the expense of extreme compromises in the range of tolerated experience (for example, the schizoid child who withdraws from relationships). Similar adaptive or maladaptive structural organizations can be observed in later childhood (the triangular phase), latency, and adolescence.

A more detailed discussion of this framework, including principles of prevention and intervention, is available (Greenspan, 1979, 1981). It should also be pointed out that through videotaped analyses of infant-caregiver interactions (Greenspan and Lieberman, 1980) these patterns evidence temporal stability and can be reliably rated and new raters trained and kept at high levels of reliability (Hofheimer et al., 1981, 1984; Poisson et al., 1981, 1983).

The ability to monitor developmental progress with explicit guidelines facilitates the early identification of those infants, young children, and families who are either not progressing in an appropriate manner or who are progressing in a less than optimal way. For example, it is now possible to evaluate infants who continue to have difficulty regulating their state and developing the capacity for focused interest in their immediate environments, or who fail to develop a positive emotional interest in their caregivers. It is also possible to assess an infant's difficulty in learning cause-and-effect interactions and complex emotional and social patterns or inability, by age two to three, to create symbols to guide emotions and behavior. In exploring the factors that may be contributing to less than optimal patterns of development, the focus on multiple aspects of development offers many advantages. Some infants, for example, may evidence a motor delay because of familial patterns where explorativeness and the practice of the motor system is discouraged. In other infants there may be a maturational variation that, together with family patterns, is contributing to a motor lag. In still other cases, genetic maturational factors may explain the delay completely. Even with a symptom as common as a motor lag, unless aspects of all contributing factors are explored, it is likely that important contributing factors will go unrecognized. The focus on multiple aspects of development, in the context of clearly delineated developmental and emotional landmarks, opens the door to a comprehensive assessment, diagnosis and preventive intervention strategies.

At-Risk Populations

The clinical approach that attempts to study infants, children, and families from multiple perspectives and assess the degree to which developmental milestones are being met allows extraction of the clinical characteristics of vulnerable infants and families. It has been known for some time that certain populations are clearly at greater risk than others for cognitive, social, or emotional development (for example, teen-age mothers, low-income families, infants with low birth weight or chronic physical illness). The impact of cumulative risk factors, which include psychological as well as social characteristics, however, has not been clearly identified. Therefore, we identified the clinical criteria seen in multirisk families with the goal of applying them to a nonintervention high-risk population, originally studied by Sameroff and colleagues in their well-known Rochester studies (Sameroff, Seifer, and Zax, 1982).

In our study of multirisk families, we observed in-depth forty-seven families who were referred by various prenatal clinics or other agencies because of their child-rearing practices (64 percent by medical facilities, 11 percent by social service facilities, and only 17 percent by mental health facilities). Multirisk families are often thought of as "social" and "economic" challenges, and, in fact, many of them have psychiatric illness, including severe developmental interferences and disturbances in psychosocial functioning. In addition, early difficulties in their interaction abilities with their infants were observed. For example, 64 percent came from families with a history of psychiatric disturbance, 34 percent had themselves experienced psychiatric hospitalization, and an additional 15 percent had some type of outpatient contact with a mental health provider.

Of these clinical infant development program mothers, 44 percent experienced physical abuse and 32 percent sexual abuse prior to age eighteen, and 93 percent reported current physical abuse and a tendency to abuse or neglect their own children. (There were significant correlates between past and present abusive patterns.) Over two-thirds (69 percent) experienced significant disruptions of a parental relationship or parent-surrogate relationship prior to adolescence. Over 75 percent had impaired psychosocial functioning in either the family, school, peer, or work setting in childhood, adolescence, or early adulthood.

Of some eighteen items considered to be unfavorable and put into an index of misfortune, 50 percent of the mothers had nine or more misfortunes (mean 0.47) compared to a low-risk comparison group which generally had none of these events (median value 0.09).

In addition, a series of objective reliable psychiatric ratings of various ego functions dealing with impulse and affect regulation, self-other boundaries, and maternal and relationship capacities predicted high-risk group membership correctly 97.8 percent of the time and low-risk group membership 84.6 percent of the time. Overall, 94 percent of cases were correctly classified. (See Wieder et al., 1984, for a more complete description of these families.)

In terms of interactional abilities, the study observed babies in the program who, during the first few days of life, were fairly well in terms of weight, size, and overall physical health status but had difficulty in regulating social responsiveness, establishing habituation patterns, and organizing their motor responses. Some of them were withdrawn and unresponsive to animate stimuli, others hyperlabile and overly responsive.

In general, babies in the program were at risk prenatally but had normal patterns of development perinatally (prenatal intervention having assured adequate nutrition and other supports, including appropriate medical care), and showed significantly less than optimal development as early as the first months of life. Pediatric, neurologic, and Brazelton neonatal examinations at one month of age, for example, showed developmental progression but not the increased capacity for orientation characteristic of a normative population. Interestingly, the group receiving comprehensive intervention was similar to normal comparison infants at birth but was slightly lower in their orientation capacity by one month. The study's high-risk group, receiving only periodic evaluations, tended to be worse in a number of areas including orientation, habituation, and motor organization (even after some of the most disturbed families left the program) than both the normal and intervention groups at one month (Hofheimer et al., 1982).

By three months of age, instead of a capacity for self-regulation, organization, and an interest in the world, a number of babies showed increased tendencies toward lability, muscle rigidity, gaze aversion, and an absence of organized sleep-wake, alert, and feeding patterns. Their caregivers, instead of having an overall capacity for offering the babies comfort, protection, and an interest in the world, either tended to withdraw from them and avoid them or overstimulate them in a chaotic and intermittent fashion.

Between three and nine months of age, in the multiproblem families, the child's behavior and affects remained under the control of internal states in random and chaotic or narrow, rigid, and stereotyped patterns of interaction. The child's caregivers, instead of offering the expected optimal contingent responsiveness to the child's varied signals, tended to ignore or misread them. The child's caregivers were overly preoccupied, depressed, or chaotic.

Toward the end of the first year of life and the beginning of the second, a child in a multiple-risk-factor family, instead of showing an increase in organized, complex, assertive, and innovative emotional and behavioral patterns (for example, taking the mother's hand and leading her to the refrigerator to show her the kind of food he wants), tended to exhibit fragmented, stereotyped, and polarized patterns. These toddlers were observed to be withdrawn and compliant or highly agressive, impulsive, and disorganized. Their human environment tended to be intrusive, controlling, and fragmented. These toddlers may have been prematurely separated from their caregivers or the caregivers may have exhibited patterns of withdrawal instead of admiringly supporting the toddler's initiative and autonomy and helping the organization of what would become more complex capacities for communicating, interacting, and behaving.

As the toddler's potential capacities continued to develop in the latter half of the second year and in the third (eighteen to thirty-six months), profound deficits could be more clearly observed. The child did not develop capacities for internal representations (imagery) to organize behavior, feelings, differentiating ideas and feelings and thoughts pertaining to the self and the nonself. These children either developed no representational or symbolic capacity or, if the capacity did develop, it was not elaborated beyond the most elementary descriptive form so that the child's behavior remained shallow and polarized. The sense of the emerging self, as distinguished from the sense of other people, remained fragmented and undifferentiated. The child's potentially emerging capacities for reality testing, impulse regulation, and mood stabilization seemed to be either compromised or extremely vulnerable to regression. In other words, patterns either consistent with later borderline and psychotic personality organization or severe asocial or antisocial impulse-ridden character disorders were observed.

At this stage, the underlying impairment manifested itself in the child's inability to use a representational or symbolic mode to organize behavior. In essence, the distinctly human capacity of operating beyond the survival level, of using internal imagery to elaborate and organize complex feelings and wishes and to construct trial actions in the emotional sphere of anticipating and planning ahead were compromised. In many of the research families, the parents simply did not have these capacities. Even when they were not under emotional distress or in states of crisis or panic, they did not demonstrate a symbolic mode, as evidenced in the lack of verbal communication (only one aspect of symbolic communication) and in the lack of symbolic play. Such families tended to be fearful and to deny and fail to meet their children's needs. They engaged the child only in nonsymbolic modes of communication, such as holding, feeding, and administering physical punishment, and at times they misread or responded unrealistically to the child's emerging communication, thus undermining the development in the child of a sense of self and a flexible orientation to reality.

Needless to say, the mastery by the children in these families of higher level developmental tasks would become even more difficult. At each new level of development, the infants and toddlers who for a variety of reasons have survived earlier developmental phases intact invariably would challenge the multi-risk-factor environment with their new capacities, for example, with their capacity for symbolic communication. The healthier the toddler, the more challenging and overwhelming the child was likely to be. In a pattern frequently observed, the child would move ahead of the parent (engaging, for example, in symbolic play around themes of dependency or sexuality), and thus the parent would become confused and either withdraw from or behave intrusively toward the child. Shortly, unless other more skillful caregivers became available, the child would begin to regress to presymbolic modes of behaving. These children may be able to consolidate higher level capacities when they begin to receive support from other systems, such as the school; and when they become capable of understanding parental limitations. These capacities, however, can only develop when the child is a little older. The youngster who experiences developmental failures, including the failure to develop a full representational or symbolic capacity (the basis for formal school experience later on) will unquestionably be handicapped in all subsequent opportunities for learning.

Application of Multi-Risk Clinical Criteria to a Non-Intervention High-Risk Population

This section reviews a collaborative study with Sameroff and colleagues of a population of multirisk families. This study demonstrated that family, psychological, and infant interactional patterns, when controlling for social economic status (SES), correlate with poor outcomes at age four. It further showed that cumulative risk patterns during infancy can be used to predict as much as a twenty-five-fold increase in the probability of poor outcomes at age four (Sameroff et al., 1984). The results of this study suggest that it is cumulative risk factors that place infants and families at greatest risk.

The findings of this study are given in some detail because of the important implication they have for predicting poor outcomes in high-risk populations. The population for this study was recruited with the original aim of looking at the effects of different types of parental emotional disturbance on development in offspring. The patterns in the population recruited, however, were consistent

Table 2–2
Variables Used for Calculating Cumulative Risk Scores for Families of Four-Year-Old Children

Risk Variable	Low Risk	High Risk
Chronicity of illness	0–1 contact	1 or more contacts
Anxiety	75% fewest	25% most
Parental perspective	75% highest	25% lowest
Interaction	75% most	25% least
Education	High school	No high school
Occupation	Skilled	Semiskilled
Minority status	White	Nonwhite
Family support	Father present	Father absent
Life events	75% fewest	25% most
Family size	1–3 children	4 or more children

with those found in the multiproblem or multirisk families described earlier. Of 215 families followed since pregnancy, all of Hollingshead's SES groupings were represented, some with greater portions in groups 3, 4, and 5. They were divided between white (131), black (79), and Puerto Rican (5), with family sizes ranging from one to ten children. Approximately 54 of the women were either single, separated, or divorced. Their education ranged from advanced college degrees to completion of the third grade. The children were well distributed between boys and girls with slightly more boys.

Ten variables that appeared to be clinically relevant from prior studies and that were measured in this study were selected to categorize the families into high-and low-risk families (table 2–2). Multi-risk status was defined operationally in this study by the number of high-risk variables in any one family (0–8). A relationship was found between the degree of risk defined by number of risk factors and verbal IQ at age four. The linear trend analysis was significant. The deviation from linear trend was nonsignificant (figure 1–1).

It is interesting to note that multi-risk patterns had far greater impact than any one risk factor alone. For verbal IQ outcomes at age four, there were two standard deviation differences between the lowest and highest risk groups. Perhaps the most important finding of this study, however, is the fact that interactive, familial, and psychological variables, as measured by multiple risk criteria, impact on later developmental outcomes even within SES groups. It is often thought that poverty or socioeconomic status more generally, in their own right, account for poor developmental outcomes. This study demonstrates that, quite to the contrary, interactive, psychological, and family patterns account for poor

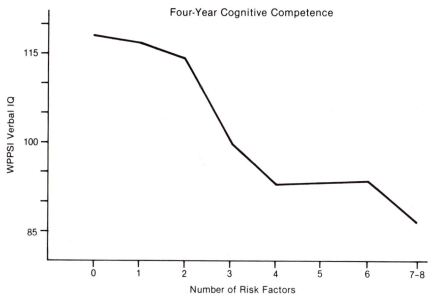

Note: Cumulative risk scores are total of high-risk factors present in each child's family.

Figure 2–1. Means of Four-Year-Old Children's Verbal IQ Scores for Each Cumulative Risk Score

developmental outcomes even when socioeconomic status is held constant. Trend analyses was significant for high ($F = 7.65$; $p = < 0.01$) and low ($F = 24.88$; $p = < 0.01$) SES groups (figure 2–2).

In another analysis, to highlight these findings, families were divided into low risk, moderate risk, and high risk depending on the number of risk factors that characterize the family (figure 2–3). A most striking finding is that if a family is in the high-risk group, characterized by four or more risk factors, they have a 25 times greater probability of falling into the low IQ category.

It should also be pointed out that the same trends described here for intellectual performance were also found for aspects of emotional and social functioning at age four (Sameroff and Seifer, 1983). However, the linear relationships, while significant, were not as dramatic. This is most likely due to the types of measures used rather than less impairment in emotional functioning.

In summary, this study applied multirisk criteria derived from in-depth clinical studies of indivdual infants and families to a nonintervention sample of multirisk families and found that familial, psychological, and interactive variables early in the first year of life predict aspects of intellectual and social performance four years later. Furthermore, familial, psychological, and interactive variables

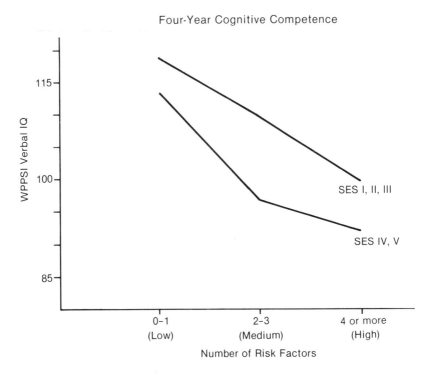

Four-Year Cognitive Competence

Figure 2–2. Means of Four-Year-Old Children's Verbal IQ Scores within High (SES I, II, III) and Low (SES IV, V) Socioeconomic Status Groups in Three Cumulative Risk Categories

operate independent of socioeconomic class. When taken together, familial, psychological, and interactive variables and social class variables can predict a twenty-five-fold increase in the probability of having a poor developmental outcome at age four. The implications of being able to identify high-risk patterns in infancy and early childhood for potential preventive programs is enormous. Further research establishing probabilities of poor developmental outcomes associated with specific familial, interactive, and constitutional patterns in infancy has the promise of bringing to developmental diagnosis and preventive intervention a degree of specificity which has only been possible for a limited number of disorders in general medicine.

Preventive Intervention Programs

Because of the developments in the clinical identification of individual infants and families who may be proceeding in a less-than-optimal fashion through the

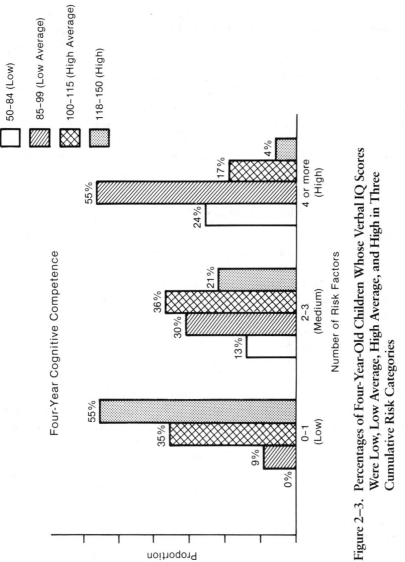

Figure 2–3. Percentages of Four-Year-Old Children Whose Verbal IQ Scores Were Low, Low Average, High Average, and High in Three Cumulative Risk Categories

age-expected, normative emotional-intellectual milestones, it is possible to identify populations who, because of cumulative risk factors, may be at greater probability for impaired intellectual or psychosocial functioning. In preventive intervention there has been great progress; yet much remains to be learned. It is useful to look at preventive interventions from several perspectives. First, it is important to have an overview of the field of preventive interventions in all areas of developmental difficulty including sensorimotor, cognitive, familial, and psychosocial problems. Second, there is a need to focus on selected successful programs. Finally, it is necessary to have a model program which is based on clinical understanding of the gradations in development for each of the multiple aspects of growth and development.

Overview of Preventive Intervention Efficacy Studies

In a collaboration with Dr. Karl White and colleagues (White and Casto, 1984) reviewing the results of their meta-analysis of all preventive intervention studies found in the literature with three-year-old and younger children, it is clear that early interventions work at the time the intervention stops. But the lack of comprehensive approaches to both intervention and evaluation in most studies limits the conclusions one can draw on the duration of effect and the type of program best for each infant and family.

Data on 162 early intervention studies have been analyzed by White and Casto. These have included studies where interventions were compared to no interventions and where one intervention was compared with another. These studies also included different types of problems and populations ranging from high-risk populations (socially, emotionally, or economically disadvantaged) to infants and children with developmental delays and handicaps. However, only 143 intervention and control studies came from work with developmentally delayed or handicapped children. The overall results were quite interesting (mean 0.44; median 0.38; standard deviation 0.68). Figure 2–4 shows that the average impact of early intervention is quite impressive. It suggests that at the time the intervention is completed, most interventions have impact. The average impact is approximately half a standard deviation. When the interventions for developmentally delayed and handicapped and disadvantaged or otherwise stressed children are looked at separately, the amount of effect is higher for the handicapped than for the disadvantaged. However, if only good-quality studies are included, the average effect size is no different for both disadvantaged (or stressed) families and handicapped infants and young children.

Perhaps the most important question is how enduring are the effects of preventively oriented interventions, but the data are insufficient to answer this (table 2–3). In looking at duration and effect, it is not only the limited number of follow-up studies, but the lack of clinically valid follow-up measures to study the diversity of long-term effects that must be highlighted. Therefore even though

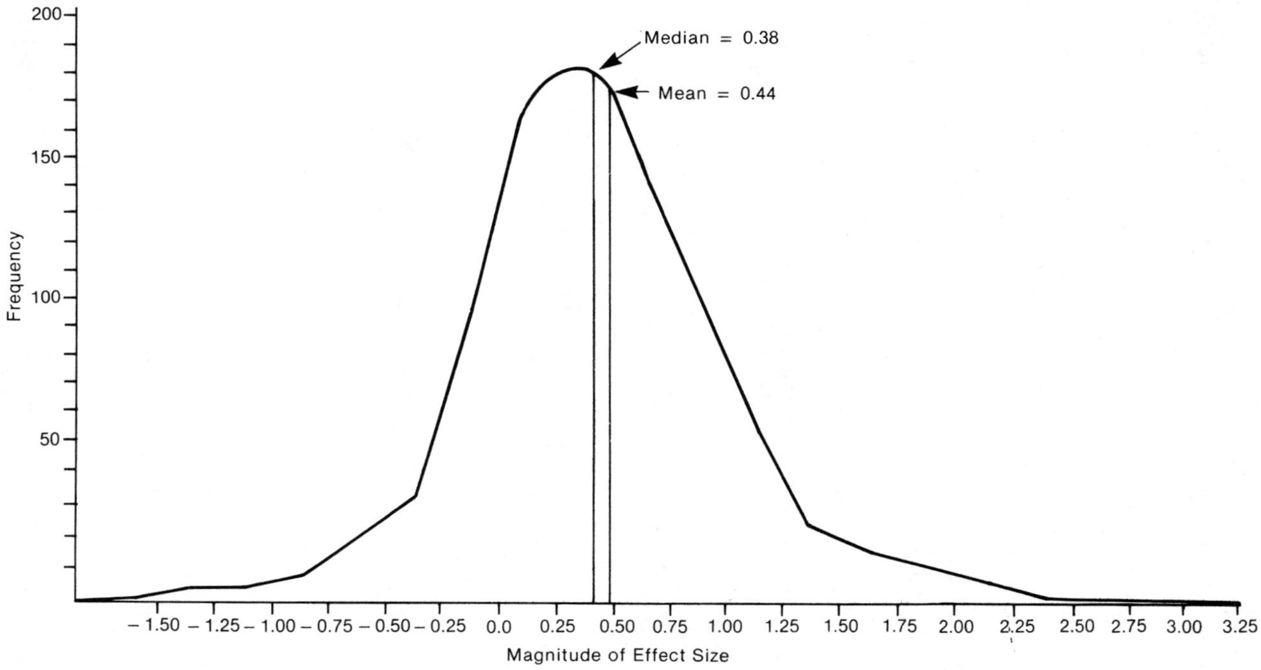

Figure 2–4. Frequency Distribution of Effect Sizes from Intervention Versus Control Early Intervention Efficacy Studies

Table 2–3
Average Effect Size for Intervention Versus Control Early Intervention Efficacy Studies (ES$_s$) for Subgroups of Data

Subgroup	Handicapped			Disadvantaged		
	ES	S_{es}	N_{es}	ES	S_{es}	N_{es}
All studies	0.56	0.06	143	0.42	0.02	751
Only good quality studies	0.39	0.13	23	0.41	0.03	188
Only good quality studies with immediate posttest	0.43	0.15	20	0.51	0.04	121

ES = mean effect size; S_{es} = standard error of the mean for ES; N_{es} = number of ESs on which a calculation is based.

studies of disadvantaged children show declining effects, the variables which do hold up in the long term, such as overall social adaptation, were usually not measured.

Limitations in Preventive Intervention Efficacy Research

One of the major limitations in preventive intervention efficacy research is a lack of comprehensiveness in both the intervention and the outcome variables. In working with disadvantaged families, for example, there is often the tendency to work only with the infant and not with the family or to work only on an educational curriculum with the family and not with day-to-day social and psychological stresses affecting the family.

In an attempt to document this impression about preventive intervention research, the existing studies were reviewed from the perspectives of types of measures used and duration and target of intervention. Additionally the review looked at the number of studies which attempted to work with multiple domains of functioning.

Tables 2–4 and 2–5 show the number and percentage of effect sizes in relationship to the type of measures used, the duration of the intervention, and the time interval lapsing after the intervention when outcome was assessed. One might have thought that studies of shorter duration would focus more on cognitive variables and those of longer duration on psychosocial and familial variables. One may have also thought that long-term follow-ups would focus more on non-IQ measures. As can be seen from Tables 2–4 and 2–5, this is not the case. There is a predominant focus on limited outcome measures regardless of the duration of the intervention or the time of follow-up.

The majority of the studies focused on the child and preschool skills. Where the parent is a major intervenor, this involves very little parent training or parent treatment. There is relatively little focus on having the parents become better

Table 2–4
Number and Percentage of Efficacy Studies Categorized by Type of Measure and Duration of Intervention

Duration of Intervention in Weeks	Type of Measure										
	IQ	Motor	Language	Soc./Emo.	ITPA	Academic	Attitude	Parent-Skill	Health	School Progress	Total
1–24	106/6.5%	42/2.6%	36/2.2%	44/2.7%	7/0.4%	3/0.2%	5/0.3%	9/0.6%	8/0.5%	2/0.1%	290/17.9%
24–52	281/17.3%	43/2.6%	118/7.3%	37/2.3%	44/2.7%	122/7.5%	10/0.6%	7/0.4%	6/0.4%	5/0.3%	720/44.3%
52–104	175/10.8%	28/1.7%	28/1.7%	27/1.7%	29/1.8%	71/4.4%	0/0.0%	6/0.4%	1/0.1%	10/0.6%	379/23.3%
104+	92/5.7%	10/0.6%	41/2.5%	19/1.2%	3/0.2%	35/2.2%	2/0.1%	4/0.2%	6/0.4%	19/1.2%	235/14.5%
Total	654/40.3%	123/7.6%	223/13.7%	127/7.8%	83/5.1%	231/14.2%	17/1.0%	26/1.6%	21/1.3%	36/2.2%	1,624/100.0%

Table 2–5
Number and Percentage of Efficacy Studies Categorized by Type and Time of Measure

Months after Intervention Completed, Outcome Was Measured	Type of Measure										
	IQ	Motor	Language	Soc./Emo.	ITPA	Academic	Attitude	Parent-Skill	Health	School Progress	Total
Immediate	339/21.1%	103/6.4%	159/9.9%	90/5.6%	70/4.4%	46/2.9%	12/0.7%	23/1.4%	19/1.2%	10/0.6%	929/58.0%
1–12	101/6.3%	16/1.0%	18/1.1%	14/0.9%	9/0.6%	31/1.9%	5/0.3%	2/0.1%	1/0.1%	4/0.2%	201/12.5%
12–24	77/4.8%	0/0.0%	17/1.1%	2/0.1%	2/0.1%	40/2.5%	0/0.0%	1/0.1%	1/0.1%	4/0.2%	144/9.0%
24–36	42/2.6%	1/0.1%	9/0.6%	0/0.0%	0/0.0%	33/2.1%	0/0.0%	0/0.0%	0/0.0%	2/0.1%	87/5.4%
36–60	42/2.6%	0/0.0%	9/0.6%	4/0.2%	2/0.1%	31/1.9%	0/0.0%	0/0.0%	0/0.0%	8/0.5%	97/6.1%
60+	44/2.7%	0/0.0%	10/0.6%	14/0.9%	0/0.0%	50/3.1%	0/0.0%	0/0.0%	0/0.0%	6/0.4%	145/9.0%
Total	645/40.2%	120/7.5%	222/13.8%	124/7.7%	83/5.2%	231/14.4%	17/1.1%	26/1.6%	21/1.3%	34/2.1%	1,603/100.0%

Table 2–6
Identification of Studies Measuring Outcomes in Four or More Areas

Study Type	Number of Outcome Measures Used						
	4		5		6		7
Experimental vs. control studies	104[a]	694[a]	128[a]	1,662	234		1,224[a]
	106	959	806	1,663	247[a]		
	274	1,221[a]	994[a]	1,665	430[a]		
	475	1,449[a]	1,478	1,666	824		
	492	1,657	1,658	1,667	1,080		
	595[a]	1,664	1,661	1,668	1,659		
Unduplicated intervention A vs. intervention B studies	694 994						

[a]Also an intervention A vs. intervention B study.

Table 2–7
Daycare Intervention: Yale Child Study Center and Infant Development Unit (New Haven—Provence)

Variable	Comments and Findings
Population	Low SES inner city families and their firstborn child
Intervention	Integrated family-oriented psychosocial, educational, and medical intervention
	Prenatal to 30-month postpartum care. Intervention team consisted of a social worker, pediatric primary daycare worker, and developmental examiner. Daycare center and home visits.
Major findings	10 year follow-up
	↑ Self-support among mothers.
	↑ Educational attainment among mothers.
	↓ Family size.
	↑ School attendance for children.
	↓ Need for special school services for boys in relation to educational and behavioral problems.
	In single follow-up year, 15 control families used $40,000 more in estimated welfare and special school service costs.

Table 2–8
Nurse Home Visitation Program: The Prenatal/Early Infancy Project
(Elmira, N.Y.)

Variable	Comments and Findings
Population	Teenagers, unmarried or low SES; 1st child
Intervention	Emotional support, factual information, facilitating linkages and support structure
Major findings	↓ Cigarette smoking
	↓ Preterm delivery
	↑ In very young adolescent group lower incidence of inadequate weight gain and higher birth weight babies
	↓ Abuse and neglect among unmarried teenagers
	↑ Return to school
	↑ Interest in finding jobs
	↑ Employment among unmarried mothers over age 18
	↑ Involvement of other family members
	↓ Welfare services
	↓ Sick visits
	↓ Repeat pregnancies in 2-year period for all age groups
	↑ Overall health improvement as indicated by higher hematocrits and less ER visits for accidents and ingestions

copers in terms of overall family adjustment or to develop their own coping skills to facilitate the development of their children. Parents tended to focus on carrying out particular curricula where the parent is the intervenor or where the child is the direct recipient of the curriculum.

As another way of looking at the degree to which comprehensive approaches were included in the studies to date, the review looked at the studies which had outcomes in four or more domains. Of the 14 out of 162 studies including outcomes in four or more domains, 12 included outcomes in five domains, six included outcomes in six domains, and 1 study included outcomes in seven domains (table 2–6). Even with multiple outcome studies (which only constitute a very small percentage of the total studies conducted), the comprehensiveness of intervention approach was quite limited. Not surprisingly, because of the narrow intervention focus, the effect sizes for programs with multiple outcome measures was consistent with the effect sizes for the overall group of studies.

Therefore, most literature on preventively oriented interventions in infancy and early childhood are educationally rather than psychosocially oriented. There is, however, an overall positive effect at the time the intervention is completed. It

Table 2–9
Early Childhood Education: High/Scope Perry Project

Variable	Comments and Findings
Population	Low SES, 50% welfare, 47% single parent, 10–20% of parents completed high school
Intervention	High quality preschool education program on site 2 ½ hr/wk for 2 years and home visits based on operative model of education
Major Findings	Follow-up through age 19 with no attrition; 95% data completion
	↓ Special education
	↑ Rates of completing high school
	↑ Job training and college classes
	↑ Self-support
	↓ Arrest rate for criminal behavior
	↓ On Welfare
	↓ Birth rate during adolescence for women in program
	Benefit to cost ratio: $4.75—$1.00 (discounted) $9.50 to $1.00 (not discounted)

seems clear, therefore, that preventive interventions have a positive effect when compared to comparison groups receiving other interventions or to control groups. What is not clear, however, is the duration of this effect and the potentially enhanced value of having individually tailored comprehensive approaches to both intervention and outcome evaluation.

There are a few studies that have been analyzed recently that do lead to optimism about the effectiveness of preventive interventions. These studies are, in part, characterized by flexible psychosocially sensitive interventions and follow-ups with a diversity of outcome measures.

Selected Programs with Follow-up

There are a few programs with follow-up in more than one area of functioning that suggest a robust and continuing effect of preventive intervention, whether educational or psychosocial. Three programs are summarized in schematic form to illustrate different models of preventive intervention that have worked quite well for the populations served. The Yale program (Provence et al., 1983) illustrates a combined educational-family psychosocial approach integrated in a day-care program for moderately at-risk, low-income families (table 2–7). The Elmira prenatal/postnatal program (Olds, 1982) illustrates a visiting nurse model with a combined infant developmental and family support approach through an outreach worker having limited availability (often once every two weeks) but cataloguing the use of other services for groups of infants and families at mixed risk (mild to severe), for example, teenagers, unwed mothers, or low SES families (table 2–8). The High/Scope program (Weikart, Bond, and McNeir, 1978) illustrates a preschool educational approach which focuses on individual differences and operative models of cognitive development, implemented through parents and peers working with groups at moderate risk for cognitive and behavioral problems (table 2–9).

Description of a Model Comprehensive Approach to Infants, Young Children, and Their Families

A model program needs to consider the multiple risks in the infant and family. The Clinical Infant Development Program (CIDP) implemented a pilot model program to develop the technology for a large-scale demonstration of preventive interventions for various groups of infants and families. The program was able to study in-depth for two or more years (oldest child age seven in 1984) 47 multi-risk-factor families with more than 200 children. Except for a few brief comments, details of the efforts made to recruit these families and of the clinical service approaches and assessments used are described elsewhere (Greenspan, 1981, 1984; Weider et al., 1984).

The CIDP approach was to develop a regular pattern of services including organizing service systems on behalf of their survival needs such as food, housing, and medical care; providing a constant emotional relationship with the family and, most importantly, offering highly technical patterns of care including approaches to deal with the infant's and family's individual vulnerabilities and strengths.

The program also had a special support structure to provide at one site partial or full therapeutic day care for the child, innovative outreach to the family, and ongoing training and supervision of the program staff.

To elaborate on these core services and to respond to the family's concrete needs, various community agencies need to be organized to build a foundation for the family's survival. However, this approach alone will not ensure a family's survival, since many of the families, for a variety of reasons, are adept at circumventing offers of traditional supports.

The second component of a comprehensive effort, and one that is absolutely necessary for these families, is a human relationship with one or more workers. Such a relationship, however, is not easy to establish, because distrust is often ingrained in each parent as well as in the family as a unit. This human relationship needs to grow in ways paralleling the infant's development and needs to help the parents facilitate that development. It must provide growing regularity, an emotional attachment, and a process that facilitates describing and examining interpersonal patterns. To provide this human relationship both a team and a single primary clinician were used. In order to give the critical ingredient, a relationship, its appropriate significance, the CIDP developed a therapeutic relationship scale that could be rated reliably, differentiate high-and low-risk groups, and correlate with other measures of caregiver functioning (Greenspan and Wieder, 1983) (tables 2–10, 2–11, 2–12, 2–13).

Agencies were alerted to send their "most difficult and challenging" cases and the CIDP became known as the group that would "go anywhere to see anyone." Calls were received from prenatal clinics regarding mothers who had missed appointments, who appeared confused and who were not adequately following medical guidance. Calls also were received from protective service case workers. The calls usually involved a family in which the mother was pregnant and evidencing a lack of interest in her yet unborn new baby and having a history of neglect of older children.

The key to recruiting and forming an alliance with these families was the staff's ability to deal with patterns of avoidance, rejection, anger, illogical and antisocial behavior, and substance abuse. Experienced clinicians were selected because of their ability not to be frightened by such behavior. For example, in the early phases of the work, it might be necessary for the primary clinician to make five or six home visits. These visits would include knocking on the door, hearing a very suspicious participant behind the door walking around, making a few comments through the door, not getting an answer, and returning three days later. This pattern would continue until the individual on the other side of the door would feel comfortable enough to open the door to let in the primary clinician. This pattern might repeat itself intermittently for a number of months.

Even more difficult were participants who eagerly embraced the offering of services and who then would flee by missing three or four appointments, without calling or returning telephone calls. The continual offering of an interested ear would in most cases eventually meet with success. Sometimes it could take a year, however, before a constant pattern of relatedness would evolve. The tendency to say, "They're not interested in help," "They told us they don't want us," "They're not motivated," "We're being a burden to them," "We're making them more crazy," and so forth was one of the key challenges the CIDP staff had to overcome.

Organizing to respond to a family's concrete needs and offering the family a human relationship, however, are not enough. That human relationship must be able to help the parents understand some of their maladaptive coping strategies and teach them how to deal with their own primary needs and those of their infant. In addition, special clinical techniques and patterns of care (Greenspan, 1981) to reverse maladaptive developmental patterns in the areas of affect and social interaction, sensorimotor development, and cognition must be available at the appropriate time.

For example, a baby with a tactile hypersensitivity and a hyperactive, suspi-

Table 2–10
Dimensions of the Therapeutic Relationship

Steps in the Therapeutic Process		
Regularity and Stability	*Attachment*	*Process*
1. Willingness to meet with an interviewer or therapist to convey concrete concerns or hear about services.	1. Interest in having concrete needs met that can be provided by anyone (e.g., food, transportation, etc.).	1. Preliminary communication, including verbal support and information gathering.
2. Willingness to schedule meetings again.	2. Emotional interest in the person of the therapist (e.g., conveys pleasure or anger when they meet).	2. Ability to observe and report single behaviors or action patterns.
3. Meeting according to some predictable pattern.	3. Communicates purposefully in attempts to deal with problems.	3. Focuses on relationships involved in the behavior-action pattern.
4. Meeting regularly with occasional disruptions.	4. Tolerates discomfort or scary emotions.	4. Self-observing function in relationship to feelings.
5. Meeting regularly with no disruptions.	5. Feels "known" or accepted in positive and negative aspects.	5. Self-observing function in relationship to complex and interactive feeling states.
		6. Self-observing function for thematic and affective-elaboration.
		7. Makes connections between the key relationships in life including the therapeutic relationship.
		8. Identification of patterns in current, therapeutic, and historical relationships to work through problems and facilitate new growth.
		9. Consolidation of new patterns and levels of satisfaction and preparing to separate from the therapeutic relationship.
		10. Full consolidation of gains in the context of separating and experiencing a full sense of loss and mourning.

Table 2–11
Reliabilities for Ratings of the Therapeutic Relationship Dimensions at Entry
Intraclass Correlations, N = 30

Regularity and stability	0.80
Attachment and affective involvement	0.80
Process level	0.84
Prediction to regularity and stability	0.84
Prediction to attachment	0.64
Prediction to process level	0.79

Table 2–12
Discrimination of Risk Level (Low vs. High) with 20 Ratings of the Therapeutic Relationship Dimensions at Entry
Multiple Analysis of Variance Univariate F-Tests with 1.56 df

	F	Probability of F If No Difference[a]
Regularity and stability	27.19	0.000
Attachment	27.0	0.000
Process level	33.94	0.000
Prediction to regularity	21.65	0.000
Prediction to attachment	21.05	0.000
Prediction to process level	27.95	0.000

[a]This would have the same meaning as the 0.001 level.

cious mother who tended to deal with stress by hyperstimulating her baby would require an approach in which the baby was provided with habituation and sensory integration approaches to overcome his or her special sensitivity. The mother was simultaneously helped to overcome her own tendency to undermine the baby's development.

Moreover, the intervention must occur over a sufficiently long period to allow the family's own strengths to take over and sustain it—in other words, not crisis intervention over a few months, but an approach that will be available to the families for several years. After working with many of these families for some two years, the mother's capacity to nurture and facilitate the development of a new baby is significantly more advanced than when she entered the program

Table 2–13
Therapeutic Relationship Scales: Mean, Standard Deviation, and Range at Entry
N = 61

| | Low-Risk Group A | | | High-Risk Groups | | | | | | ANOVA with 2.55 df F^a |
| | | | | B | | | C | | | |
	Mean	SD	Range	Mean	SD	Range	Mean	SD	Range	
Regularity	72.25[b]	9.33	84.50	46.81	14.44	66.14	50.40	16.92	22.74	11.57
Attachment	65.25	6.15	76.54	44.31	13.41	70.22	44.56	13.71	63.21	13.18
Process Level	62.25	7.92	84.46	42.69	12.44	67.20	38.30	14.83	63.16	14.60
Predictions to:										
Regularity	74.33	4.07	87.70	57.43	12.31	79.14	54.73	15.23	85.65	10.15
Attachment	73.08	8.82	83.68	54.81	10.07	73.29	55.17	15.46	83.65	9.15
Process Level	77.00	7.15	85.65	57.94	12.87	79.33	53.73	16.44	85.65	11.89

[a] All were significant at 0.004 or below.
[b] Ratings were visual analog scales utilizing an unbroken line of 100 mm. Scores indicate number of millimeters marked at rating.

pregnant with an earlier child (S. Wieder and S.I. Greenspan, in preparation). In other words, when the helping relationship is offered over a period of time, the frequently observed trend of multiproblem families to deteriorate further upon the birth of each subsequent baby (a trend that often starts when the parents are still teenagers) begins to be reversed.

Another way to visualize the model discussed above is from a developmental perspective. The tasks at each stage of development (Greenspan, 1981) imply that certain components of the service system must be available to assure appropriate support for the functions of that stage. One might visualize preventive service approaches as a pyramid. Figure 2–5 portrays the three levels of care in the service pyramid. It emphasizes that specialized services, be they physical or occupational therapy, psychological counseling or parent-infant interactional guidance, must be based on a foundation that deals with concrete survival issues and the formation of a regular, stable working relationship. This service pyramid, however, must contain ingredients which are sensitive to the changing developmental needs of infants and families. There are different service patterns within the pyramid for each stage of development.

In most of the families maladaptive trends were observed. By carefully pinpointing the area in which a child's development first begins to go awry and by using organized and comprehensive clinical techniques and service system approaches, the families often become capable of more adaptive patterns. For example, the CIDP found significant differences in a variety of measures of maternal functioning prior to and after two years in the program and in the functioning of children in such basic areas as the ability to experience pleasure, deal with impulses, and form relationships.

Many parents in the program began their childrearing as teenagers and have commonly experienced further deterioration in their own functioning and that of their infants with each subsequent birth. In most instances, however, even when a woman has had four or more children this pattern of deterioration reversed itself by means of appropriate clinical techniques and services. In a number of multi-risk-factor families, after they enter the program, a gradual improvement takes place in the mother and a modest but positive change in the first baby born thereafter. Then, if the family remains in the program and a second baby is born, the change in the family is more dramatic and is reflected in the new baby's more optimal development from the beginning.

For example, Mrs. E. was pregnant when she came to our attention. At first glance she appeared to the team social worker to be "beyond help" after she was found sleeping on the street. All her children had been removed from her care by the County Department of Protective Services because of abuse and neglect. Mrs. E. appeared unable to think except in concrete terms, was at times psychotic, could not communicate her thoughts and plans, and seemingly lived by impulse and her talent for survival. Shortly before the birth of her child a few months later, however, she entered the program, prompted by extensive outreach efforts.

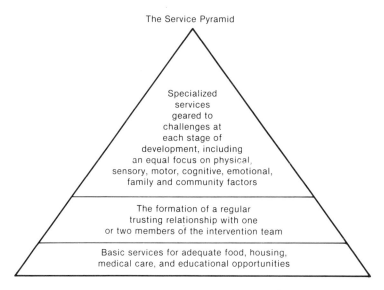

Figure 2–5. The Service Pyramid

All the collective efforts to induce Mrs. E. to use a support structure (for example, to obtain housing, food, or clothing) failed. Nevertheless, subsequently, of her own accord, she requested foster care for the new infant. Mrs. E. maintained contact with this child and made a great deal of progress in treatment over a two-year period. When she became pregnant again, not only could she care for the newest baby but she was able to work and support an apartment. Thus far, with therapeutic support, she has nurtured a competent 11 month old and also has become contructively involved with her older children.

Infants in the intensive intervention group also showed a capacity to recover from early perinatal stress or developmental deviations (Hofheimer et al., 1984). Even when an infant's development had deteriorated during the first three months of life (as evidenced by lack of human attachment, chronic gaze aversion, muscle rigidity, and affect lability), appropriate interventions were often associated with adaptive homeostatic and attachment capacities within one to four months (Greenspan, 1981, 1984; Wieder and Greenspan, 1984). The process of therapeutic work involved first figuring out the types of experiences that were aversive and satisfying for the infant and the underlying feelings of the parents that might be interfering with their providing comforting and pleasurable interactions. Often it was then possible to help a family deal with their special individual differences where the infant had unique differences such as auditory or tactile sensitivities or extreme state or mood lability or where there was severe psychopathology or patterns of rejection or overstimulation in the parents. The clinical work was challenging, and often the staff found the most challenging cases the most rewarding.

Summary and Conclusions

While a great deal of progress has been made, there are also enormous challenges ahead. It has been demonstrated that preventive interventions are generally efficacious in spite of the narrow focus of most programs. Yet little is known about the degree to which preventive interventions hold up over time and the efficacy of specific types of interventions for specific types of problems. Furthermore, models which demonstrate how to work with multiple aspects of development, that is, physical, cognitive, emotional, and social and familial, are few and far between. The application of such models to a range of common challenges in primary care settings for infants, children, and their families including motor and language delays, high-risk parenting situations, and emotional-social disorders have not been implemented and evaluated with sufficient rigor.

In addition, while the normative developmental landmarks have been well delineated, studies documenting disturbed patterns in development have been relatively scarce. Such basic questions as the relative contributions of fine and gross motor delays to emotional problems or the contributions of difficulties in sensory processing to emotional, social, and intellectual difficulties have not been well studied. The demarcation of a developmental timetable involving cognitive, emotional, and social functioning now permits the study in greater detail of the factors that determine poor versus optimal developmental outcomes in both short- and long-term studies. In addition, the ability to follow development from each phase to the next will permit short-term studies to have more meaning for longer term ones.

It is time to undertake new programs of research that could simultaneously look at the efficacy of comprehensive approaches to preventive intervention and offer the prospect of further understanding of the pathogensis of psychomotor, cognitive, and emotional difficulties. Obviously the latter would help fine-tune the former. While it may be thought that one should fully understand pathogenesis before one embarks on intervention, the history of medicine, in fact, is to offer the best state of the art available and through clinical programs of research refine diagnostic and intervention strategies.

Therefore, it is suggested that research programs begin to look at various groups of at-risk or developmentally disordered infants and families, especially those seen in primary health care settings. These would include infants with motor, sensory, sensorimotor, cognitive, emotional, and social delays, infants in at-risk families or other at-risk environmental settings, infants experiencing combinations of the above, and infants with chronic physical illness and low-birth-weight or genetic risk for emotional or cognitive disorders (offspring of schizophrenics, manic-depressives, learning-disordered parents, and parents with unique sensitivities to environmental stress).

The assessments of these populations should be so designed to further understand the pathogenesis of disturbed development. Of particular interest is the relationship between biological, constitutional, maturational, and experiential-environmental factors. Studies might include:

The role of irregularities in sensory processing in early psychophysiologic regulation on cognitive and psychosocial delays.

The role of the infant's emotional status and interactive patterns (with caregivers) on overall developmental progress.

The role of parental personality functioning and family patterns on the infant's developmental progress.

The role of cumulative risk on developmental outcome.

The role of specific, genetic-biologic risks in the context of different interactive and family patterns (including sensory and motor lags or irregularities, offspring of schizophrenics and multirisk families, offspring of parents with manic-depressive illness, families with history of learning difficulties, as well families especially sensitive to environmental stresses).

Another major challenge is the further development of clinical tools and training approaches. While there are a number of research instruments that have been developed to assess various aspects of cognition and affect, there are relatively few clinical tools that can be used in primary care settings to assess psychosocial as well as intellectual development and disturbance.

The types of studies suggested will permit exploration of specific hypotheses. It also will, however, facilitate within each of these studies exploratory hypothesis-generating investigations that are necessary to define individual differences in patterns of sensory processing, fine and gross motopatterns, social interactions, and family functioning that contribute to various types of difficulties. These studies are essential for improving the specificity of diagnostic and preventive intervention strategies.

References

Ainsworth, M., Bell, S.M., and Stayton, D.: Infant-mother attachment and social development: socialization as a product of reciprocal responsiveness to signals. In Richards, M. (ed.): *The Integration of the Child Into a Social World*. Cambridge, Cambridge University Press, 1974.

Bakwin, H.: Loneliness in infants. *Am. J. Dis. Child. 63*:30, 1942.

Bell, S.: The development of the concept of object as related to infant-mother attachment. *Child Dev. 41*:219, 1970.

Bergman, P., and Escalona, S.: Unusual sensitivities in very young children. *Psychoanal. Study Child 3–4*:333, 1949.

Bowlby, J.: *Maternal Care and Mental Health*. WHO Monograph No. 2. Geneva, World Health Organization, 1951.

Bowlby, J.: *Attachment and Loss*. New York, Basic Books, 1969.

Brazelton, T.B., Koslowski, B., and Main, M.: The origins of reciprocity: the early mother-infant interaction. In Lewis, M. and Rosenblum, L. (eds.): *The Effect of the Infant on Its Care Giver*. New York, Wiley, 1974.

Burlingham, D., and Freud, A.: *Young Children in Wartime*. London, Allen and Unwin, 1942.

Cameron, H.C.: *The Nervous Child*. London, Oxford Medical Publications, 1919.

Charlesworth, W.R.: The role of surprise in cognitive development. In Elkind, E., and Flavell, J.H. (eds.): *Studies in Cognitive Development: Essays in Honor of Jean Piaget*. London, Oxford University Press, 1969.

Cravioto, J., and DeLicardie, E.: Environmental correlates of severe clinical malnutrition and language development in survivors from kwashiorkor or marasmus. In *Nutrition, the Nervous System and Behavior*. Publ. No. 251. Washington, D.C., PAHO, 1973.

Ekman, P.: Universals and cultural differences in facial expressions of emotion. In *Nebraska Symposium on Motivation*. Lincoln, University of Nebraska Press, 1972.

Emde, R.N., Gaensbauer, T.J., and Harmon, R.J.: Emotional expression in infancy: a biobehavioral study. In *Psychological Issues*. Monograph No. 37. New York, International Universities Press, 1976.

Escalona, S.K.: *The Roots of Individuality*. Chicago, Aldine, 1968.

Fraiberg, S.H.: *The Magic Years: Understanding and Handling the Problem of Early Childhood*. New York, Scribner, 1965.

Freud, S.: Formulation on the two principles of mental functioning (1911). In *Standard Edition*, Vol. 12. London, Hogarth Press, 1958.

Gewirtz, J.L.: A learning analysis of the effects of normal stimulation, privation and deprivation on the acquisition of social motivation and attachment. In Foss, B.M. (ed.): *Determinants of Infant Behavior*, Vol. 1. London, Methuen, 1961.

Gewirtz, J.L.: The course of infant smiling in four child-rearing environments in Israel. In Foss, B.M. (ed.): *Determinants of the Infant Behavior*, Vol. 3. London, Methuen, 1965.

Gerwitz, J.L.: Levels of conceptual analysis in environment-infant interaction research. *Merill-Palmer Q.* 15:9, 1969.

Gouin-Decarie, T.: *Intelligence and Affectivity in Early Childhood: An Experimental Study of Jean Piaget's Object Concept and Object Relations*. New York, International Universities Press, 1965.

Greenspan, S.I.: Intelligence and adaption: an integration of psychoanalytic and Piagetian developmental psychology. In *Psychological Issues*. Monograph 47–48. New York, International Universities Press, 1979.

Greenspan, S.I.: Psychopathology and adaption in infancy and early childhood: principles of clinical diagnosis and preventive intervention. In *Clinical Infant Reports*, No. 1. New York, International Universities Press, 1981.

Greenspan, S.I.: A model for comprehensive preventive intervention services for infants, young children and their families. In Greenspan, S.I., Wieder, S., Lieberman, A.F., Nover, R.A., Lourie, R.S., and Robinson, M. (eds.) *Infants in Multi-Risk Families;*

Case Studies of Preventive Intervention. Clinical Infant Reports No. 3. New York, International Universities Press, 1984.

Greenspan, S.I., and Greenspan, N.T.: *First Feelings: Milestones in the Emotional Development of the Infant and Young Child.* New York, Viking Press (in press).

Greenspan, S.I., and Lieberman, A.F.: Infants, mothers and their interactions: a quantitative clinical approach to developmental assessment. In Greenspan, S.I., and Pollock, G.H. (eds.): *The Course of Life: Psychoanalytic Contributions Toward Understanding Personality Development.* Vol. 1. *Infancy and Early Childhood.* DHHS Publ. No. [ADM] 80–786. Washington, D.C., Government Printing Office, 1980.

Greenspan, S.I., and Lourie, R.S.: Developmental structuralist approach to the classification of adaptive and pathologic personality organization: application to infancy and early childhood. *Am. J. Psychiatry* 138:6, 1981.

Greenspan, S.I., Lourie, R.S., and Nover, R.A.: A developmental approach to the approach to the classification of psychopathology in infancy and early childhood. In Noshpitz, J. (ed.): *The Basic Handbook of Child Psychiatry,* Vol. 2. New York, Basic Books, 1979.

Greenspan, S.I., and Wieder, S.I.: Dimensions and levels of the therapeutic process. *Psychotherapy* 21 (1), 1984.

Hartmann, H.: *Ego Psychology and the Problem of Adaptation.* New York, International Universities Press, 1939.

Hofheimer, J.A., Strauss, M.E., Poisson, S.S., and Greenspan, S.I.: *The Reliability, Validity and Generalizability of Assessments of Transactions between Infants and Their Caregivers: A Multicenter Design.* Working paper, Clinical Infant Development Program. NIMH, 1981.

Hofheimer, J.A., Lieberman, A.F., Strauss, M.E., and Greenspan, S.I.: Short term temporal stability of mother-infant interactions in the first year of life. Unpublished paper, 1984.

Hunt, J.M.: Infants in an orphanage. *J. Abnor. Soc. Psychol.* 36:338, 1941.

Izard, C.: On the development of emotions and emotion-cognition relationships in infancy. In Lewis, M., and Rosenblum, L. (eds.): *The Development of Affect.* New York, Plenum, 1978.

Klaus, M., and Kennell, J.H.: *Maternal-Infant Bonding: The Impact of Early Separation or Loss on Family Development.* St. Louis, Mosby, 1976.

Lipsitt, L.: Learning processes of newborns. *Merrill-Palmer Q.* 12:45, 1966.

Lourie, R.S.: The first three years of life: an overview of a new frontier for psychiatry. *Am. J. Psychiatry* 127:1457, 1971.

Lowrey, L.G.: Personality distortion and early institutional care, *Am. J. Ortho.* 10:546, 1940.

Mahler, M.S., Pine, F., and Bergman, A.: *The Psychological Birth of the Human Infant.* New York, Basic, 1975.

Meltzoff, A.N., and Moore, K.M.: Imitation of facial and manual gestures by human neonates. *Science* 198:75, 1977.

Murphy, L.B., and Moriarty, A.E.: *Vulnerability, Coping, and Growth.* New Haven, Yale University Press, 1976.

Olds, D.: The prenatal/early infancy project: an ecological approach to prevention of developmental disabilities. In Belsky, J. (ed.): *In the Beginning.* New York, Columbia University Press, 1982.

Olds, D.L., Henderson, C.R., Tatelbaum, R., and Chamberlin, R.: *Improving Maternal Health Habits, Obstetrical Health, and Fetal Growth in High Risk Populations: Results of a Field Experiment of Nurse Home-Visitation.* Rochester, University of Rochester, Department of Pediatrics, 1984.

Olds, D.L., Henderson, C.R., Chamberlin, R., and Tatelbaum, R.: *The Prevention of Child Abuse and Neglect in a High-Risk Population: Results of a Field Experiment of Nurse Home-Visitation.* Rochester, University of Rochester, Department of Pediatrics, 1984.

Piaget, J.: *Structuralism* (1968). New York: Basic Books, 1970.

Piaget, J.: (1962). The stages of the intellectual development of the child. In Harrison, S.I., and McDermott, J.F. (eds.): *Childhood Psychopathology.* New York, International Universitites Press, 1972.

Poisson, S.S., Hofheimer, J.A., Strauss, M.E., and Greenspan, S.I.: Inter-observer agreement and reliability assessments of the GLOS measures of caregiver infant interaction, NIMH. Unpublished manuscript, 1983.

Poisson, S.S., Lieberman, A.F., and Greenspan, S.I.: Training manual for the Greenspan-Lieberman Observation System (GLOS), NIMH. Unpublished manuscript, 1981.

Powell, M.B., and Monahan, J.: Reaching the rejects through multifamily group therapy. *Int. J. Psychother. 19*:35–43, 1969.

Provence, S. (ed.): *Infants and Parents: Clinical Case Reports.* Clinical Infant Reports No. 2. New York, International Universities Press, 1983.

Provence, S., and Naylor, A.: Working with disadvantaged parents and their children. In *Scientific and Practie Issues.* Yale University Press, 1983.

Rachford, B.K.: *Neurotic Disorders of Childhood.* New York, E.B. Treat and Co., 1905.

Rheingold, H.: The development of social behavior in the human infant. *Monogr. Soc. Res. Child Dev. 31*:1, 1966.

Rheingold, H.: Infancy. In: Sills, D. (ed.) *International Encyclopedia of the Social Sciences.* New York, MacMillan, 1969.

Sameroff, A.J., and Seifer, R.: Paper presented at Society for Research in Child Development meeting, April 1983.

Sameroff, A.J., Seifer, R., and Zax, M.: *Mono. Soc. Res. Child Dev. 47* (serial No. 199), 1982.

Sameroff, A.J., Seifer, R., Baracas, R., Greenspan, S.: I.Q. scores of 4-year-old children reduced by environmental risk factors. *Science* (in press).

Sander, L.: Issues in early mother-child interaction. *J. Am. Acad. Child Psychiatry 1*:141, 1962.

Seitz, V., Rosenbaum, L.K., and Apfel, N.H.: Day care as family intervention. Paper presented at the biennial meeting of the Society for Research in Child Development, Detroit, 1983.

Spitz, R.A.: *The First Year of Life.* New York, International Universities Press, 1965.

Spitz, R.A., Hospitalism. *Psychoanal. Stud. Child. 1*:53, 1945.

Spitz, R.A., Emde, R., Metcalf, D.: Further prototypes of ego formation. *Psychoanal. Study Child 25*:417, 1970.

Sroufe, L., and Waters, E.: Attachment as an organizational construct. *Child Dev. 48*:1184, 1977.

Sroufe, L., Waters, E., and Matas, L.: Contextual determinants of infant affective response. In Lewis, M., and Rosenblum, L. (eds.): *The Origins of Fear.* New York, Wiley, 1974.

Stern, D.: Mother and infant at play: the dyadic interaction involving facial, vocal, and gaze behaviors. In Lewis, M., and Rosenblum, L. (eds.): *The Effect of the Infant on Its Caregiver.* New York, Wiley, 1974a.

Stern, D.: The goal and structure of mother-infant play. *J. Am. Acad. Child Psychiatry* 13:402, 1974b.

Stern, D.: *The First Relationship: Infant and Mother.* Cambridge. Harvard University Press, 1977.

Tennes, K., Emde, R., Kisley, A., and Metcalf, D.: The stimulus barrier in early infancy: an exploration of some formulations of John Benjamin. In Holt, R., and Peterfreund, E. (eds.): *Psychoanalysis and Contemporary Science.* Vol. 1. New York, Macmillan, 1972.

Thomas, A., Chess, S., and Birch, H.G.: *Temperament and Behavior Disorders in Children.* New York, New York University Press, 1968.

Tomkins, S. *Affect, Imagery, Consciousness.* Vols. 1 and 2. New York, Springer, 1962, 1963.

Weikart, D.P., Bond, J.T., and McNeir, J.: *The Ypsilanti Perry Preschool Project: Preschool Years and Longitudinal Results.* Monograph No. 3 of the High/Scope Educational Research Foundation. Ypsilanti, Mich.: High/Scope Press, 1978.

Weikart, D.P., Epstein, A.S., Schweinhart, L., and Bond, J.T.: *The Ypsilanti Preschool Curriculum Demonstration Project.* Monograph No. 4 of the High/Scope Educational Research Foundation. Ypsilanti, Mich.: High/Scope Press.

Werner, H., and Kaplan, B.: *Symbol Formation.* New York, Wiley, 1963.

Werner, H., and Kaplan, B.: The stages of the intellectual development of the child. In Harrison, S., and McDermott, J. (eds.): *Childhood Psychopathology.* New York, International Universities Press, 1972.

White, K.R., and Casto, G.: An integrative review of early intervention with at-risk children: implications for the handicapped. In *Analysis and Intervention in Developmental Disabilities,* 1984.

White, K.R., Casto, G., and Mastropieri, M.: *A Meta-analysis of the Efficacy of Early Intervention with the Handicapped and At-risk Child.* Logan, Utah, Early Intervention Research Institute, 1983.

Wieder, S., and Greenspan, S.I.: Effects of interventions with multi-risk families. In Greenspan, S.I., Wieder, S., Lieberman, A.F., Nover, R.A., Lourie, R.S., and Robinson, M. (eds.): *Infants in Multi-Risk Families: Case Studies of Preventive Intervention.* Clinical Infant Reports No. 3. New York, International Universities Press, 1984.

Wieder, S., Jasnow, M., Greenspan, S.I., and Strauss, M.: Identifying the multi-risk family prenatally: antecedent psychosocial factors and infant developmental trends. *Infant Mental Health J.* 4(3), 1984.

Williams, D., Nover, R.A., Castellan, J.M., Greenspan, S.I., and Lieberman, A.L.: An infant, family and the service system. In Greenspan, S. et al. (eds.): *Infants in Multi-Risk Families; Case Studies of Preventive Intervention.* Clinical Infant Reports No. 3. New York, International Universities Press, 1984.

Winnicott, D.W.: *Clinical Notes on Disorders of Childhood.* London, Heineman, 1931.

3

Developmental Framework of Infants as an Opportunity for Early Intervention for Pediatricians

T. Berry Brazelton

New parents today are beseiged by overwhelming cultural pressures—the breakdown of the family (58% of children in the United States live in a single-parent family for a significant part of their lives), rapidly changing sex roles, ecological misuse, the threat of nuclear warfare, the disillusionment of youth, and increasing technological discoveries without concomitant humanistic advances. All these confuse caring parents at a time when they are making important decisions about the future of a small child, for these changes signify a kind of breakdown in cultural expectations that leaves them high and dry about the futures of their new babies. And most seriously, there are no successful backups for new, inexperienced parents to replace the loss of the extended family. Not only is the extended family likely to be at a distance physically, but our generation gap has contributed to a kind of psychological distance between generations that leaves new parents without clear direction around a crisis like a new baby. Most parents have had no experience in observing or participating in childrearing before they come to their own. All of the animal literature points to the importance of prior experience (observational as well as behavioral) in fitting an inexperienced mother for her new role (Suomi and Harlow, 1978).

In pediatrics, we are offered a choice today between two roles, that of the specialist who deals with physical diseases of infancy and childhood and that of a physician who is interested in and responsible for the child's entire well-being. Since the latter role implies a familiarity with the child's environment, and participation with the parents in rendering it as favorable as possible to his or her well-being, many pediatricians in practice are pressed into a role equivalent to the old family doctor. This is a dual role because we have an opportunity to be the physician to the child's physical growth, development, and aberrations, and to his emotional health. We have an opportunity to participate in the ongoing development of an immature organism at a time when support and guidance may have real potential for influencing the outcome of this development.

I find that over 85 percent of my time in a 60- to 70-hour week is made up of advice, guidance, and counseling about psychological or development problems; only 10 to 15 percent is spent in straight somatic examination and advice. This 15 percent is fascinating and vital, but it is facilitated by antibiotics, good clinical facilities, and referrals to experts in related fields. It leaves 85 percent of the time free to practice what I consider the art of medicine. A case of colic in an infant is far more demanding of a pediatrician's resources nowadays than is a hearty strep throat, and more exciting to control if it is approached as a psychosomatic disease.

The consequences of intrauterine conditions such as malnutrition (Cravioto, DeLicardie, and Birch, 1966), drug ingestion, infection, and toxemia, which may be the result of inadequate prenatal supervision, point to another kind of responsibility to which physicians concerned with the futures of children are still responding ineffectively (Brazelton, 1968). Our attempts to reach out to and maintain relationships with pregnant women are grossly inadequate. For the most part, we stick to an antiquated medical model of waiting for the pregnant patient to present herself for care and an expectancy that she will follow the regimen we offer her from our rather exalted and dictatorial position as medical advisor (Brazelton, 1983). We have fooled ourselves into believing that this approach has served a purpose for a large segment of the population and that it can and should work for all of it, if they are deserving, as evidenced by their motivation. In the model used by most prenatal clinics, the real needs of potential mothers for individualized support and understanding are rarely met. The regimens offered are not understood by the target population, nor are they appropriate to the conditions of most of the population they serve. More important, this approach ignores some of the obvious deterrents to seeking prenatal care that exist in the very populations we need to reach: those whose fetuses are at highest risk. We need to develop a model for reaching people at critical times (figure 3–1).

Prenatal Visit

Preparing to become a parent forces a kind of self-evaluation that can be stressful and even painful. A marriage or a couple's relationship may have been settled, but the expectation for a new kind of giving that will be required of a mother and father is uncovered during pregnancy. I believe that the anxiety and tension, which seem at an almost pathologic level in pregnancy, serve a major purpose: that of unwiring the old set of connections (the locked-in memories of relationships with parents and life experiences) and freeing up a couple's coping or stress mechanisms for a new, fresh, more flexible adjustment to the new baby. The ambivalence seen during pregnancy (morning sickness, overeating, and all sorts of symptoms finally underlying the anxiety about "Have I damaged my baby?") is also preparation for the demands of parenthood. The assessment of "Will I be a good enough parent?" and "I don't want to reproduce the old pattern of my parents" is preparation for trying to render old patterns more flexible. Even the

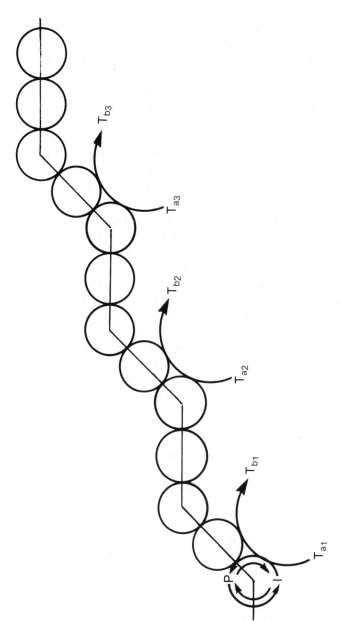

Figure 3–1. Touchpoints for Intervention

fantasy of what they would do with an impaired infant serves the purpose of preparing young parents for the eventuality of such an infant. We see many of the negative or ambivalent feelings in young parents as an asset. Can they be put to more positive use by any maneuvers on our part as professionals?

We are now becoming aware of the special vacuums we have created in our culture: (1) the institutionalization of pregnancy and delivery, treating the process as though it were a disease and forcing young parents to submit to a kind of depersonalization, a submission to authority that is both insensitive and oriented toward illness, not the coping strengths that are and should be a primary concern to prospective parents: (2) separation of a young woman and her mate at the time of delivery, forcing them into a system that says, "You're inadequate, you're helpless," and (to the man) "Stay away, you're dirty." Its deeper significance is ignored in our present insensitive, lumbering medical system; (3) the relative lack of support for a new, anxious, caring parent; (4) the thinking of the 1940s that the environment shapes the child and that anything that goes wrong is the parents' fault. This is coupled with a deluge of literature about child rearing that implies that there is a perfect way to rear a baby. If parents do not conform to the image of perfection that is being created, they inevitably feel inadequate and helpless; (5) the reinforcement of vulnerability by a real lack of experience with what it means to be a parent and what the ingredients of early child care might be, as well as by inadequate knowledge of early development of children. In our families, a young person is indeed fortunate (and unusual) if he or she has participated in the care of younger siblings. At the onset of pregnancy, some young people have literally never held a baby or seen one diapered. The incidence of success in breastfeeding in women is tripled if their own mothers have nursed and they have witnessed nursing of younger siblings (Newton and Newton, 1967).

I have been interested in the early parent-infant interaction as an example of a period when the pediatrician can be of major importance in diagnosis, support, and intervention in preventing future psychopathology. A young woman comes into mothering based on her genetic endowment, her past experiences with her own mothering, and the life circumstances that put pressures on her at the time of delivery. But the kind of infant she produces essentially shapes her particular energy to respond. If the baby is active and demanding, she is pushed to respond very differently from the way she might if the infant were quiet and sensitive. In the white, affluent, intellectual middle class with whom I practice, I see mothers who can adjust to one kind of infant but not to another. If positive interaction between mother and child is as fragile as this in the middle class, I wonder how it can develop in more pressured circumstances.

As the potential for early intervention increases, it becomes increasingly important that we be able to evaluate infants at risk as early as possible, with an eye to more sophisticated preventive and therapeutic approaches. Early intervention may prevent a compounding of problems that occurs all too easily when the environment cannot adjust appropriately to the infant. Premature and minimally brain-damaged infants seem to be less able to compensate in disorganized, deprived environments than well-equipped neonates, and their problems of organization in development are compounded early (Greenberg, 1971). Quiet, nondemanding infants do not elicit necessary mothering from already overstressed parents and are selected by their neonatal behavior for kwashiokor and marasmus in poverty-ridden cultures such as are found in Guatemala and Mexico (Cravioto et. al., 1966; Klein, Habicht, and Yarbrough, 1971). Hyperkinetic, hypersensitive neonates may press a mother and father into a kind of depression that produces child-rearing responses that reinforce the problems of the child, so that he or she grows up in an overactive, hostile environment (Heider, 1966). Parents of children admitted to the ward of the Children's Hospital in Boston for clinical syndromes such as failure to thrive, child abuse, repeated accidents and poisonings, and infantile autism are often successful parents of other children. By history they associate their failure with the one child to an inability to "understand" him or her from the neonatal period on, and they claim difference from the other children in his or her earliest reactions to them. If we are to improve the outcome for such children, assessment of the risk in early infancy could mobilize preventive efforts and programs for intervention before the neonate's problems are compounded by an environment that cannot understand him or her without such help.

Concentration on the parents—understanding and accepting their personalities, their relationships with the child, their feelings and fears, and their needs in relation to the child—is of first importance in setting up goals for the child. In practice, it has become my routine to concentrate initially on the mother and father, with as much understanding and acceptance of their parenting as possible, and to endeavor to foster a positive working relationship with them.

The value of a prenatal visit with prospective parents cannot be underestimated (Brazelton, 1968; Senn, 1947; Wessel, 1963).

In very little time, a pediatrician can establish a working knowledge and a healthy, reliant relationship with a young couple. Obstetricians are understandably reluctant to share their relationship with patients during pregnancy, but it is to the advantage of the prospective parents, as well as to their pediatrician-to-be, that a relationship be established before the baby comes and the working pressures of parenthood set in.

When a mother-to-be calls me, I urge her to come in for a brief interview at a time when her husband also can come. A prospective father usually is eager to come, and will participate with me in taking care of the child much more readily after he has met me. This invitation is so unexpected and so needed at this turbulent time that he feels I am his as well as his wife's ally.

The interview lasts ten to twenty minutes (Brazelton, 1975); in addition to taking a routine family history and a history of the pregnancy, I ask the mother a few open-ended questions, for example, "How are you?" "Do you expect to deliver with or without anesthesia?" "How do you plan to feed your baby?" "Do you think it's a girl or a boy?" It always surprises and gratifies me that parents will indeed use these questions as easy springboards to express wishes, fears, and anxieties about what kind of parents they will be. We can form an alliance at this crucial time, which makes a great difference when I see their new infant in the hospital. We are already a team.

I always direct one question to the father, to include him more actively: "Do you plan to have him circumcised if he's a boy?" This often causes the father to start, blush, turn to his wife, then draw himself up and begin to participate in our team. The confession of his anxiety and his wishes to be an adequate father to his new baby, whatever the sex, comes rushing forth. As a result of his one pre-natal visit, 80 percent of the fathers come in at least four times during the first year for their baby's routine visits. The value of having included the father early is inestimable to me when an illness or a psychological problem arises in the later rearing of the child. Additionally, I know a good deal more about the family's dynamics from having had both parents' participation in the early well-baby visits, when attitudes of child rearing can be shaped by pediatricians.

Neonatal Period

The neonatal period is the second opportunity in the new family's adjustment for the pediatrician to become involved. I spend thirty minutes at most with a new patient and see new mothers in the hospital two or three times totaling no more than three-quarters of an hour. This initial time is the best investment either of us makes in the future of our relationship. Bronfenbrenner (1974) points to the isolation of the young. Unless we can offer new parents an opportunity to have their own dependent needs met, we cannot expect that they will do well by the next generation.

I have been struck by the tremendous energy available in young parents for early attachment to their neonates. The current efforts of such pediatricians as Klaus and Kennell (1970) to capture this energy for premature and other infants at high risk are founded on excellent research and on our increasing awareness that risk is enhanced when new parents do not feel at ease with their difficult infants. It is a time when medical supervision might help them to understand their roles in nurturing these babies during prolonged recovery periods.

The Neonatal Behavioral Assessment Scale (Brazelton, 1973) was originally created to evaluate and highlight a neonate's capacities to respond to his or her environment. The infant's ability to shut out the disturbing aspects of the new environment is coupled with marvelous capacities to choose, become alert to, and respond to objects and caretakers. The scale documents all the state changes and the autonomic and affective changes that accompany response to a caregiver and reflects the kind of soft signs to which pediatricians have always responded as they routinely examine neonates. These are the same soft signs on which we rely to make an unspoken prediction.

This examination couches behavioral tests of such important central nervous system mechanisms as (1) habituation, or the neonate's capacity to shut out disturbing or overwhelming stimuli, (2) choices in attention to various objects or human stimuli (a neonate shows clear preferences for female voices and for human visual stimuli), and (3) control of his or her state in order to attend to information from the environment (the effort to complete a hand-to-mouth cycle in order to attend to objects and people) (figure 3–2). These are all evident in the neonate, even the premature infant, and seem to be more predictive of central nervous system intactness than are reflex responses (Tronick and Brazelton, 1975). The amazing capacities for recovery even from CNS insults in an immature system are as follows:

vicarious functioning
equipotentiality of redundant pathways
behavioral substitution
regrowth and supersensitivity
diaschisis
recovery from trauma

It is critical that we provide appropriate experiences for an immature infant, for a hypersensitive infant, or an infant recovering from such a CNS insult. These are critical to his or her recover.

We can predict whether the normal baby will be easy or difficult to care for, whether he or she has striking individual assets or deficits, and even such important behaviors as whether the infant will eat and sleep well or cry excessively or whether he or she will be comforted easily and be responsive to the parents. My most valuable act as a pediatrician in the neonatal period has been my attempt to utilize these assets (or difficulties) in the neonate (based on the use of the assessment scale over the years) to personify him or her to the parents and to ally myself with them as they learn how to interact with this new baby.

Recently, researchers have been using the scale to demonstrate the neonate's behavior to mothers of at-risk mother-infant pairs (Heider, 1966; Anderson, 1979; Ryan, 1973). I also demonstrate the neonate's social responsiveness to the new parents after the infant has recovered from the effects of delivery. They are usually amazed at the infant's capacity to become alert to and turn repeatedly toward the human voice, to fix on and follow their faces, to watch and follow a red ball. They "knew" but could not quite believe that the infant was responding to them and to their own caring behavior. Even more important to the thesis that we should entrench ourselves as members of their team, when we demonstrate that we too see this neonatal behavior, we underscore that we value the parents as skilled observers and the importance of their interaction with the baby.

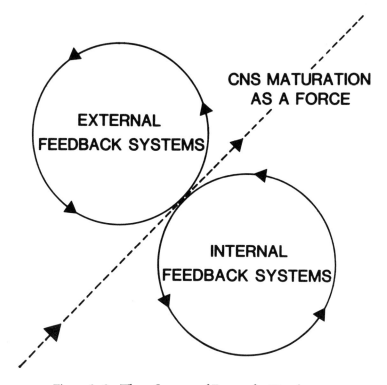

Figure 3–2. Three Sources of Energy for Development

Stressing the baby's strength and individuality and pointing to the way in which he or she is shaping them, rather than vice versa, provide a powerful means for entry into the parent-child relationship (Brazelton, 1975). Another maneuver is to stress the age-locked and normal aspects of the child's contribution. Our relationship with young parents is enhanced, and they now see us as sensitive to the infants' individual needs and demands as well as to their own.

While a mother is still in the hospital with her new baby, she is particularly eager for such a relationship. The crisis of the delivery has heightened her anxieties, her sensitivities, and her needs. She must have an understanding person to whom she can transfer the dependency she has had on her obstetrician. She is eager at this time to share her feelings, her wishes, and her fears about the new baby.

A supportive relationship is further fostered by urging the mother to accept a telephone "umbilical cord" in times of stress. A new mother is urged to call at least once a week, or more often at first, so that she can be helped with all her questions, important or unimportant. A telephone hour every morning is set aside just for this purpose, and parents are urged to use it. It is striking how quickly their need to call drops after they are sure this need for dependency will be met. They can and do develop their independent resources.

One valuable tool that we ignore these days in our busy practices is the value of a home visit, at about three weeks—the third touchpoint—not for an illness but for diagnosis and prevention of psychological difficulties. I have had several successive phone calls from young parents about their colicky baby, and if after I have attempted to reassure them about the infant's need to cry part of every day (Brazelton, 1962) the crying increases in intensity and duration, I try to see them. Not only do my diagnostic capacities increase as I see the dynamics and the reality of their lives at home, but they recognize my interest in them and my willingness to take their anxiety seriously.

The home visit allows for an examination of the child with the concerned family present (father, mother, grandparents, nurse) and provides a dramatic release for family tension that has built up around a normal baby's crying periods (Brazelton, 1962). This has saved me more phone calls than any single therapeutic effort.

In allowing the mother this sort of dependent, caring relationship with the pediatrician, it would seem easier to accomplish several therapeutic goals in her relationship with the child.

1. Implicitly, such a relationship sanctions dependency, and when she can allow herself to become dependent on a figure in authority, perhaps it frees her for a healthier acceptance of the child's dependency. Certain mothers are so deprived that they must deprive their child as a sort of retribution. This sort of dependent relationship with the pediatrician may minimize that need on her part.
2. As a mother can ventilate her anxieties, fears, and limitations in relation to the child in the first few weeks, they become less unrealistic and less frightening. Then she and the pediatrician may be able to redirect some of this anxiety and work around her limitations.
3. As the mother's dependency is accepted, and as her limitations and anxiety are worked through, the mother can begin to become more self-sufficient and develop outlets for her problems and anxieties, which leaves the child more or less unscarred. As she sees this growth in herself and the child, her self-confidence and independence flourish. I find that very few mothers misuse this dependency, and the need for it tapers surprisingly after the first three weeks.
4. Another important preventive role of the pediatrician is to outline for the parents the mechanisms and dynamics of the normal child's development. With knowledge of the parents' concerns, the pediatrician can foresee the normal variations in this development that will affect them. Forewarning

parents about the normalcy of such variations and helping with their feelings about them may alleviate their anxiety when the child demonstrates them.

5. With impaired or high-risk infants, showing the baby's organized and responsive behaviors has an amazing effect on the parent. Caught in her own grief about having produced an impaired infant, she (and the father) can see the organization as potential for future development. They can lock onto this responsive behavior as representing their role for fostering the development of even a severely impaired infant. I am amazed at how powerful this can be as an intervention. Demonstrating the lowered sensory threshold and the poor state controls of a hypersensitive infant gives the parent a chance to understand their role with such an infant in providing him or her with an environment, appropriate to that infant's lowered threshold for experiencing environmental experiences.

In a longitudinal study of the development of temperament in children, Thomas, Chess, and Birch (1968) found that the relationships with families established by the professionals (psychiatrists, pediatricians, social workers, psychologists) who observed them over the many years of the study proved to be amazingly effective in alleviating potential disorder: 68 percent of the patients in whom mild or moderate symptoms were identified were noted to recover or markedly improve over the period of observation, and 50 percent of patients with severe symptoms of psychopathology also seemed to improve with the preventive approach and early intervention that resulted from the team's working relationship with these families.

Although we are all aware that children recover from many symptoms that appear to be of a pathologic nature, without any intervention other than time and a nurturing environment, I believe that pediatricians are in a unique position to provide the kind of relationship, insight, and therapeutic support of which Thomas and co-workers have written. This implies that a priority in the delivery of care becomes an understanding of normal children and their development, as well as of the value and mechanisms of establishing a supportive working relationship with their families.

Conclusion

The impact of the pediatrician on a child's development can be measured by the importance to him or her of the relationship with the child and the parents. That the pediatrician can be of value in preventing developmental problems for the child and in supporting young parents as they nurture the child seems obvious to most who see this as a major responsibility in their day-to-day practice of pediatrics. Recent work in the area of attachment points to the importance of early intervention. Pediatricians can capture the energy available in parents to attach to their small child for use in their own work with new parents who care and the coping strengths that all normal children have, pediatricians can see their role as a vital member of the parent-child team. As such, they can strengthen the developmental potential for many children, and although they may not prevent all problems, they may offer children and their parents an opportunity for a richer experience. This is a challenge to the pediatricians of the future.

References

Anderson, C.: Informing mothers about the behavioral characteristics of their infants: effects on mother-infant interaction. Presented at Society For Research in Child Development, San Francisco, 1979.

Brazelton, T.B.: Anticipatory guidance. *Pediatr. Clin. N. Am.* 22:533, 1975.

Brazelton, T.B.: Behavioral competence of the newborn infant. *Semin. Perinatol.* 3:35, 1979.

Brazelton, T.B.: Crying in infancy. *Pediatrics* 29:579, 1962.

Brazelton, T.B.: Developmental framework of infants and children: a future for pediatric responsibility. *J. Pediatr.* 102:697, 1983.

Brazelton, T.B.: Neonatal Behavioral Assessment Scale, London, Wm. Heinemann, 1973.

Brazelton, T.B.: Prenatal care: the pediatrician's role. In Green, M., and Haggerty, R.J. (eds.): *Ambulatory Pediatrics*. Philadelphia, W.B. Saunders, 1968.

Brazelton, T.B.: The origins of reciprocity. In Lewis, M., and Rosenblum, L. (eds.): *Effect of the Infant on the Caretaker*, Vol. 1. New York, Wiley, 1975.

Bronfenbrenner, U.: The origins of alienation. *Sci. Am.* 231(8):53, 1974.

Cravioto, J., DeLicardie, E.R., and Birch, H.G.: Nutrition, growth and neurointegrative development: an experimental and ecologic study. *Pediatrics* 38:319, 1966.

Eisenberg, R.B., Griffin, E.J., Coursin, D.B., et al.: Auditory behavior in the human neonate: a preliminary report. *J. Speech Hear. Res.* 7:245, 1964.

Greenberg, H.N.: A comparison of infant-mother interactional behavior in infants with atypical behavior and normal infants. In Hellmuth, J. (ed.): *Exceptional Infant*, Vol. 2. New York, Bruner Mazel, 1971.

Heider, G.M.: Vulnerability in infants and young children. *Genet. Psychol. Monogr.* 73:1, 1966.

Klaus, M.H., and Kennell, J.H.: Mothers separated from their newborn infants. *Pediatr. Clin. N. Am.* 17:1015, 1970.

Klein, R.E., Habicht, J.P., and Yarbrough, C.: Effect of protein-calorie malnutrition on mental development. *Adv. Pediatr.* 1:571, 1971.

Lester, B.M.: A synergistic process approach to the study of prenatal malnutrition. *Int. J. Behav. Dev.* 2:377, 1979.

Newton, N., and Newton, M.: Psychological aspects of lactation. *N. Engl. J. Med.* 177:1179, 1967.

Ryan, L.J.: Maternal perception of neonatal behavior. Master's thesis, University of Washington School of Nursing, 1973.

St. James, and Roberts. Neurological plasticity. *Adv. Child Dev. Behav.* 13, 1979.

Senn, M.E.: Anticipatory guidance of the pregnant women and her husband for their roles as parents. Transcript of the first conference, J. Macy Foundation, March 3 and 4, 1947.

Suomi, S.J., and Harlow, H.F.: Early experience and social development in rhesus monkeys. In Lamb, M.E.: *Socio-personality Development,* New York, Wiley, 1978.

Thomas, A., Chess, S., and Birch, H.G.: *Temperament and Behavior Disorders in Children.* New York, New York University Press, 1968.

Tronick, E., and Brazelton, T.B.: Clinical uses of the Brazelton Neonatal Behavioral Assessment. In Frielander, B.Z., et al.: *Intervention.* New York, Brunner Mazel, 1975.

Wessel, M.A.: The prenatal pediatric Visit. *Pediatrics 32:*926, 1963.

4

One to Six: The Pediatrician's Role in Mastery and Individuation

Richard H. Granger

I n the years between one and six, children gradually extend voluntary control over their bodies and much of the environment to personal interactions with both peers and adults. They slowly differentiate themselves from their parents and establish themselves as individuals. These are the processes we refer to as mastery and individuation. This chapter addresses those processes and describes how pediatricians can work with parents to help children fulfill their developmental imperatives.

A full review of the developmental tasks in this period is beyond the scope of this chapter, but an impressionistic overview will illustrate their variety and complexity. They may be divided into four general areas:

1. gross motor functions
2. fine motor functions
3. cognitive functions
4. social-emotional functions

1. *Gross motor functions* are the activities made possible by maturation of the large muscle groups of the body and include walking, climbing, running, riding wheeled vehicles, and sphincter control. They are somewhat less sensitive than others to the deleterious effects of mild deprivation or emotional upsets. But parents who prize coordination and athletic skills may be put off by a child who is awkward or clumsy and the parent-child relationship may suffer. Pediatricians can help parents understand their expectations and come to terms with their disappointment. Then they appreciate their child for his or her real strengths rather than mourning what the child is not. The pediatrician also should know that there are, in many communities, reputable programs designed to help children enhance their motor performance. One issue worth mentioning is that the gross motor skills and strength of boys and girls are quite similar throughout this entire period—if anything the girls are likely to be a little better.

2. The term *fine motor functions* refers primarily to the development of hand skills. It is helpful to remember that the hand does not manage all sized

objects equally well at the same time in development. The skill of unbuttoning is much easier than buttoning, and a year or more may elapse between the acquisition of these skills. Parents often get quite angry at what they see as stubbornness that is actually only developmental unreadiness.

The ability to use tools for writing and drawing which comes late in the preschool period is an important precursor for school. Because the inability to perform skillfully with the hands at school entrance may be a handicap to the child, it should be watched for carefully.

3. *Cognitive functions* include such areas as language development, memory, and problem solving. Pediatricians have not seemed to be extensively informed about cognitive development. For instance, they too often pay insufficient attention to delayed language even though it is possible that the cause of the delay may be as strictly medical as impaired hearing. Language is most sensitive to the nuances of parent-child interactions. Delayed language development may be one of the earliest intimations of a seriously impaired home emotional environment for the child.

The Swiss psychologist Piaget is the major theoretician of cognitive development. The two Piagetian stages in this age group are sensorimotor and preoperational. The former extends from birth to two years. By one year infants are well on the way to learning that objects are permanent—even when out of sight—and they have begun to have a primitive sense of cause and effect. In the early part of the second year the toddler experiments deliberately, repeating actions over and over and watching the results closely. By the end of that year the child has developed the beginnings of symbolic thought allowing some problems to be solved in his or her head without repetitive experimentation.

The preoperational stage begins at two and ends at six. It is characterized by the full development of symbolic thought and language. The child begins to understand the concept of numbers—but not yet those of mass, space, shape.

4. *Social-emotional development* is a broad area including topics such as separation, individuation, gender identity, peer relations, the use of fantasy and play, and the development of self-control. As parents come from smaller families and are less informed about children, as they move more often and do not have family or other support groups, and as their own lives become more stressful and disorganized—they need the help of a knowledgeable professional more than ever. These dislocations are hard for both parents and children. The pediatrician should ask about such stresses and be alert to their impact on the family and the child.

From one to six years of age children continue to need the feeling of support, but they also need to be helped to deal with separation and to feel confidant and good about themselves. They need to learn how to relate to other children and to adults outside their families. They have to learn to control their early antisocial behaviors (such as temper tantrums) in favor of interactive behavior more facilitative of good social relationships. Parents' expectations of their childrens' behaviors often deviate markedly from the age-appropriate reality, and they need help with this.

Parents are often disturbed by the child's use of fantasy—especially when it extends beyond the boundaries of play into the routines of daily life—as in the case of the imaginary playmate. Many parents become concerned over what they see as the child's lying and deal harshly with what for the child is in reality a normal developmental activity. Children in this age group rarely, if ever, lie, and pediatricians can minimize or prevent much parental concern by helping parents understand this.

Parents also often fail to understand how much of the child's developing sense of relationships, of right and wrong, of self-control, and of cooperation is worked out through play. Parents can be helped to realize that play is the child's work and to help facilitate it.

In stressing a theme of separation and individuation, I do not mean to downplay the role of parents. Parents still need to be parents—providers, nurturers, anchors in the seas. But they also need to have the strength and the foresight to understand that their children must become relatively independent as early as developmentally appropriate and that they, the parents, can facilitate this not by pushing them away, but by not keeping them too closely tied; by encouraging exploration, applauding their achievements, and minimizing the effect of mistakes; and by offering support and helpful interpretation rather than criticism and angry punishment. Discipline is one of the most frequently asked-about issues, so pediatricians need to have thoughtful, age-appropriate, nonjudgmental ways of helping parents find personal answers.

The child's developmental status and behavior are very sensitive indicators of the health and well-being of the parent-child relationship and of the family structure as a whole. Globally delayed or uneven development may derive from many things including genetic problems, physical illness, and malnutrition, but it may also point unerringly to problems in the child's life, usually to some important trouble in the child's ongoing relationship with one or both parents. The problem might arise from something as dramatic as child abuse or neglect, but usually the difficulties are much more subtle than that and can be elicited only through developed interviewing skills coupled with a working understanding of family dynamics.

A representative list of common psychopathologies of childhood will illustrate the point.

language delay

sleep disturbances

enuresis

encopresis

retarded development

bullying behavior

social inappropriateness

separation problems

psychobiologic symptoms

school unreadiness

learning disabilities

withdrawal

These problems are familiar to any experienced pediatrician, to whom they often seem somewhat disruptive intrusions in the day's work—perhaps beyond the pediatrician's ability to help or work with; nonetheless, the interested and informed pediatrician can help as the two following case vignettes illustrate. The cases begin with the same symptom, but then diverge enough to illustrate the two important ways in which the pediatrician can intervene.

Case One. Jason, the six-year-old son of two white school teachers, had been toilet-trained at an appropriate age without difficulty, but at five and a half he began to soil his pants. School seemed to be going well. He did not soil there but only when he arrived at daycare from school. His parents reported they had tried both ignoring and punishing the symptom, but neither approach had worked.

The mother was not greatly concerned because her son had responded with the same symptom at other times when there had been stress in his life, for example, first starting school, and she thought that his one-year-old sister had recently become more of a problem for him. However, previous episodes had never lasted more than a day or two, and the present problem had persisted for weeks.

The pediatrician spent a few sessions with the boy in which the child through play revealed considerable anger and aggression, although the source was not clear. Conferences with both parents yielded only denials of other difficulties in the household. The boy enjoyed his visits with the pediatrician. After several weeks the symptoms disappeared, and the visits were discontinued by the parents.

Six months later, however, the parents separated angrily and announced that the breakup was irreconcilable. There is little doubt that the marital difficulties precipitated the child's regressive behavior. Although the pediatrician's intervention was not able to be of help to the parents, it was certainly successful in providing the child a sympathetic audience and a safety valve for his feelings.

Case Two. Warren was a four-year-old white boy who had been both withholding stool and soiling his pants increasingly over a three-month period. At times he seemed depressed, and he had begun to suck his thumb, which he had not done for more than two years. At other times he seemed very angry and would argue and start fights, especially with his mother. His mother wondered if his six-month-old sister had something to do with his problem.

The pediatrician saw the boy twice and found his behavior much as the mother had reported. The first two interviews with the mother turned up little new information. She said things were going well, but she seemed edgy. On the third visit, she suddenly told the pediatrician she had a question. She then revealed that ten years earlier, when she was eighteen and before her marriage she had had a baby girl who she had given up for adoption. She had never told anyone about this before, not even her husband.

The birth of her new daughter had reactivated feelings about the first girl, and the mother had become obsessed by the thought of seeing her. She had gone so far as to find out where the child lived. Her question to the pediatrician was whether she should, in fact, make herself known to her daughter.

Wisely the pediatrician did not answer that question. Instead, he engaged the mother in a dialogue over several more interviews to explore with her more fully her feelings and motivations for pursuing her plan. It was his goal to get the mother into psychotherapy where she could deal with the feelings that had never been worked through when the first child was born. A month later the mother did start treatment and within two weeks her son stopped soiling and regained his former sunny disposition.

In this case the mother's depression and inner turmoil clearly was tremendously stressful to the son with whom she had been close before her daughter was born. The pediatrician's task was to ferret out the family secret and then help the mother to find treatment in order to help the boy recover.

These cases demonstrate two routes of intervention, one is working directly with the child to relieve symptoms and ease pain and discomfort and the second is helping parents to recognize their etiologic role and working to solve their problems. In both cases, however, the basic process is the same: careful, open-ended interviewing of important family members to illuminate the nature of the problem and then helping the family assume its responsibility for working to resolve it. Although formula questions and curricula are helpful introductions to this work, there is no substitute for a basic understanding of dynamics and the ability to individualize each case.

In general, the pediatrician's role is to facilitate the parents' recognition of, and responsiveness to, the child's development and psychological state, but there are also many times when the pediatrician must be alert and responsive to the parent's psychological state. Often a parent introduces a concern that does not seem real to the pediatrician. Nevertheless it is a problem worthy of attention just because it is in the parent's mind. The facile and unconsidered "Don't worry—he'll outgrow it" is never a useful or constructive response. Few concerns are alleviated by being told not to worry, and few children outgrow anything but their clothes.

Most often, the parent's question is a surrogate for another concern, not easily stated or focused, which the pediatrician can elicit with an open-ended response that allows a dialogue to develop. The usual pontifical reassurance has the opposite effect of bringing conversation to an immediate dead end. Even when the question begins with the classic, "Oh, by the way, doctor . . .", with one hand on the doorknob, the pediatrician is better advised to hold his or her temper, take the question seriously, recognize the difficulty the parent had in bringing it up at all, and then, resisting the temptation to give a quick answer, invite the parent, or both parents, back for a subsequent visit just to discuss that problem. Parents are usually surprised and almost always grateful. They do make the appointments, and they do show up.

The new pediatrics requires a redefinition of well-child care which will provide a better and more satisfactory use of pediatric time and more appropriate services for children and their families. The well-child visit needs to be refocused to concentrate on the child's development and activity as well as on the parent's feelings about their children and their interactions with them. The payoff in both patient well-being and pediatrician satisfaction is enormous. And the work can be learned and done by pediatricians.

That's not just one opinion. More and more the pediatric literature is reinforcing the importance to children and to pediatricians of the psychosocial domain. It will be useful here to undertake a brief review of that literature. It can be divided into four broad areas of study:

1. the prevalence of psychosocial problems
2. pediatrician-parent interactions
3. intervention programs
4. training and education programs

The Prevalence of Psychosocial Problems

The early pediatric literature, even as late as the 1940s and 1950s, contained few articles on developmental or psychological issues. The prevalence of psychosocial issues in those days was usually reported at 1–3 percent. But over the years the percentages have been slowly climbing, not, I believe, because the problems are more pervasive, but rather because we are looking more carefully and with better understanding.

Goldberg et al. (1979, 1984) and Starfield and her co-workers in 1980 reported that between 5 and 15 percent of children seen at pediatric visits had developmental or psychosocial problems. Starfield now (1984) reports from a health maintenance organization (HMO) in Maryland that 25 percent of all the children seen there were diagnosed as having a psychosocial problem. These figures agree with those from studies by mental health professionals who have for years been reporting much higher prevalences.

Rutter Tizard, and Whitmore's (1970) study of children on the Isle of Wight and Werner and Smith's (1977) study of the children of Kauai both document long-term problems in sizable percentages of the child population.

In a small study Raymond Sturner and I reported in 1980, three pediatricians each studied 100 consecutive routine well-child visits and found that in these supposedly problem-free visits 39 percent of the children had a definable developmental or psychological problem which needed attention.

Beautrais, Ferguson, and Shannon (1982) demonstrate another aspect of psychosocial research. He and his co-workers in New Zealand looked at "The relationship between family life events and rates of childhood morbidity . . . illness, accidents, and accidental poisoning." They found a strong correlation that held through all social strata between those childhood problems and such family events as moving, death, job problems, separation and divorce, parental illness, and marital discord.

Pediatrician-Parent Interaction Studies

Korsch, Guzzi, and Francis (1968), Korsch et al. (1971), Reisinger and Bires (1980), and Duff (1982) have all reported serious discrepancies between what parents want from pediatricians and what they get. They report that pediatricians are ill-equipped to recognize and deal with most developmental or psychosocial issues.

A report by Hickson, Altemeier, and O'Connor (1983) indicates that "of 207 mothers seeking care in private pediatric offices . . . only 30 percent were most worried about their child's physical health. The remaining 70 percent were most concerned about problems in six categories of parenting, behavior and development." Only 28 percent of those mothers had discussed this concern with their pediatrician because they "were not aware that he could help, or they questioned his ability or interest in assisting them." Bass and Cohen (1982) also reported parental anxiety as a major factor in 33.8 percent of visits to one pediatric office.

In an ongoing study, Fearn (1984) is studying audio recordings of prenatal interviews. She is looking not only at content and types of statements, but also at the process of the communication. She has found, as have most others, that pediatricians tend to dominate the interviews. In general, they spend most of the time giving rather than gathering information, talking rather than listening. Most of the information they give is about physical care, medical issues, or the business arrangements of the practice. They often cut off the patients' attempts to open up other areas of discussion.

What stood out in this study, though, was a subgroup of pediatricians with special interest and training in developmental and psychosocial issues. This group of psychologically sophisticated pediatricians (PSPs) spend almost equal time giving and gathering information, ask more open-ended questions that seem to facilitate the flow of the interview, and talk much more about issues related to feelings and fears about parenting than do their colleagues.

Intervention Studies

Intervention studies are hard to do and to evaluate, but they are beginning to form a more important part of the literature. Chamberlin and Szumowski (1980), in a longitudinal study of practicing pediatricians in Rochester, New York, reported that physicians' unfocused efforts to teach about child development increased parents' knowledge somewhat but did little to affect children's behavior.

In contrast to these results are three randomized controlled studies. Gutelius et al. (1977) and Casey and Whitt (1980) both offered health supervision and anticipatory guidance to high-risk mothers. They found that the study mothers interacted with their children in such a way as to facilitate development much more than did the controls. And, under observation, the children in the study groups behaved in a more mature way and had fewer maladaptive behaviors. In a very different setting, Cullen (1976), a pediatrician in rural Australia, also demonstrated that counseling parents could reduce the incidence of preschool children's behavioral problems.

Rutter (1982) evaluates the rationale for, and the pitfalls in, doing intervention work. He maintains that "there is a potential for effective primary prevention but it remains largely unrealized."

Education and Training Studies

In its report, *The Future of Pediatric Education* (1978), the Academy of Pediatrics' Task Force took special note of the gap in training in the biosocial and developmental aspects of pediatrics and made major recommendations for upgrading in this area. In the same year the academy's Manpower Committee (1978) said, "Pediatricians will be devoting a greater portion of their time to serving those patients for whom the primary problem requires the enhancement of the psychosocial adjustment, intellectual development, and the quality of the child's life."

In 1980, Leventhal and Stashwick reported that pediatric residents assessing mothers at well-child visits failed to collect important data about parenting attitudes and skills and relied instead on maternal compliance with medical directions and appointments. Jewett et al. (1982) and Brent (1983) both discuss the importance of teaching pediatricians to help parents and children deal with emotional crises. Reports from the academy's Committee on Psychosocial Aspects of Child and Family Health (1983, 1984) point out the importance of further attention to the prenatal interview and propose a curriculum for detecting and managing psychosocial issues in the first few years of life. In 1975 I reported on a curriculum for fellowship training in the developmental and psychological aspects of pediatrics that was designed for pediatricians who wanted to remain in primary care pediatrics.

We are involved in our own five-year effort to examine some issues about pediatric care and to test an intervention into a common pediatric problem—enuresis. The idea and plan for the study were stimulated and determined by our having available to us a unique clinical tool. That tool is a group of eleven pediatricians in both academic and community practice who meet every week to discuss the psychological and developmental aspects of cases from their practices and to have the ongoing support of a closely knit group of colleagues. The group has been meeting for eight years. It is an offshoot of another group which has been meeting with Dr. Albert Solnit for more than twenty-five years.

Our group has coleaders, myself and Dr. Julian Ferholt, a child psychiatrist. All the other members were at one time fellows working in or with my postresidency training program. Five members of the group who are in community practice provided the patient cadre for the study group and did the intervention. Two of them are members of the pediatric section of a large health maintenance organization (HMO) in New Haven. Two of the others practice in four-person partnership groups, one based in a local community hospital and the other in a town forty miles from New Haven. The fifth member is in individual practice in a suburban town in the greater New Haven area.

The study began with two hypotheses: (1) Primary nocturnal enuresis is primarily caused by confused parental expectations and training practices and not by genetic or intrinsic developmental factors; and (2) With a relatively simple and practicable intervention—addressing the issue of night dryness directly, along with toilet training information, pediatricians can significantly reduce the incidence. These two hypotheses were worked out, agreed on, and understood by all the participants in the study. Once the study got under way, however, John Leventhal and I, who are the coinvestigators and are not clinical participants in the project, decided to add a hypothesis unknown to the study group. (3) Pediatricians specially interested in, and trained in, practicing the "new pediatrics" will be demonstrably more effective in working with parents to help children achieve mastery and individuation.

The study was planned as a prospective intervention study with a cohort design. The intervention was to be a preventive rather than a therapeutic one. Although there is no clear consensus in the literature, the most commonly reported figures indicate a prevalence of primary, nocturnal enuresis of 13 to 15 percent of five year olds. Based on this we decided to enroll 250 children in the study cohort and an equal number in the control group. The study group would receive the intervention and the control group would not. The follow-up of both groups would be the same.

Children in the study group were enrolled by the five pediatricians. At the onset, they enrolled all the children in their practices between twelve and twenty-four months of age and then continued to enroll children who reached that age or entered the practice in that age group, until the group as a whole had enrolled 250 patients. The control group children were enrolled similarly from the practices of the partners in the same group or HMO. In the case of the solo practitioner, controls were enrolled from two neighboring solo practices in the same town.

The pediatricians doing the intervention have a similar approach to toilet training: It is primarily an educational rather than a disciplinary process, and it largely involves helping the parents understand that the children retain control and the parents are enablers. The intervention began with a history of the parents' own toileting experience and of their expectations for their own children. After exploring this briefly with the parents, the pediatricians then include a statement indicating their own belief that children who achieve daytime dryness are capable of being night dry at the same time or very soon thereafter. We prepared a small printed handout on toilet training, including the same statement. The whole intervention took no more than three to five minutes and was repeated at subsequent visits when necessary.

The data collection was done through telephone interviews by research assistants blinded to the actual design and goals of the study. Ninety percent of the interviews were completed between forty-one and forty-five months. The research assistants made every attempt to follow up and locate the families even if they had moved out of state, and our loss rate is under 5 percent. We are presently beginning a second round of telephone interviews, with a new set of questions, to reach the projected endpoint of the study with the five-to six-year-old child.

This is not the place to present a carefully detailed research report, but a preliminary analysis of half the cases, 228 children representing 114 matched pairs of study and control cases, reveals some interesting results. These results are from our three-and-a-half-year-old interview only.

Of our total sample, study and control children alike, 98 percent are dry in the daytime and 91 percent are dry at night. Of this group, 84 percent had become dry by the age of thirty-six months, 57 percent within one month or less of becoming dry in the daytime, and 10 percent became dry at night even before becoming dry in the daytime. Fortunately for our hypothesis, the number of children in the control group still bedwetting is two-and-a-half times the number in the study group, which works out to a high level of significance. What's more, the study children became night-dry closer to the time they were day trained, also at a significant level. And all this at three-and-a-half years with our real endpoint at five. If these trends continue through our total sample, the results will all be highly significant.

In relation to our third hypothesis, we had even more striking results. Eighty-five percent of the mothers reported that pediatricians from the study group had discussed child rearing with them as compared to only 38 percent of the mothers' reporting on other pediatricians. Only 5 of 114 mothers said they had not had such a discussion with one of the study pediatricians. In this case the differences are significant at a p value less than 0.0001.

In order to test the issue further we next asked what aspects of child raising had been discussed and wrote down all the subjects the mothers listed in the order in which they were given. For this report I merely counted the number of specific issues each mother reported remembering as having been discussed. Of the mothers who had used one of the PSPs, 92 percent remembered at least one specific item that had been discussed and 76 percent remembered two. By contrast only 64 percent of the mothers reported remembering any specific subject which had been discussed with them by the pediatricians from the control group.

Once again, the data are highly significant at a p value less than 0.0001 and reinforce the impression that the PSP group not only discuss child-rearing issues more often with their patients but do so in a way which helps the parents remember the discussion and retain the information. Increased information does not necessarily mean changes in behavior or performance, but the enuresis results encourage us to feel that changes in performance have also occurred through our interventions. At the very least we feel we can state these preliminary conclusions:

1. Pediatricians can be trained to understand and use knowledge and skills which deal with the psychosocial aspects of child and family life and development.
2. Pediatricians so trained do use their knowledge and skills in actual primary care practice.
3. They intervene positively so as to improve developmental outcomes for children in a way that facilitates the processes of mastery and individuation.

If we accept these conclusions for the sake of discussion, we then need to ask what it is that pediatricians need to know that they are not taught now and what they need to do that they are not usually trained to do at the present time. Our experience indicates that the most useful areas of information they can have are the following:

1. All aspects of development—social, emotional, communicative and cognitive—as well as the usual areas of motor and physical growth
2. A reasonable grasp of family dynamics, the complex interactions which

commonly occur in families between parents, among generations, and between parents and children

3. The effect of family and other environmental influences on child growth and
   development, both those which enhance development and those which foster maladaptive responses
4. Familiarity with those community resources which offer special kinds of
   help to parents and children with special needs
5. Some self-knowledge, some insight into their own personalities and awareness of what they bring into their relationships with parents and children,
   and how to use that insight and awareness to facilitate their role as helping
   and not harmful persons

To facilitate the use of that knowledge they need enhanced skills in the following areas:

1. Interviewing as opposed to history taking. The art of asking open-ended,
   facilitative questions and then listening to the answers in order to give patients a chance to say what they want and need to say and that the pediatrician needs to hear and know in order to be helpful.
2. Observation of infant and child behavior and of parent-child interactions.
3. Performance of a screening type of developmental assessment.
4. Collaboration with professionals from other disciplines in the child mental
   health fields.
5. Making referrals that work. Parents are quite sensitive about seeking help
   for children with developmental or psychosocial problem. The pediatrician
   who has their trust needs to work with the family for a while and help them
   explore their feelings about this before referring them for further evaluation
   or treatment. Failure to do so most often results in referrals that are not
   consummated.

These issues must be introduced at all levels of training—medical school,
residency, fellowship, and continuing education, but I want here only to put for-
ward a brief description of one model for the last level.

Not until most pediatricians leave their training years and enter practice do
they recognize the huge demand for dealing with psychosocial issues and the inadequacy of their training in helping them do so. And then it seems to be too late.
Educators have been saying for years that short-term continuing education programs, occasional lectures, day-long seminars, or even longer special programs,
serve to stimulate interest and increase knowledge somewhat, but not to change
behavior or performance in practice.

I believe the best model is that of the ongoing small study group of no more
than twelve who are willing to bring for discussion cases from their own practice.
The members of the group must feel comfortable enough with each other, and

trusting enough, to discuss cases honestly. A good clinical mental health professional should be part of the group, not as a consultant but as a regular member. The group must meet regularly, and the members must make a commitment to it.

Such a group should establish its own guidelines for the work it wants to do. Every member will learn and teach a great deal. If pediatricians are to have a significant influence on the development and well-being of children, they must take on the psychosocial sphere. If they do not do this, I am convinced, there will be no need for primary care pediatricians. The work is hard, but it is challenging, intellectually stimulating, and incredibly rewarding. And it greatly widens the positive influence pediatricians can exert on behalf of children.

References

Bass, L.W., and Cohen, R.L.: Ostensible versus actual reasons for seeking pediatric attention: another look at the parental ticket of admission. *Pediatrics* 70:870, 1982.

Beautrais, A.L., Ferguson, D.M., and Shannon, F.T.: Life events and childhood morbidity: a prospective study. *Pediatrics* 70:935, 1982.

Brent, D.A.: A death in the family: the pediatrician's role. *Pediatrics* 72:645, 1983.

Casey, P.H., and Whitt, J.K.: Effect of the pediatrician on the mother-infant relationship. *Pediatrics* 65:815, 1980.

Chamberlin, R.W., and Szumowski, E.K.: A follow-up study of parent education in pediatric office practices: impact at two and a half. *Am. J. Publ. Health* 70:1180, 1980.

Committee on Manpower of the Academy of Pediatrics: Projecting pediatric practice patterns. *Pediatrics* 62(Suppl.):628, 1978.

Committee on Psychosocial Aspects of Child and Family Health: Guidelines to health supervision. Unpublished paper, 1983. Committee on Psychosocial Aspects of Child and Family Health: Statement on the prenatal visit. *Pediatrics* 73:561, 1984.

Cullen, K.J.: A six-year controlled trial of prevention of children's behavioral disorders. *J. Pediatr.* 88:662, 1976.

Duff, R.: Study of primary pediatric care. Unpublished paper, 1982.

Fearn, K.: The pediatric prenatal visit: the state of the art. Unpublished paper, 1984.

Goldberg, I.D., Regier, D.A., McInerny, T.K., et al.: The role of the pediatrician in the delivery of mental health services to children. *Pediatrics* 63:898, 1979.

Goldberg, I.D., Roghmann, K.J., McInerny, T.K., and Burke, J.D., Jr.: Medical health problems among children seen in pediatric practice: prevalence and management. *Pediatrics* 73:278, 1984.

Granger, R.H.: A training program in the developmental and psychological aspects of pediatrics. Paper presented at the meetings of the Society for Research in Child Development, Denver, 1975.

Gutelius, M.F., Kirsch, A.D., MacDonald, S., et al.: Controlled study of child health supervision: behavioral results. *Pediatrics* 60:294, 1977.

Hickson, G.B., Altemeier, W.A., O'Connor, S.: Concerns of mothers seeking care in private pediatric offices: opportunities for expanding services. *Pediatrics* 72:619, 1983.

Jewett, L.S., Greenberg, L.W., Champion, L.A.A., et al.: The teaching of crisis counseling skills to pediatric residents. *Pediatrics 70:*907, 1982.

Korsch, B.M., Guzzi, E.K., Francis, V.: Gaps in doctor-patient communication. I. Doctor-patient interaction and patient satisfaction. *Pediatrics 42:*855, 1968.

Korsch, B.M., Negrete, V.F., Mercer, A.S., et al.: How comprehensive are well child visits? *Am. J. Dis. Child 122:*483, 1971.

Leventhal, J.M., and Stashwick, C.A.: Pediatric residents assessments of parenting. *Pediatr. Res. 14:*435, 1980.

Reisinger, K.S., and Bires, J.A.: Anticipatory guidance in pediatric practice. *Pediatrics 66:*889, 1980.

Rutter, M.: Prevention of children's psychosocial disorders: myth and substance. *Pediatrics 70:*883, 1982.

Rutter, M., Tizard, J., and Whitmore, K.: *Education, Health and Behavior.* London, Longmans, 1970.

Starfield, B., Gross, E., Wood, M., et al.: Psychosocial and psychosomatic diagnoses in primary care of children. *Pediatrics 66:*159, 1980.

Starfield, B., Katz, H., Gabriel, A., et al.: Morbidity in childhood—a longitudinal view. *N. Engl. J. Med. 310:*824, 1984.

Sturner, R.S., Granger, R.H., Ferholt, J.B., and Klatskin, E.H.: The routine "well child" examination. *Clin. Pediatr. 19:*251, 1980.

Task Force on Pediatric Education: *The Future of Pediatric Education.* Evanston, American Academy of Pediatrics, 1978.

Werner, E.E., and Smith, R.S.: *Kauai's Children Come of Age.* Honolulu, University Press of Hawaii, 1977.

5

Family Support Programs: Partners to Pediatricians

Bernice Weissbourd

The family support movement is an exciting new star on the social horizon. This new star has many overlapping names: family support, family resource, parent support, parent education, and mutual aid, to mention only a few. Since we in the area of human services do not always have the scientific bent for specificity, our words frequently have many meanings; sometimes the same meanings are expressed by different words. This new star is no exception. Not only are there many words to describe family support, there are new words in our approach to family and family structures. Some have already become so commonplace we do not realize they are not yet in the dictionary. One such word is *parenting*, as in parenting programs, parenting education, parenting as an important task, and careful parenting. I think it reflects an approach to being a parent as a job, a skill to be learned, a process of acting upon children. *Parenthood*, the word of previous years, is a state of being, whereas *parenting* is a word of action. There are other new words: *blended* family, used to describe the situation when parents divorce, remarry, have another set of children, so some children have two sets of parents, four sets of siblings, and four sets of grandparents. Combining these two is another new term *stepparenting*. Books appearing on this subject abound, and a national organization for stepparents has been formed. The word *stepmother* is no longer associated with the mean, ugly woman in our fairy tales, and children often refer to their stepmother with respect and affection.

We use the phrase *single-parent home*, not *broken home*; and we say "children of a single parent," not "children born out-of-wedlock," or "illegitimate." *Female-headed households* has supplanted the more denigrating *matriarchal family*. Fortunately we never hear the word *bastard* applied in its literal meaning to a child. It is interesting to note that terms such as *broken home* or *illegitimate* applied when the phenomena were primarily characteristic of the poor and minority population. The words changed when the circumstances became more commonplace in the majority white middle-class culture. The most recent word *POSSLQ* (pronounced poss-el-que) describes families and is derived from our latest census report. It is an acronym for people of the opposite sex sharing living quarters.

This is another way of picturing the vast changes in attitudes toward families and in structures of families. Another way is with such familiar statistics as 50 percent of marriages end in divorce, one out of seven children spends part of his or her life in a single-parent home, one in six children in America live in families whose income is below the poverty line, and by 1990 there will be more stepfamilies than nuclear families.

We do know that whether the structure of the family is single, blended, or nuclear it remains the primary support for raising children. It is through the family that children get the care, love, and attention that enable them to grow into responsible, healthy members of society. It is in the family that the child learns a system of values, and develops a sense of self and of identity. Robert Frost has captured the bedrock importance of the family in these inimitable words: "Home is the place where or when there is no other place to go, they have to take you in."

Today, there are thousands of family support programs across the country, and they are a community-based response to the concern about the future of American families. Their phenomenal growth can be attributed to a number of factors, including loneliness. There is not a day that goes by without my receiving letters from across the country asking, "Do you know of any program for families in my neighborhood?" or "I'm a father alone taking care of two children" or "How can I start a family support program?"

"We have a society that claims love and concern for its young, yet it leaves parents to raise their children virtually unprepared and alone." The author of that sentence is not a sociologist, but a young parent. She is expressing the sense of isolation and loneliness prevelent in our society. When Mother Theresa visited the United States, she said, "The disease in India is poverty; in America, it is loneliness." The average family moves fourteen times. Twenty percent of the American population moves each year. The support of extended family is seldom present. Whatever its problems were, and there were many, the extended family, nevertheless, was a haven for venting feelings, a system of ties and relationships that created a sense of belonging.

The changing structure of families has also contributed to the growth in family support systems. The high divorce rate and number of children living in single-parent families has altered the family environment for many.

A third reason for this growth is the financial inequities in our society, and the fact that children born into families in financial stress will inevitably suffer basic deprivations. Poor children generally live in communities with poor housing, poor schools, and poor services.

The changing role of women is the fourth reason. A subtle revolution is occurring for women, reflected in the changing roles of women in relation to work, careers, marriage, and motherhood. I think it is subtle only if the word revolution encompasses the meaning of violence. To me and to others, it is not so subtle—it is a dramatic, swift, drastic change within one generation. Today there are more mothers working than in the home. Concurrently, attitudes have changed: in 1930, when asked the question, "Do you believe that married women should have a full-time job outside the home," 18 percent of the population said yes. In 1972, in answer to the same question, 73 percent said yes. The revolution for women has caused a subtle revolution for men as well. There is a wider recognition of the impact of fatherhood on men as well as of the significance to the child of the father's participation, starting at birth.

There has also been a revolution within one generation of our understanding of the capabilities of infants. We know today that infants are born into the world able to see, to turn to the sound of their mother's voice, and to be responsive, and we know that each is an individual with a characteristic pattern of activity, crying, sleeping, and wakefulness. While the impact of infant research on parents and programs for parents is enormous, the new information on infants is yet to become common knowledge. A recent film, *Right from the Start*, opens with an interview of persons on the street in which they are asked, "When do you think a baby sees?" Somebody says, "I don't know, three months, six months?" "When do you think a baby hears?" "Oh, I don't know, maybe at about a year."

Underlying the family support movement is a gradual change in ideology. Independence is no longer associated with isolation, and dependence is no longer associated with deficiency. The family support movement is propelled by the growing recognition of our interdependence, of our basic desires to be social, giving, and connected human beings. These programs have emerged, not because something is wrong with people, but because something is right with people. The family does not function in a vacuum. It is totally dependent on the institutions of the community—on the presence of health care facilities, on the quality of the schools, on the availability of daycare. Asking families to be independent and self-sufficient is like asking fish to swim out of water. A new definition of *self-sufficiency* is one which acknowledges that being able to function independently springs from being able to relate to others. It actually follows our child development principles: The child first develops trust in others, and the security of those relationships enable separation and individuation.

Today, families of all kinds are declaring their existence, their strength and value, and their desire for support. Family support programs arise in many forms and settings. Some are in educational facilities—preschools, public schools, universities; some are in mental health facilities; some are voluntary service agencies—programs sponsored by nurse-midwives and pediatric social workers; some are programs on military bases—army, navy, air force; and large numbers are community parent mutual-aid programs, parent cooperatives, and church, temple, and community center groups. Professional social service agencies have expanded to include family support services in addition to therapy.

The wide variety of services offered by parent programs includes drop-in centers, parent discussion groups, parent education classes, peer-support groups, information and referral, parent-child joint activity groups, warm/hot lines, health care, and education, crisis intervention, and advocacy. Many programs include special support groups for single parents, divorced parents, parents of handicapped, parents in mourning for a lost child, or older parents. Some programs are focused on one type of service such as parent education or information and referral. Many combine services and act as a central resource. There is a similar diversity in budgets, ranging from $2,000 annually to over $1 million. Some programs are 100 percent volunteer operated, others 80 percent professionally staffed.

These programs could be generally defined as falling into two broad categories: parent education and parent support. The philosophies on which they are based differ in that one assumes education of parents to be the primary factor in change of behavior, while the other emphasizes experience of parents as a focal point. Parent education proponents stress teaching parenting skills and assume that correct information motivates parents to respond appropriately. These programs provide scheduled classes, topic-oriented discussions, skill training, and parent curricula. They derive from our parent education history and tend to refer to parents as teachers.

In contrast, parent support programs evolve from the belief that the parents feelings of competence and confidence directly effect their behavior with the child, and that this has the greatest impact on parent-child interaction. These programs have informal peer support groups, open-ended discussion, modeling by staff, and varied social (potluck suppers, family basketball teams), educational, and advocacy activities. Though programs tend to fit into one or another of these categories, most have overlapping characteristics: parent support programs include scheduled child development information sessions, and parent education classes provide a resource for peer interaction and support.

Underlying the family resource movement are some basic assumptions:

1. All families need support, regardless of race, economic status, religion, or ethnic origins. Though in our country such an assumption appears radical, other Western countries provide services based precisely on this premise. In a recent visit here of thirty social workers from Denmark, financed by their government, to observe social services for children in the United States, they were surprised and perplexed by the concern repeatedly expressed for the need to prove the value of programs for families of young children. Their response was, "We assume—and know—families need support services."

2. The varying kinds of support provided are determined by the needs of parents and are responsive to the cultural and social characteristics of the community in which families live. When communities represent varied cultures, conflicts often arise. For example, in a family focus center located in a heterogeneous community, the Hispanic mothers involved in weekly craft group keep their children with them. There are other parents in the room, mothers who share their cultural rule that each parent is responsible for her

own child. The Spanish women will keep eye contact on their child until the child goes to another adult in the room, then assume the other adult will watch the child. Their cultural rule is that children are everyone's responsibility. The other mothers say of them, "They don't care about their children." In a similar setting, a group of Japanese parents attend a session on toddlers. They are quite strict, expect obedience, and will not tolerate tantrums. They are very critical of the other mothers, whom they perceive as too permissive, and whose children they think get away with everything, have bad manners, and are "wild." Situations like these require astute awareness and sensitivity to the norms and patterns of other cultures on the part of program staff, with expectations for conflict, and a plan for conflict resolution. They also necessitate an honest search into one's own cultural biases, and a willingness to recognize that they exist. One pediatrician I spoke to said, "We too often advise families from our own experience. If we are not black, we do not understand what goes on in black families."

3. Parents want to be good parents, and if they are not, it is due to their life situation, and their own experiences as children. We are all familiar with the terror of the child-abusing mother, who herself had been an abused child. We believe most parents are capable of "good-enough" mothering, in the words of Winnicott, and to this we add in "good-enough" circumstances.

4. The physical and mental health of children is closely related to that of their parents, and the parents' sense of confidence, competence, and self-worth have a direct impact on the child's self-image. This surely does not require expanded definition. A depressed mother is hard pressed to communicate good feelings to her child. Pediatricians are familiar with the depressed mother who is looking but not listening, who is hearing but not acting on advice and instructions.

5. The availability of social networks, mutual aid, and peer groups is essential to the family's ability to enhance the child's development. Current research validates the value of support systems, indicating that social networks that provide support are essential to the mental and physical health of all people, not only those who happen to have acute needs. We know that: (a) support systems ameliorate abuse in high-risk families; (b) families belonging to more extensive networks are more open to change than families belonging to restricted networks; (c) support systems significantly affect the rate of second pregnancies to teenage parents; (d) a higher incidence of illness and accidents has been associated with limited social networks. Pediatricians, by being sensitive to the effects of isolation, can assist and encourage parents to make the connections that can alleviate loneliness by linking up with community resources.

6. Early life experiences have a significant effect on a person's later development. Family support programs are primary prevention services, many focusing on the early years. This is not to say that it is all over by three years

of age, but that it is far better to give children a healthy start than to focus on the management and repair of problems created in the early years.

7. Information on child development, both formal and informal, assists families in their child-rearing role. Today, pediatricians also assume the role of authorities on questions related to child development. Parents often tell us, "I asked my pediatrician about his sleeping, and he said . . ."

8. Since the family cannot be seen as separate from the community, support is provided in the context of community life and through links with community resources. Schools, hospitals, mental health centers, recreational centers, and pediatricians are essential community supports.

9. Being a parent is a most important job. One of the unfortunate side effects of the women's movement is the low status given to motherhood, a position now greatly modified. However, its remnants remain. Family resource programs say being a parent is important.

10. Support enables parents to be advocates for their families. The confidence that has resulted from support in family programs encourages parents to speak out in their own behalf.

Today there are forceful concepts emerging in the study of parents and children, and setting the directions of the family support movement. They are symbiotic and interrelated, as if their existence emanates from the same wellspring of understanding. One is primary prevention. Definitions of primary prevention have commonly focused on preventing the occurence of disease. In the health field, cause and effect are easily discernible—there are inoculations to prevent diseases. In addition, we accept the fact that preventing illness necessitates providing a healthy environment, good nutrition, regular exercise, and adequate rest. And we act on that assumption. When we talk of primary prevention as the prevention of mental illness, of emotional disturbances, of delinquency, of pathologic behavior, we are immediately asked "How can you prove you have prevented anything?"

If we cannot prove what we have prevented in a child's development, we do know what happens when certain conditions are not met. We have ample negative proof that infants who do not get loving, responsive care become depressed and withdrawn and fail to thrive. We do know that toddlers who are neglected or whose natural motivation to be curious and into everything is punished become school children resistant to and unable to learn. We do know that children who are seriously deprived of normal love in their early years frequently become adults who cannot give love to others. There is, I believe, a way to formulate a positive definition of primary prevention—as "providing an environment conducive to promoting the optimal development of the child." We call ours a definition of *optimalism*. We are concerned with promoting optimal development for all children through the support of the family and the maintenance of viable communities. Knowledge and understanding of prevention can contribute to the strengths of family support programs.

Definitions of primary prevention also promote a different view of parents. Today we recognize that it is not sufficient to view parents solely as vehicles for raising children—or, from the pediatrician's point of view, solely as vehicles for assuring their child's health maintenance. Parenthood today is seen as a pivotal stage in the life cycle, as a function of the adult years. It is that stage of generativity of which Eric Erikson speaks—a time of expansion of ego interest. Being a parent is an organizing factor of our adult lives; it reflects the events of our childhood and shapes the later periods of our lives. Some sayings incorporate these views—"The child's play rehearses the adult that he will become, and the adult's play memorializes the child that he has been."

The way a small child is treated starts the socializing process that influences the parent he or she will become. When children become parents they either repeat their parents' practices and patterns or consciously do exactly the opposite of what their parents did. Those who repeat their parents' practices may be angry at themselves for doing so. "I always hated when my mother did that, and here I am doing the same thing" is a frequently heard statement as parents reexperience their past and relive old conflicts. They also generate new hopes and countless dreams. For example, there is the parent who says, "I want something better for my kid," "I ended up doing something I don't like because my father wanted me to. My kid is going to make his own decisions."

We are learning that stages in parenting may parallel the stages in the child's growth, and as a child reaches a certain developmental stage the parents' attitudes, feelings, and childhood experiences determine his ability to respond. Some parents are particularly gratified with infancy. They enjoy the total dependency of the child and will talk of always wanting the warmth of an infant in their arms. They may keep having babies! Others, equally loving, experience ambivalence between the desire to fulfill the demands of the infant and the frustration of being completely at the beck and call of another. Still others, speaking frankly, do not like infancy and cannot wait until their babies become "little people."

Parents of toddlers who are striving for independence and autonomy begin to face the child's first steps toward moving away and have to deal with their own issues of control and separation. The mother who had been most gratified with the dependency of her infant may feel threatened by the child who explores, runs around, says a defiant no. The mother who experiences infancy as an intolerable burden may now delight in a child who is assertive and independent and may at this time first begin to feel competent as a mother.

And so on through development. For all parents there is a constant adjustment required, an understanding of the child's growth needs at any particular time, what those needs ignite in their own personalities, and what they rekindle from the past.

Furthermore, the notion that the mother alone is responsible for the child's behavior and personality has been replaced by an understanding of the interaction between the child's temperament and the mother's. Perhaps, however, we are beginning to see something new. I heard a mother say of her difficult toddler, "Well, we are just a bad match." I hope this does not represent a trend!

The family support movement emphasizes that parents are people. They are people with a past that has shaped their personalities, directed their responses, and affected their coping skills. They are people who cannot be viewed outside of their culture, their economic status, or their community.

Another concept forging the family support movement is that of community. Over a century ago, Alexis de Tocqueville visited America in order to see this unique example of a free democracy. He found the spirit of American society in active citizens who used and developed their own energy, skills, and resources in every aspect of community life. He was speaking of community as neighborhood or town. Now, community encompasses local institutions, that is, schools, hospitals, mental health boards, social service agencies. But it also refers to the social network that parents create among themselves. Even the term *social network* does not capture the cohesion of a community of parents in which there is a sense of belonging, of shared concerns, of practical support (babysitting, clothing exchanges), and of working for a common good. Having created such a community, a feedback is started by which parents become competent with each other and with their children and start acting together to influence programs, themselves, their children and families, their neighborhood and local institutions, and their state and federal governments.

The community of parents is dynamic and reaches out to affect the larger society. Whether a program is using a theoretical model based upon health, education, or support, that network building process that occurs by virtue of having such programs, of having a place to be together, starts the important process of change. Parents speak out on many levels: changing hospital practices around birth procedures, interviewing pediatricians before choosing one, visiting daycare centers before enrolling their children. Just as there are excellent pamphlets on what to look for in a quality daycare program, there should be pamphlets on what to look for in a good pediatrician. These are healthy signs and point to the possibility of new and stronger relationships between parents and their pediatricians. As one group of mothers said, "Our child is more than a stomach and we are more than a birth canal, and the child is best served by our efforts together—our partnership."

Finally, family support programs represent a belief in the basic strength of families. Ninety-eight percent of children in America are in families of varying forms, and our challenge is to think in terms of the strengths, not the deficits, of these families. The assumption is that every parent has some strengths. It may be the strengths in personal characteristics or attitudes, such as optimism or determination, or it may be external strengths evidenced through family ties, or the strength coming from a strong sense of cultural and ethnic identity. Sometimes the only strength apparent is that required to join a program or keep an appointment. Whatever it is, this approach begins with the question, "What does this family have going for them?" not "What's their problem?"

The community of caring people that families are seeking, that has given rise to and continues to stimulate the growth of family support programs include the pediatrician as a major actor. In the interviews Phyllis LaFarge, an editor of *Parents* magazine, had with parents around the country, she learned that parents look to their pediatrician as authorities but also accept their counsel more willingly when the physician is friendly and sensitive to the their concerns. Those concerns are exemplified in the assumptions upon which family support programs are based, and these parallel approaches for effective pediatricians. Pediatricians are essential to creating the "good-enough" circumstances in which children grow up.

A dominant theme emerging from Phyllis LaFarge's interviews was the mother's need for confirmation in their role as mothers. The sense of confidence which a mother can communicate to her child is enhanced by a family support program, and by her pediatrician. She learned that parents want to be seen as authorities about their own children. How often we have parents who know something is wrong with their child before the doctor does! The pediatrician's statement, "He'll grow out of it—don't worry" may temporarily relieve parents, but the underlying anxiety will persist until the probelm is resolved. It is a remark best used only when the meaning of the behavior is genuinely understood and known to be a developmental stage that will pass. Even then, suggestions on how to deal with it are incumbent on the pediatrician.

The linkage between family support programs and pediatricians is obviously a natural one, precisely because the goals of both are healthy children. A few specific activities for pediatricians are leading discussion groups on health issues for parents or just dropping in to say hello and increasing understanding by interacting with families in a community setting. According to Barbara Korsch, the inevitable response from practitioners of the health professions when confronted with this kind of approach is to exclaim in horror, "Who has the time to go into all that?" Be it in private practice or at a medical center, the time set aside for patients seems too brief for the task at hand even before the introduction of what seem like extra frills. However, if parents need not struggle to get their ideas across, they will have been won over to the doctor's concern, and will be ready to listen and understand because they feel understood.

For pediatricians in training, family support programs provide an unusual opportunity to be with normal families and observe children and parents, together and separately. There could be no better way to understand healthy development and typical parent-child interactions. Being involved helps pediatricians understand the culture of different families and permits parents to overcome the gap that exists when a parent says, "I didn't want to get on the bad side of her and have her develop an attitude about me."

Pediatricians are partners with family support program staff, and both are partners with parents. Being partners does not imply denying one's knowledge and experience, but applying it in a context of respect and understanding. It means viewing children as part of a system, in their own setting of families and community, knowing whether it is an environment which breeds confidence and hope or one which epitomizes despair and futility.

From our mutual assumptions, the role of pediatricians can be derived, and the diverse avenues through which pediatricians can interact with parents will emerge. Now is the time to examine and explore the potentials of the pediatrician-parent partnership possible through the family support movement, and to develop the linkages that will strengthen the capabilities of families to raise healthy, productive, and caring children.

The family support movement is a star on the horizon, but it is also a challenge on earth. As family support programs emerge in communities, they present the unique opportunity for a community of people working together for families—the concept of community that parents build for each other is extended to professionals building with parents. The bottom line we share is the well-being of children and it can only exist as we embrace our interdependence and as we join parents in insisting that society support their efforts.

In the words of Otto Pollach, "Here is a new issue for family life in modern times: the defense of its own power against becoming a dependent variable of changing opinions in the field of education, health care, and public welfare. The discovery that all experts can make mistakes, that one may have the right to be poor, and the right to be sick is one of the challenges of the future for the American family, confronted by experts who can and do change their opinions as a matter of normal professional development."

6
Hyperactivity: Symptom and Disorder

Esther H. Wender

H yperactivity has become an emotionally loaded word, often suggesting that a pejorative label has been applied incorrectly to a healthy active child. Yet, there exist behavioral syndromes—of which hyperactivity is the most noticeable, but not the most important part—that constitute the most common serious behavioral disturbances in childhood. Though controversies surrounding definition are a central theme here, assuming varying definitions, prevalence figures repeatedly arrive at between 5 and 10 percent of the childhood population so affected. And if one still remains sanguine because of the assumption that these disorders constitute a passing phase of development, one need only review the increasing number of studies following these children into adolescence and young adulthood to realize that, at worst, a significant percentage develop serious personality disorders or end up in the population of juvenile delinquents and adult criminals (Hecktman, Weiss, and Pearlman, 1981; Satterfield, Hoppe, and Schell, 1982) and at best, virtually all continue to have difficulty completing tasks and suffer from low self-esteem (Hoy et al., 1978; Weiss et al., 1979). Though controversies remain regarding etiology and management, the evidence clearly indicates that the disorders should not be ignored. Yet those primary health care providers who are probably nodding in agreement with this statement may well be, in effect, ignoring this condition by insisting that it be managed entirely by mental health specialists, and feel their job is finished when they refer to already overburdened mental health facilities. These disorders are too common and too serious in their potential impact on children and families to be relegated solely to tertiary care. Prevention, early detection, counseling, medical management, and coordination of multidisciplinary care—all lie within the appropriate scope of primary health care.

Hyperactivity: The Symptom

The title of this chapter highlights the complexity in understanding and evaluating these disorders. Overactive behavior is a symptom that may or may not indicate an underlying disorder. The child may be excessively active but within the range of normal and misperceived as hyperactive by the caretaker. Or the child's overly active behavior may be a manifestation of a psychological disorder other than one of the hyperactive syndromes. Initially, therefore, the clinician needs a framework to use in the evaluation of hyperactivity as a presenting symptom. The essentials of such a framework follow.

Normal Development and Problem Behavior

Activity level is normally high in very young children and gradually decreases with age. As normal hyperactivity decreases, it is accompanied by an increasing ability to concentrate and stay with a task. Therefore, the normal hyperactivity of the young child can also be described as aimless and non-goal-directed, which is similar to the quality of this symptom in the behaviorally disturbed, older child. Also children, from birth and in utero, vary considerably in activity level according to temperament (Thomas, Chess, and Birch, 1968).

The normal activity level of very young children can become a symptom, producing problems within the family when that behavior is troublesome to the caretaking adult. The most common reasons for misperception of normal behavior are (1) lack of understanding, as in a new parent or a very young adolescent parent; (2) a preoccupation with psychological problems such as depression, environmental stresses such as financial problems, other children, and illness and death, and psychodynamic issues such as an unwanted child or a "vulnerable" child; and (3) temperamental "dissonance." Normal variation in activity as a component of temperament can become a symptom when that temperament is dissonant with the biological rhythms of the caretaker (Thomas et al., 1968). Thus, a very active child being raised by a phlegmatic, slow-moving parent, may be perceived as troublesome.

The primary health care provider should evaluate these possibilities, first by determining if the child's behavior is indeed deviant. If the problem is one of misperception of normal behavior, it is likely that the child will not be seen as deviant in the environment of other caregivers. Therefore, it is necessary to obtain information from other important caregivers in the child's environment. For example, if the parent is the source of complaint, how has the child been viewed by teachers and babysitters? Even this information, however, can be misleading, because children with a developmentally based behavioral disorder, may vary in behavior in different environments. Also, other observers may be biased in their perception of the child. Both these factors should be taken into account when evaluating the history. The clinician can be assisted by the use of questionnaires standardized on populations of normal children (Goyette, Connors, and Ulrich, 1978). Because questionnaire responses are subjective data influenced by the perceptions of the teachers or parents who complete them, they must be interpreted with caution.

In order to determine the attitudes, stresses, and psychological problems of the caregiver, a portion of the interview should be devoted to these issues. Parents (and other caregivers) may become guarded when the interview turns from a focus on the child to questions that clearly relate to the adult's own attitudes and experience. Initially, the parent may express relief that the clinician will now assume a role in the child's problem, since the parent has been worried and felt guilty about his or her contribution to the child's difficulty. This guilt, however, may turn to anger and defensiveness when the information gathered is translated into expectations for the parent to change. Therefore, this aspect of the interview should be preceded by a face-saving explanation. When children's behavior is difficult, an important part of treatment is for the parent to become one of the therapists by learning new ways of responding to the child, thus implying that the old ways may not have solely produced the problem.

History should also address the temperament of both child and parent. The child who is overly active, only as a component of the normal range of temperament, will not possess the other behaviors characteristic of significant behavior disorder.

Hyperactivity Secondary to Anxiety and Depression

Children who suffer from depression may manifest this disorder, in part, by excessive motor restlessness and impaired ability to concentrate and attend. Also, when a child has an anxiety disorder, excessive activity is considered to be a manifestation of anxiety, rather than the symptom of another behavior disorder. The relationship between hyperactivity and symptoms of anxiety and depression, however, are more complex than appears on the surface because some symptoms of anxiety and depression coexist with or may appear later in the course of development in a child who initially demonstrates characteristics of a hyperactive behavior disorder. What distinguishes children with the primary diagnosis of depression or anxiety disorder is the severity and the onset of these behaviors early in the child's history. In summary, children who initially and primarily manifest signs and symptoms of depression or anxiety and qualify for these diagnoses usually also are described as overly active and inattentive. It is much more common, however, for children to manifest initially and primarily signs and symptoms of hyperactivity and inattention and to display symptoms of anxiety and depression during the course of development. In order to distinguish between these possibilities, the history should focus on the earliest manifestations of the child's problem. The clinician should also be familiar with the criteria for diagnosis of primary depression and anxiety disorder in children (table 6–1).

Table 6–1
Diagnostic Criteria for Anxiety Disorder and Primary Depression in Children

Anxiety Disorder	Primary Depression
Generalized, persistent anxiety or worry (at least four of the following):	Must have one of the following:
1. Unrealistic worry about future	1. Dysphoric mood
2. Preoccupation with past behavior	2. Loss of interest or pleasure in all usual activities
3. Overconcern about competence	Must have at least four of the following:
4. Excessive need for reassurance	1. Poor appetite or weight loss
5. Somatic complaints	2. Insomnia or hypersomnia
6. Marked self-consciousness	3. Psychomotor agitation or retardation
7. Marked feelings of tension	4. Loss of interest or pleasure in usual activities
Must have persisted 6 months	5. Loss of energy; fatigue
	6. Feelings of worthlessness; self-reproach; guilt
	7. Decreased ability to think or concentrate
	8. Thoughts of death; suicide

Source: Adapted from *Diagnostic and Statistical Manual of Mental Disorders* (Third Edition), 1980.

Hyperactivity: The Disorder

Hyperactivity is one component of, and the label most frequently used to designate, a behavioral syndrome or syndromes. In the most recently revised diagnositic nomenclature, a single disorder is described and is called attention deficit disorder (ADD). This syndrome is operationally defined as problems with concentration and attention and excessively impulsive behavior, either with or without hyperactivity (Table 6–2). Problems must have been present for at least six months and the onset must have been before the age of seven. These later refinements in the criteria help ensure that the behavioral symptoms are not due solely to recent life stresses. The child must also be free of the major psychiatric conditions of depression or schizophrenia. However, overlap with other disorders in the diagnostic nomenclature are not excluded, and several studies, employing a structured diagnostic interview based on the revised nomenclature, reveal the overlap between ADD and other childhood disorders, especially, conduct and oppositional disorders.

The criteria for attention deficit disorder are quite general. Prior to publication of the revised (*Diagnostic and Statistical Manual of Mental Disorders*

Table 6–2
Diagnostic Criteria for Attention Deficit Disorder

Inattention. At least three of the following:

1. Often fails to finish things he or she starts
2. Often does not seem to listen
3. Easily distracted
4. Has difficulty concentrating on schoolwork or other tasks requiring sustained attention
5. Has difficulty sticking to a play activity

Impulsivity. At least three of the following:

1. Often acts before thinking
2. Shifts excessively from one activity to another
3. Has difficulty organizing work (this not being due to cognitive impairment)
4. Needs a lot of supervision
5. Frequently calls out in class
6. Has difficulty awaiting turn in games or group situations

Hyperactivity. At least two of the following:

1. Runs about or climbs on things excessively
2. Has difficulty sitting still or fidgets excessively
3. Has difficulty staying seated
4. Moves about excessively during sleep
5. Is always "on the go" or acts as if "driven by a motor"

Onset before the age of seven

Duration of at least six months

Not due to schizophrenia, affective disorder, or severe or profound mental retardation

Source: Adapted from DSM-III.

(DSM-III)) nomenclature a similar disorder or disorders were characterized by other behaviors in addition to inattention, impulsiveness, and hyperactivity. The most frequently employed additional criterion was (and still is) a score that is two standard deviations or more above the mean on the ten questions that constitute the hyperkinesis index from the Conner's teacher or parent questionnaire. This teacher-parent questionnaire and scoring procedures are shown in figure 6–1. These ten questions inquire not only about the child's activity level and ability to concentrate, but also about temper outbursts, quick and drastic mood changes, pouting and sulking, being demanding, and disturbing others. Thus, half the ten questions used to help diagnose children with behavior disorder as-

	0 Not at All	1 Just a Little	2 Pretty Much	3 Very Much
1. Restless in the "squirmy" sense.				
2. Demands must be met immediately.				
3. Temper outbursts and unpredictable behavior				
4. Distractability or attention span a problem.				
5. Disturbs other children.				
6. Pouts and sulks.				
7. Mood changes quickly and drastically.				
8. Restless, always up and on the go.				
9. Excitable impulsive.				
10. Fails to finish things that he starts.				

Source: Adapted from Goyette and Conners 1978. Add scores for all 10 questions. Cut off = score ≥ 15.

Figure 6–1. Revised Conner's Teacher–Parent Questionnaire

sess behaviors other than those that define the disorder according to the current nomenclature. British child psychiatrists, particularly Michael Rutter, have been most critical of these inconsistencies.

Rutter asserts that problems with concentration and excessive activity are a component of many different childhood disorders and do not constitute a distinct diagnostic entity. The criteria for attention deficit disorder established in the third revision of the *Diagnostic and Statistical Manual of Mental Disorders* (DSM-III) are broad and, I believe, constitute a nonspecific marker of several different behavior disorders, including the following:

1. hyperactivity syndrome(s)
2. other psychiatric disorders
3. other developmental deviations
4. diffuse neurologic pathology
5. psychological stress

First, these criteria describe in part one or more behavioral syndromes, often referred to as hyperactivity. Whether this is a single syndrome or two or more different disorders is still a subject of debate. Some evidence suggests that this disorder is strongly affected by genetic predisposition (Cadoret et al., 1975; Cantwell, 1972). Second, problems with concentration and attention and impulsivity frequently accompany other psychiatric disorders. This was recognized in developing the criteria, and two such psychiatric disorders are specifically excluded, namely, schizophrenia and depression. The primary health care provider should, however, recognize the possibility that symptoms are secondary to another psychiatric condition and consider the possibility of schizophrenia, depression, manic-depressive, or bipolar, disorder, and overanxious disorder. Third, the criteria for attention deficit disorder also frequently characterize children with specific developmental disorders such as reading disability or speech and language delay. What is not clear and requires further research is the nature of the association between behaviors of attention deficit and developmental disorders. Problems with concentration and attention, by definition, are a component of perceptual and cognitive dysfunction, that is, if a child has difficulty learning and retaining certain kinds of information, that difficulty is, in part, manifest by poor powers of concentration which in turn leads to restless, fidgety behavior. However, in addition to this phenomenon, many children with specific developmental disorders also seem to have the same patterns of behavior that characterize the behavioral syndrome or syndromes referred to as hyperactivity. Fourth, children who have neurologic disease or disorder that affects the nervous system diffusely often demonstrate subsequent behavior consistent with attention deficit disorder. Examples of such nervous system insults include seizure disorder, fetal alcohol syndrome, lead toxicity, postmeningitic or postencephalitic syndrome, and factors producing small-for-gestational-age (SGA) babies. Again, because of confusion over behavioral criteria and nomenclature, it is not known whether the be-havioral disorder that often follows such neurologic dysfunction is different from the behavioral syndrome or syndromes described in the first paragraph of this section. Finally, problems with concentration and attention, excessive activity levels, and impulsivity constitute a potential response to psychological stress. This causal connection is most clearly demonstrated in those cases where a child's behavior changes after a stressful event such as a stormy divorce, and then re-turns to the initial normal adjustment in response to counseling or therapy. When behavior consistent with the behavioral syndrome(s) called hyperactivity, which means the behavioral pattern has been present since early childhood, is seen in a child whose environment is also stressful, it may not be possible to determine which factor accounts for the problem.

From this list of factors that may be associated with attention deficit disor-der, neurologic insult and psychiatric disorder are uncommon. The specific de-velopmental disorders are common and should be systematically evaluated in all children presenting with hyperactivity and inattention. Hyperactivity produced solely by emotional stress may be common in socioeconomically disadvantaged environments. The prevalence of attention deficit disorder in such environments may be as high as 25–30 percent of school-age children (Berger, Yule, and Rutter, 1975). However, one must be cautious in attributing this increase in prevalence entirely to environmentally associated emotional factors. The hyperactivity syn-drome or syndromes described in this section may be due, in large part, to genetic factors that are much more prevalent in lower socioeconomic populations, owing to the downward drift in economic status that is the result rather than the cause of these disorders.

Subgroups of Attention Deficit Disorder

In the past five to ten years, research has increasingly focused on attempts to characterize more specifically syndromes within the broad framework of atten-tion deficit disorder. So far, this research has focused primarily on different symp-tom patterns. Ultimately, the validity of distinct and separate syndromes must be based upon differing etiologies. In the absence of an established cause, such syn-dromes must be shown to have different prognoses or responses to treatment. This aspect of subgroup research is only beginning.

Conduct Disorder. The greatest amount of investigation has centered around the relationship between conduct disorder and attention deficit disorder. Before de-scribing the results of this research, the term *conduct disorder* should be ex-plained. According to the revised American nomenclature (DSM-III), conduct disorder is a behavioral syndrome characterized by a pattern of disobeying rules and defying authority that varies along two dimensions as outlined in table 6–3. First, the child may be unsocialized or socialized, a dimension that focuses on

Table 6–3
Conduct Disorder

Undersocialized. Failure to establish normal affection, empathy, bond. No more than one of the following:

1. Peer group friendship over six months

2. Extends self even when no immediate advantage likely

3. Feels guilt or remorse (not just when caught)

4. Avoids blaming others

5. Shows concern for friends' welfare

Socialized. Shows at least two of above

Aggressive. Repetitive, persistent pattern of aggressive conduct. Basic rights of others violated, as indicated by at least one of the following:

1. Physical violence against person, or property

2. Thefts, outside home, confrontation with victim

Nonaggressive. Repetitive, persistent pattern of nonaggressive conduct. Basic rights of others or major, age-appropriate societal norms violated, as indicated by at least one of the following:

1. Chronic violations of important rules

2. Repeated running away

3. Persistent lying, in and out of home

4. Stealing, no confrontation

Source: Adapted from DSM-III, 1980.

the child's interest in and attachment to other people. Second, the behavior may be agressive or nonagressive, which refers to whether, in the process of breaking rules and defying regulations, the child uses physical aggression. The socialization dimension appears to indicate the presence or absence of a schizoid quality. The aggressive, nonaggressive dimension has not been adequately characterized from a developmental point of view. That is, what are the earliest beginnings of aggressive behavior in children, and, therefore, how do we understand the etiology and natural history of this behavior?

In fact, the evolution of all aspects of conduct disorder are not understood. The socialized, nonaggressive form of conduct disorder appears to be the least serious of the four versions of this condition. However, even this version indicates fairly severe behavioral deviation. The description of this disorder is "a repetitive, persistent pattern of conduct where the basic rights of others or major, age-appropriate societal norms are violated." Then the child must be characterized by at least one of four examples, including: (1) chronic violation of important rules; (2) repeated running away; (3) persistent lying, in and out of home; and (4) stealing, but without physical confrontation. A possible developmental basis for conduct disorder is suggested in the new diagnostic nomenclature by the listing of a syndrome called oppositional disorder (table 6–4). This syndrome is characterized by disobedient, negativistic, and provocative opposition to authority that appears after the age of three, but falls short of violation of basic rights of others or of major age-appropriate societal norms. Therefore, oppositional disorder appears to identify similar, but less serious behavior than that which characterizes conduct disorder and behavior that appears earlier in the course of development.

A number of studies using symptom cluster analyses have shown an extensive overlap between conduct disorder and attention deficit problems (Roberts, Milich, and Loney, 1981; Loney, Langhorne, and Paternite, 1978; Lahey, Green, and Forehand, 1980; Prinz, Conner, and Wilson, 1981). This overlap is not surprising when one looks at the measures used to identify these two disorders. As mentioned previously, the most frequently used independent measure of hyperactivity or attention deficit disorder is the score on the Conner's parent-teacher questionnaire. These ten questions include one item that clearly could indicate conduct disturbance—"disturbs other children." Three other items appear to identify negative emotion that could precede or accompany defiance of authority—"temper outbursts and unpredictable behavior," "pouts and sulks," and "mood changes quickly and drastically." A fifth item also suggests defiant behavior—"demands must be met immediately." As the British psychiatrists have pointed out, when conduct disturbance is the behavior pattern being sought, a high percentage (60–70 percent) are also described as hyperactive or inattentive (Rutter, Tizard, and Whitmore, 1970). According to Rutter and his research group, the term *hyperkinetic syndrome* applies only when no conduct problem behaviors are present. Based upon these definitions, in their excellent epidemiologic studies, hyperkinetic syndrome occurs in less than 0.5 percent of nine- to 10-year-old children, while conduct disorder characterized 4 percent of the same age group. These figures suggest that conduct disorder, as they define it, is by far the most common condition.

This extensive overlap in diagnoses was noted early in the history of research in and reviews of what was then called minimal brain dysfunction or postencephalitic syndrome. These early descriptions have been ignored in much of the later literature largely because these conduct problems are seen as "emotional," which to most people means that they are learned behaviors, acquired by difficult children in response to feedback from peers or caretakers. It is also possible that these conduct problems follow from temperament, or biologically based traits, a possibility that is suggested by much clinical observation.

Specific Developmental Disorder. Specific developmental disorders are so frequently accompanied by problems with concentration and attention that learning disorders have, in the past, been listed as one of the defining criteria of the hyperactivity syndrome. The failure to include learning disability as a defining

Table 6–4
Oppositional Disorder

Pattern of disobedient, negativistic and provocative opposition to authority, as indicated by at least two of the following:

1. Violation of minor rules

2. Temper tantrums

3. Argumentativeness

4. Provocative behavior

5. Stubbornness

No violation of basic rights of others. Major age-appropriate societal norms.

Source: Adapted from DSM-III, 1980.

criterion in the revised nomenclature of the DSM-III indicates recognition that inattention, impulsivity, and hyperactivity are also frequently seen without any of the perceptual problems that define specific developmental disorders, suggesting separate, but frequently associated, syndromes. There continues to be, however, confusion, on the part of both parents and teachers regarding the reasons for school problems that characterize both disorders. In the case of the behavioral syndrome(s) most often called "hyperactivity," disturbance in school performance is due to unwillingness to persist in the repetitive effort required in completing tasks, behavior that is usually characterized as poor motivation. Again, confusion occurs because lack of motivation is seen as an emotional problem secondary to inadequate stimulation or poor supervision. However, it is more consistent with clinical findings to view lack of motivation as due to the defiance of authority or resistance to conditioning that is characteristic of attention deficit disorder. By contrast, the academic disturbance typical of specific developmental disorder is due to perceptual problems that impair the child's ability to acquire and retain such specific information as the spelling of words, arithmetic processes, and the recognition (reading) of specific words. Careful history and educational testing will distinguish between these two possible sources of academic difficulty.

"Pure" Hyperactivity. In the studies describing the overlap between attention deficit disorder and conduct disorder, a specific subgroup emerged, called pure hyperactivity (August and Stewart, 1982). These children were exceptionally restless, overactive, and inattentive but did not defy rules and regulations and did not suffer from perceptual problems typical of children with specific developmental disorder. This small subgroup was characterized by a lower IQ and more impaired coordination than other children with ADD, suggesting that diffuse brain dysfunction is a more likely etiology in this subgroup.

In summary, though much work remains to be done, some subgroups of the broadly defined attention deficit disorder have been further characterized by symptom pattern. The conduct-disordered subgroup clearly constitutes the major clinical problem, both because it so frequently is associated with hyperactivity and inattentive, impulsive behavior, and because follow-up studies suggest that the poorest prognosis of attention deficit problems is found in the conduct-disordered subgroup (Satterfield, Hoppe, and Schell, 1982; August, Stewart and Holmes, 1983). There is a need, however, for a better understanding of the possible developmental evolution of conduct disorder. For example, do children who qualify for oppositional disorder go on to have conduct disorder?

It is not known whether these subgroups differ in etiology or in response to treatments such as stimulant medication, behavior modification, or psychotherapy. In the past, however, studies have failed to yield symptom patterns that predict different stimulant medication response (Werry, 1968). Two other lines of research focused on attention deficit behaviors promise useful information and should be further pursued. First, some work has been done characterizing autonomic nervous system responses that may differentiate children with severe conduct disorder from others with attention deficit problems but less serious conduct disturbance. Second, some research has demonstrated an improved (more compliant) response to discipline as one effect of stimulant medication in children with attention deficit disorder. (Humphries, Kinsbourne, and Swanson, 1978; Barkley & Cunningham, 1979). Even more important than a changed response in the child is an altered parenting behavior pattern, following stimulant-produced changes in the child's behavior.

Implications. What is the important message for the health care provider who is committed to the goal of maximizing each child's potential for functioning as an adult in our society? Most experts would agree that attention deficit disorder is not a single condition. However, there exist behavioral syndromes in childhood marked most obviously by problems with concentration and attention that result in significant emotional morbidity and are the most prevalent behavior disorders of childhood. Long-term follow-up studies, plus the highly speculative research on adults with what DSM-III calls "attention deficit disorder, residual type," indicate that this emotional morbidity includes the following potential problems: (1) significant academic underachievement, or what Levine terms low output failure; (2) a persistent and pervasive low self-concept which may be the source of much behavioral dysfunction in adult life; (3) substance abuse which may be initiated and sustained by its affect on self-concept and the alleviation of emotional distress; (4) antisocial behavior that is, in part, due to poor control of angry emotions and may include a greater susceptibility to child-abusing behaviors as an adult; and (5) interactional dysfunction resulting in impaired interpersonal relations. Examples of this last problem include more frequent loss of jobs, marital conflict and divorce, and lowered economic productivity.

Another view of the potential for emotional morbidity during adult life is revealed by studies showing that certain personality disorders are commonly preceded by attention deficit problems in childhood. Those disorders include hysteria, or Briquet's syndrome in women and psychopathic personality in men.

The ultimate challenge for the several disciplines that study and evaluate these disorders is to develop effective treatment. However, much additional research is needed before truly effective treatment can be developed. First, we need to know what is different about these children, at the earliest possible age. As mentioned previously, much attention has been focused on activity level and attention, but very little is known about the emotional characteristics of these children, particularly when very young. Second, we need to have a better understanding of the impact of these behaviors on the caregiver and, in turn, the impact of different caregiving behaviors on the child with these problems. Such interactional research is difficult, but vital. Third, we need to continue to attempt to characterize the biological component of these disorders in an attempt to develop an effective biological treatment. Meanwhile, we should continue to responsibly employ biological treatment, that is, stimulant medication, which should be justified primarily on the basis of effectiveness. As long as a treatment is beneficial (and helpfulness is always, in the practice of medicine, a decision based upon the individual patient's response), it should not be withheld on philosophical grounds alone but only if it is biologically or psychologically harmful. Finally, we need to understand more about the effect of these behavioral differences on the inner life of the child as the basis for developing more effective psychological therapies.

We have clearly moved beyond the notion that hyperactivity is the most salient feature of a single disorder that can be effectively treated by a single modality. Multiple approaches to treatment should be urged and several disciplines need to be involved. The primary health care provider is an important, if not the most important, member of that team. Pediatricians and others who deliver primary health care to children cannot afford to hide behind ignorance and lack of interest in the care of these children.

References

August, G.J., and Stewart, M.A.: Is there a syndrome of pure hyperactivity? *Br. J. Psychiatry 140*:305, 1982.

August, G.J., Stewart, M.A., and Holmes, C.S.: A four-year follow-up of hyperactive boys with and without conduct disorder. *Br. J. Psychiatry 143*:192, 1983.

Barkley, R.A., and Cunningham, C.E.: The effects of methylphenidate on the mother-child interactions of hyperactive children. *Arch. Gen. Psychiatry 36*:201, 1979.

Berger, M., Yule, W., and Rutter, M.: Attainment and adjustment in two geographical areas. *Br. J. Psychiatry 126*:510, 1975.

Cadoret, R.J., Cunningham, L., Loftus, R., et al.: Studies of adoptees from psychiatrically disturbed biological parents. II. Temperament, hyperactive, antisocial and developmental variables. *J. Pediatr.* 87:301, 1975.

Cantwell, D.P.: Psychaitric illness in the families of hyperactive children. *Arch. Gen. Psychiatry* 27:414, 1972.

Goyette, C.H., Conners, C.K., and Ulrich, R.F.: Normative data on revised Conners parent and teacher rating scales. *J. Abn. Child Psychol.* 6:221, 1978.

Hecktman, L., Weiss, G., and Pearlman, T.: Hyperactives as young adults: past and current antisocial behavior (stealing, drug abuse) and moral development. *Psychopharmacol. Bull.* 17:107, 1981.

Hoy, E., Weiss, G., Minde, K., et al.: The hyperactive child at adolescence: cognitive, emotional and social functioning. *J. Abn. Child Psychol.* 6:311, 1978.

Humphries, T., Kinsbourne, M., and Swanson, J.: Stimulant effects on cooperation and social interaction between hyperactive children and their mothers. *J. Child Psychol. Psychiatry* 19:13, 1978.

Lahey, B.B., Green, K.D., and Forehand, R.: On the independence of ratings of hyperactivity, conduct problems, and attention deficits in children: a multiple regression analysis. *J. Consult. Clin. Psychol.* 48:566, 1980.

Loney, J., Langhorne, J.E., and Paternite, C.E.: An empirical basis for subgrouping the hyperkinetic, minimal brain dysfunction syndrome. *J. Abn. Psychol.* 87:431, 1978.

Prinz, R.J., Conner, P.A., and Wilson, C.C.: Hyperactive and aggressive behaviors in childhood: intertwined dimensions. *J. Abn. Child Psychol.* 9:191, 1981.

Roberts, M.A., Milich, R., and Loney, J.: A multitrait-multimethod analysis of variance of teachers' ratings of aggression, hyperactivity, and inattention. *J. Abn. Child Psychology* 9:371, 1981.

Rutter, M., Tizard, J., and Whitmore, K.: *Education, Health and Behavior.* New York, John Wiley & Sons, 1970.

Satterfield, J.H., Hoppe, C.M., and Schell, A.M.: A prospective study of delinquency in 110 adolescent boys with attention deficit disorder and 88 normal adolescent boys. *Am. J. Psychiatry* 139:795, 1982.

Thomas, A., Chess, S., and Birch, H.G.: *Temperament and Behavior Disorders in Children.* New York: New York University Press, 1968.

Weiss, G., Hechtman, L., Pearlman, T., et al.: Hyperactives as young adults: a controlled prospective ten-year follow-up of 75 children. *Arch. Gen. Psychiatry* 36:675, 1979.

Werry, J.S.: Studies on the hyperactive child: an empirical analysis of the minimal brain dysfunction syndrome. *Arch. Gen. Psychiatry* 19:9, 1968.

7

The New Pediatrics and the School-Age Child

Judith S. Palfrey
Barry G. Zallen

Over the past three decades in pediatrics, there has emerged a growing appreciation of the importance of developmental dysfunction in school-age children (Green, 1975). Alerted to the major psychological consequences of inadequate school performance, pediatric researchers have joined other child-oriented specialists in taking a fresh look at the impact neurodevelopmental factors can make in the lives of school-age children.

Attention, memory, behavioral organization, motor planning, motor execution, and language have increasingly been recognized as contributors to the well-being or the disability of five- to fourteen-year-old children. Since school is the main arena of performance for children and since assessment, monitoring, and comparison are such integral components of school, psychological stress frequently arises as a by-product of the school experience. It is not uncommon for such stress to result in acting out, encopresis, enuresis, school dropout, or family conflict.

When pediatric clinicians are asked to assess school-age children with developmental disabilities and consequent behavioral problems, the differential diagnosis is long and the evaluation process is often complex. In part, the difficulty arises because a vast array of heterogeneous factors (attention problems, language disability, sequencing problems, cognitive impairment, memory problems, perceptual dysfunction, behavioral disorganization as well as certain psychiatric disabilities such as depression) manifest themselves with a small number of relatively undifferentiated symptoms: namely, poor school output, poor school attendance and unhappiness with school (Levine et al., 1980). The other part of the doctor's dilemma is that the knowledge base regarding many aspects of childhood developmental disabilities is incomplete. Further, most of the methodologies available for expanding that knowledge base are themselves relatively primitive (Pless, 1981). Fortunately, a number of investigators have taken this problem as a challenge and have worked vigorously to bring a better understanding to both basic research questions and to clinical applications.

It is well beyond the scope of this chapter to review every aspect of the newly emerging literature or to explore the rich historical background of each developmental theory. Therefore, we focus our attention on five topics relevant to clinical practice, discussing the work which has addressed these areas most recently and commenting, when appropriate, from our own research and experience. The five topics are: (1) prevalence, (2) associations, (3) etiology, (4) clinical phenomenology, and (5) community response.

Prevalence

A perplexing question has plagued the field of developmental pediatrics: Just how many children are there with school-age developmental dysfunction? This question has obvious policy and clincial relevance. For policymakers, it is critical to have a reasonable estimate of the occurrence of a condition or (conditions) in order to make coherent and systematic plans for children and their families. For clinicians, a sense of prevalence gives a helpful guide for assessing the adequacy of case findings within a given practice.

Why has it been so difficult for researchers and other analysts to estimate the prevalence of developmental problems in the school-age period? To a large extent, the difficulty is with definitions. What constitutes a developmental problem? What constitutes developmental variation? What are the components of a behavioral problem and how is that differentiated from an unconventional temperament or an innovative behavioral style? Furthermore, until recently, the natural history of developmental disorders was so poorly understood, that there was considerable question about whether a learning or behavioral problem seen at one point in time really constituted a condition or was instead a transient situational response.

The definitional issues have led to countless reviews, congresses, and meetings of pediatricians and other child developmental specialists, all absolutely convinced that clinical entities of school-age problems exist, but varying in their descriptions of the children and in their sense of the scope of the problem (Gaddes, 1976; Eisenberg, 1978; Johnson and Mylkebust, 1967). The estimates for learning disabilities, for instance, have varied, from 2 percent to 20 percent. For few (if any) other conditions in pediatrics has there been so much uncertainty about the nature and extent of the problem.

Over the past ten to fifteen years, two types of inquiry have attempted to bring some order to the reigning confusion. The first has involved studies of community data bases. The second has addressed the natural history of developmental and learning problems.

Population-Based Studies

Studies of Special Education Populations. With the passage of the federal statute PL 94–142 (Education for All Handicapped Children Act of 1975) came a major opportunity for the collection of data on children with developmental disabilities. Since federal funding was contingent on accurate child counts by diagnosis, an immediate and accessible data base was created for the collection and analysis of information about children with educational handicaps.

Now that PL 94–142 has been in effect in the United States for half a decade, such analysis from the school special education population has begun. Major studies commissioned by the federal government provide the basis for cross-sectional and time trend comparisons (SRI International, 1979; Education Turnkey Systems, 1978).

The overall prevalence of school-age developmental problems by state has been documented at around 8–10 percent (U.S. Department of Health, Education and Welfare, Office of Education). Within this, the largest proportion of children are those with learning disabilities (2.5–3.0 percent) and children with speech problems (2.8–4.0 percent). Children classified as mentally retarded constitute the next largest group (2.1–2.3 percent), with the designation "emotionally disturbed" following at 1.3–2.0 percent. Children with sensory impairments account for little more than 0.5 percent as do children with significant physical impairment and multiple handicaps.

While the national data base is helping researchers define the group of children with learning problems somewhat more systematically than previously, three problems continue to hamper these efforts. First there are major inconsistencies from site to site with regard to the prevalence of certain conditions. Second there is overlap and fluidity between a number of the conditions, since children do not come as neatly packaged as bureaucrats and epidemiologists might wish. Third, studies of already identified children may mask the true community prevalence of the conditions.

Most studies of the prevalence of developmental problems in school-age children have shown both inconsistencies and fluidity between the various diagnostic classifications. With regard to inconsistencies, for instance, in the five sites our group is currently studying, the designation "learning disabled" varies from 30 to 58 percent of the special education population; the designation "emotionally disturbed" from 2 to 16 percent and "mentally retarded" from 7 to 20 percent. This variation is of particular concern since the underlying prevalence of disability seems to be relatively stable and similar site to site (Walker et al., 1984).

With regard to fluidity, the most permeable barriers seem to be between speech and learning disabilities and between emotional disturbance and learning disabilities. There is also considerable movement of children within school systems back and forth between the categories educably mentally retarded and learning disabled. The movement between these categories belies the inherent artificially of the unidimensional diagnoses used by school systems for funding and program planning purposes and has led a number of investigators and policymakers to suggest that more generic or functional terminology would be more meaningful for both educational and epidemiological purposes (Hobbs, 1975; Hallahan and Kauffman, 1977).

Studies from the General Population. A variety of institutional and political pressures influence the identification process which places children in special education. As a result, studies of the already identified special education population may not adequately reflect the entire group of children with school age developmental difficulties (SRI International, 1979), making it important to derive estimates from the general population as often as possible. Clearly such a community-based approach is the most scientifically meaningful if the population base is representative. Rutter's landmark study on the Isle of Wight allowed an early appreciation of the epidemiology of childhood developmental disability. While mounting such studies is a collosal effort, without such an approach it is impossible to be completely informed about the prevalence, phenomenology, or associated characteristics of childhood developmental disability. Currently, a series of community studies is being conducted to derive population-based estimates of neurodevelopmental symptoms in school-age children. The results from this type of research will help establish more rigorously defined prevalence estimates. One anticipated issue, however, is that population-based studies will find many new developmental signs among children who are in fact functioning well. Thus, analysis of the clusters of strengths and dysfunctions may be crucial to understanding why some children fail and others succeed.

Studies of Natural History

Until recently there has been considerable question about the seriousness and the consequences of learning problems because of the paucity of studies of the long-term outcomes of children with learning difficulties. Fortunately for clinicians and investigators, that knowledge gap is quickly being filled, but unfortunately for the children, the findings of the studies are relatively bleak.

Schonhaut and Satz (1983) reviewed all the long-term follow-up studies on children with reading/learning problems. They specifically excluded studies that labeled children "M.B.D." or "hyperkinetic" because of the ambiguity of the terms. Among the eighteen studies chosen for analysis, there were favorable outcomes in four, unfavorable outcomes in twelve, and mixed outcomes in two. The unfavorable outcomes included poor reading ability, excessive school dropout rates, and increased rates of psychological problems.

While Schonhaut and Satz excluded children with attendant behavioral concerns, a number of follow-up studies have concentrated their attention on children with hyperactivity, or in more current terminology, attention deficit disorder. In Weiss and co-workers (1979) ten-year prospective follow-up of a group of 75 hyperactive children, they found that the young people with attention deficits attained lower educational levels, were involved in more car accidents, made more geographic moves, and manifested impulsivity more frequently than a group of matched controls. However, they found no more antisocial behavior among the subjects than among the controls. Studies by Milich and Loney (1979), Huessey and Cohen (1976), and others have come to conclusions similar to the Weiss study.

The issue of the relationship of learning disabilities to juvenile delinquency has been actively studied and hotly debated for some time (Karniski et al., 1982). There appears to be no question that young people in trouble with the law have significant, across-the-board learning problems. Most studies show these youngsters to be at least one and a half to two years delayed in reading and math. What is less clear, however, is whether there is any causal link between developmental difficulties and juvenile delinquency. Only through very careful prospective work can such an hypothesis be tested. Satterfield's recent prospective study (Satterfield, Hoppe, and Schell, 1982) is helpful in that regard since his group has been able to follow 110 boys with attention deficit disorder diagnosed from the time of diagnosis until age seventeen and to compare their delinquency rate with that of 88 adolescents without attention deficit disorder. Their findings are striking. For youngsters of low socioeconomic status the rates of serious offenses was five times that of controls; for boys in the middle socioeconomic group the rate was four times that of the controls; and for youngsters with attention deficits in the highest socioeconomic group the offense rate was twenty-six times that of the mtached controls.

A recent study of juvenile deliquency completed by our group at Boston Children's Hospital (Levine et al., in press) has shown the importance of multiple risk factors in the etiology of delinquency. Learning problems often contribute to a cluster of problems whose synergistic effect is more powerful than that of any single risk factor.

Follow-up studies of children with more substantial developmental delays focus primarily on life skills and vocational opportunities. In contrast to the studies of children with learning disabilities where negative outcomes are highlighted, the studies of mildly retarded children are often designed to illuminate the potential of the children and to lend support to the argument that the designation mentally retarded holds only so long as youngsters are required to perform school-related tasks. On follow-up into adulthood, many of the mildly retarded individuals function successfully in society where the behavioral and occupational options are far more plentiful than within the school environment (Charles, 1953; Cobb, 1972; Kennedy, 1966). Nonetheless, the role of developmental dysfunction is adequately documented by the fact that few of these individuals are able to compete for high-paying jobs.

Finally, follow-up studies of children with moderate to severe retardation document their serious long-term disability and total dependency needs (Saenger, 1957; Stanfield, 1973). These studies show that the prognosis for children of IQ 30–50 is that they will need near-constant supervision throughout their lives and have few opportunities for meaningful or productive activities.

Associations

Developmental disability in school-age children rarely stands as an isolated finding. Children who are chronically failing in school or who are frequently absent or developmentally maladjusted often carry with them a constellation of other problems that confound or exacerbate their basic condition. Rarely does a single factor constitute a 100 percent risk. Rather, the cumulative impact of a variety of factors combines to determine a given child's academic performance. Risk factors in addition to neurodevelopmental weaknesses include individual psychological dysfunction, disorientation of family dynamics, chronic illness, problems with physical environment, and peer group and subcultural influences. The interaction of these factors is not two-dimensional. Rather, the effect of one factor on another may shift the ultimate balance. It is the awareness of these associations and the disentangling of the secondary complications that can often be the pediatrician's major contribution to a school-age child with developmental disability.

Socioeconomic Associations

One of the most common associations with developmental problems is low socioeconomic status. It is impossible to read the literature on developmental disabilities without being struck repeatedly by the high loading of socioeconomic stress that some children with developmental disability suffer. Studies show over and over again, for instance, that classes for children with mild or educable mental retardation are disproportionately composed of poor children and often overrepresentive of minority groups. This finding has been so consistent, pervasive, and disturbing that the National Research Council recently appointed a special panel to review all studies (Heller, Holtzman, and Messick, 1982). The panel was charged with determining whether these findings reflected unfair classification and placement practices or whether there was, in fact, a significant correlation between poverty, social disadvantage, and developmental attainment of school-age children. The panel acknowledged that the problem was culturally and politically very complex, but concluded that the association was real, not apparent and suggested that the other correlates of poverty including malnutrition, poor prenatal care, poor ongoing medical care, low maternal education, and lack of necessary supports could probably explain much of the association (Shonkoff, 1982). Since many of these factors are amenable to policy manipulation (and some of them to health policy reform), future intervention research may be directed at lessening the occurence of these problems. For the present, the recommendations of the National Research Council are aimed at classification and curricular reform. The report suggests that children with mild educational handicaps should be removed from the regular classroom setting only when it is clearly documented that they are not benefiting in regular class placements despite appropriate modifications and special service provision.

Studies relating to the socioeconomic correlates of learning problems other than mild mental retardation show a less clear picture. Moderate to severe retardation appears to be less environmentally bound than mild retardation, but there is still a suggestion throughout the developmental literature that children of poverty are at significantly higher risk than other children. Perhaps the best explanation of this phenomenon is to be found in the signal work of Bierman, and French; Werner, *The Children of Kauai* (1971). In that study, Werner and her group explored the synergistic effect of environment on other developmental stressors, particularly perinatal events. The findings of her work, which others have corroborated (Escalona, 1982), strongly suggest that the developmental outcome of equivalent perinatal traumatic events will be directly proportional to the accompanying degree of socioeconomic hardship the child's family faces. This concept, termed "the continuum of caretaking casualty" (Sameroff and Chandler, 1975), postulates that in families of poverty any individual cross-sectional event such as a traumatic delivery or neonatal sepsis is compounded by a set of longitudinal risk factors (including poor maternal nutrition, working late during pregnancy, inadequate or sometimes nonexistent prenatal care, poor maternal health and habits, less than optimal obstetric care, prematurity risk, poor mothering concepts, little opportunity for parenting education, heavy social burdens including single parenthood, work schedules, demands of large families, and social isolation). The concept of "impaired resiliency" which is currently quite popular suggests that a child or family can often snap back from a given insult if there are adequate physical, fiscal, and emotional resources, but that there may be a critical level of those resources without which a child and family simply cannot heal the wound completely.

For learning disabilities, the issue of socioeconomic correlates is somewhat confusing. Some studies have shown wide socioeconomic heterogeneity (Levine, 1979), while others have pointed to the prominence of lower socioeconomic groups (Eisenberg, 1978).

In part the federal policies designed to provide educational services to children at social disadvantage (e.g. Title 1), have contributed to the notion that the learning problems of poor children are somehow different from the learning problems of nonpoor children. In fact, the PL 94-142 definition of "learning disability" specifically excludes environmental determinants as potential contributors to learning disabilities. As funds for educational programming for children at socioeconomic disadvantage are being rescinded, poor children may either be forgotten altogether or begin to comprise a greater and greater proportion of the learning-disabled population. In addition, as the recommendations from the National Research Council regarding the classification of poor, developmentally delayed children become more widespread, there may be a more clear-cut association of socioeconomic factors with learning disabilities.

Another socioeconomic issue has been the disentanglement of school problems from problem schools. In areas where as many as 40–50 percent of children fail basic competency tests, the issue is often raised whether the problem is not with the children, but rather with the instructional services themselves. This situation most frequently pertains in urban areas where there is a high density of extremely needy families and children. In exploring this issue, Rutter (1983) determined that in fact there are major school level influences which affect the educational development of children and which can in turn be affected by enlightened programming—even in the face of devastating social risk situations. The key elements identified by Rutter are organization of curricular material with precisely articulated academic goals, clear-cut and accepted school rules, emphasis on the value of education, respect for children, and positive staff morale. Rutter identifies the school principal as the individual with the greatest potential for creating an environment conducive to children's learning or, on the other hand, for stifling the spark of childhood imagination and zeal.

A final disturbing (and challenging) association of low socioeconomic status and school-age learning problems is the relatively low rate of preschool experiences of children of poverty. Despite the vigorous pioneering efforts of Richmond (1966) and Caldwell (1975), and despite the highly suggestive findings of Bronfenbrenner (1975), Lazar (1977), and others that early intervention really does work and works best for children at social disadvantage, the opportunities for preschool experiences for poor and minority children are still extremely limited. Quality daycare is in short supply and funding to pay the woefully inadequate salaries of those currently involved in preschool work is vulnerable at best. In our recent review of special education, inequities in preschool opportunities were clearly demonstrated. Interestingly, the lowest rates for preschool attendance were among children who ultimately were designated "learning disabled" (Walker et al., 1984).

Experimental studies are needed to find ways of extending schooling downward into the preschool years. One study which has attempted to do this was the Brookline Early Education Project (BEEP). Children enrolled from the community at three months prior to birth, were provided with diagnostic and educational services with the hope that developmental and behavioral problems could be identified early and that intervention could begin as soon as possible. In this project, the good news was that there was the virtual elimination of reading problems among the upper socioeconomic group. For the lower socioeconomic groups, there were some successes, but there was an absolute requirement for a high level of services and aggressive outreach for the children from the poorest groups (Palfrey, Levine, and Pierson, 1984).

Behavioral Associations

It is the behavioral associations which most often bring children with learning problems to clinical attention. The well-documented association of attention deficit disorder and learning problems is discussed in chapter 6. Other behavioral correlates include serious mood effects and physiologic manifestations.

Often it can be very difficult to disassociate depression from school problems and determine which is primary and which is secondary. A child who is unable to keep up in school, or more fundamentally, is really incapable of understanding the world in ways that other children can is at profound risk of severe depression. Being out of touch is an extremely uncomfortable feeling for anyone, but for a child who needs peer acceptance so desperately, this can be a major issue. In the authors' study, as many as 30 percent of children with learning problems seemed to be having additional emotional problems.

The individual psychological profile of a youngster may contribute to or help prevent an impaired outcome in one functional area or another. The child's individual coping strategies may be an important balancing mechanism. Inefficient coping strategies may leave a child more at risk and exposed to other factors.

Enuresis and encopresis frequently accompany school problems. To what extent they represent secondary consequences and to what extent they suggest a different maturational sequence of the central nervous system is unclear. However, they are such frequent fellow-travelers that it is incumbent on the clinician to inquire about them.

Family Problems

Finally, family problems are often found in association with learning problems. Neither the nature nor the direction of this relationship is perfectly or adequately understood, but the current hypothesis is that some children are more vulnerable than others and that in such children, family disruption constitutes a major risk factor. In a recent study of the persistence of preschool developmental problems into school age, family disruption was a strong correlate (Palfrey, Levine, and Pierson, 1984).

Family problems could be interacting with school dysfunction in a number of ways. Direct conflicts between parents and children (for whatever reason) might lead to a negative cycle in the family. This, in turn, might lead to lowered self-esteem, a sense of abandonment, overidentification with peer group, and ultimately to significant academic impairment. A second mechanism might not involve parent-child conflict, but rather the school-age child's anxiety regarding family circumstances. During periods of separation and divorce, it is not unusual for school performance in the affected children to suffer as the youngsters manifest preoccupation with the painful social crisis in their lives. Finally, for some children, the absence of family financial and social supports may mean that they are bearing significant responsibilities in the home with babysitting, cooking, and other necessary chores. The growing number of latchkey children attests to the isolation these children face and the added burden placed upon them by unfortunate family circumstances.

Social Associations

Childhood learning problems often include difficulties with social cognition. As children have perceptual difficulties in other spheres, they may not adequately read the cues they are receiving from the other children in their class or neighborhood. As a result, they may be considered the class clown or worse persona non grata. They may often be left out of playtime activities, birthday parties, and the like. The pain of this exclusion may be significantly worse than any academic failure. Recognition of this association by families, schools, and physicians may lead to directed interventions that build in positive social experiences for school-age children with learning problems.

Etiology

The etiology of developmental and behavioral problems has been the object of intensive study in recent years. Investigations have proceeded on a number of parallel fronts with the recognition that developmental disability is not a single entity, and that there are doubtless many different causes, each explaining only a small part of the functional variance seen in disabled children.

Two major theorectical questions that have tantalized investigators continue to be problematic. The first question is whether trauma to the central nervous system (CNS) is delivered in an all-or-none or in a continuous fashion. The second question relates to the interaction of multiple factors.

It is well documented that physical trauma, birth injury, CNS infection, asphyxia, and other pathologic events can cause devastating results in CNS function. What is not as well known is whether minor head trauma, less severe CNS infections, or minor episodes of biochemical imbalance can cause less severe functional impairment. This notion of a continuum led to the concept of minimal brain damage and continues to be a central issue in the study of developmental disability. As graduates of intensive care nurseries are avoiding major devastation, a number of investigators have postulated that they will instead manifest mild learning and other developmental problems.

The second issue is that of the multiplicity of risk factors. Although most investigators continue to pursue leads about unifactorial causation, it is also acknowledged that many children are at risk not on one but on multiple fronts. Borrowing from current work in immunology, questions are being raised about "inciting agents" and "host factors."

The areas in which significant work on etiology have been undertaken are perinatal influences, nutrition, genetics, focal neurologic trauma, faulty wiring, toxins, and biochemical abnormalities.

Perinatal Factors

Many studies have reported significant relationships between perinatal events and later developmental outcome (Abramowicz and Kass, 1966; Drillien, 1972; Fitzhardinge and Steven, 1972; Lilienfeld and Pasamanick, 1955, 56; and Natelson and Sayers, 1973). On the other hand, some researchers have raised serious questions about the predictive validity of perinatal complications (Denhoff, Hainsworth, and Hainsworth, 1972; Dinwiddie et al., 1974; Niwander et al., 1966; Smith et al., 1972; and Wiener, 1970). The inconsistencies in the studies derive to some extent from differences in interpretation, but to a larger extent they reflect the major methodologic differences in the studies in terms of the types of children and conditions studied and in terms of timing and type of outcomes used.

Davie, Butler, and Goldstein (1972) identified four factors that have held up in most studies as important predictors of later dysfunction: social class, birth order, birth weight/gestational age, and traumatic delivery. However, Davie and his group emphasized the fact that the relationship between these factors and academic performance was not one to one and that many other factors must contribute (Alberman and Goldstein, 1970).

Nutrition

Disorders of nutrition have been shown to affect learning in a variety of studies (Winick, 1976). However, the relationship is not straightforward. Infants who had in utero exposure to the famine in the Netherlands of 1944–45 showed differences in height, weight, and head circumference at birth compared to those born in unaffected areas (Smith, 1947), but a follow-up study of the males 19 years later found no differences in mental function compared to controls (Howard and Cronk, 1983).

Studies of postnatal malnutrition have found decreased head circumference, IQ, language skills, and visual-motor integration skills. However, the relationship between the degree of malnutrition and outcome does not fit a mathematical model unless other factors affecting outcome are considered (Howard and Cronk, 1983). In malnutrition from pyloric stenosis, Klein et al. (1975) suggested a relationship with subsequent short-term memory and attention problems in school-age children.

Chronic malnutrition may impair learning in a variety of ways. Children so afflicted may have chronic illnesses, decreased attention, and increased lethargy at crucial times for acquisition of skills (such as language) and decreased responsiveness to the environment. All these factors may affect outcome. Studies of the effects of improving nutrition in chronically malnourished infants (prenatal and postnatal) have demonstrated improvements in motor, language, and attention skills (Howard and Cronk, 1983).

Oski and co-workers (Oski, 1983) suggested that a nutritional deficiency of iron may affect learning and behavior in infants and in adolescents. While these studies have been subjected to some methodological criticism (Pollit, Greenfield, and Leibel, 1978), they open the way for serious investigation of specific nutritional components which may be missing, particularly in the diets of socioeconomically deprived children.

Genetics

Many researchers have noted an apparent male superiority when dealing with tasks involving visual-spatial perception (MaCoby and Jacklin, 1974). Therefore, attempts have been made to determine a sex-linked pattern of inheritance for visual-spatial abilities (Hartlage, 1970; Bock and Kolakowski, 1973; Goodenough, et al. 1977). However, a number of researchers have pointed out flaws in such a model. For instance, as Garron (1970) and Money and Granoff (1965) have shown, patients with Turner's syndrome who possess only one X chromosome and, therefore, could express a recessive sex-linked trait, do not show increased competence with visual-spatial tasks. In addition, Broverman and Klaiber (1969) have pointed to evidence for decreasing spatial abilities with increasing phenotypic evidence for androgenicity. Moreover, Masica et al. (1969) found that individuals with testicular feminization syndrome (male karyotype and female phenotype) performed worse with spatial tasks than either females or males. Bouchard and McGee (1977) studied a number of the reports of sex-linked visual-spatial abilities and found no pattern suggestive of a recessive, sex-linked trait.

While studies have refuted a direct X-linked effect on the differential performance of males and females, it may be that testosterone acts in some way to aid the development of superior spatial abilities. Of course, testosterone may be only a piece of the puzzle, and environmental influences may also be significant.

Recently, evidence has been presented for the association between mental retardation and the presence of a "fragile" X chromosome (Turner et al., 1980). This chromosomal abnormality has been found in individuals who have no other apparent cause for their developmental delay. Of course, there is no known etiology for the majority of retarded individuals. Thus, the presence of the fragile X chromosome may help explain retardation in a substantial number of individuals.

The discovery of an association between a subtle chromosomal defect and cognitive function raises hope for the detection of other genetic markers for risk factors for learning disorders. The degree of penetrance of a genetic defect, the presence or absence of other risk factors and the presence or absence of compensatory strengths will all determine the role such a defect might have in the expression of a learning disorder.

Focal Lesions and "Wiring"

The search for focal neurologic lesions as a cause of developmental dysfunction began with neurologists working with adults. The classic work by Broca and Wernicke (Benson, 1979) established the concepts of speech and language centers predominantly in the left hemisphere. Neurologists studying the victims of neurologic disease have defined a variety of clinical syndromes with specific focal lesions. Several of these clinical descriptions are of interest to those working with pediatric developmental dysfunction.

Luria (1980) proposed that lesions in the postcentral and premotor portions of the cortex might lead to disturbances of the so-called kinetic melodies or automatic motor patterns involved in writing. Marcie and Hecaen (1979) described cortical lesions responsible for agraphia in association with a variety of associated clinical findings (asphasia, apraxia, alexia). It is possible that similar functional lesions in children may account for some types of writing difficulties. Albert (1979) described lesions in the angular gyrus thought to contribute to forms of alexia. Levin (1979) discussed acalculia in adults afflicted with neurologic disease. He noted the relative importance of the left hemisphere for acalculia. Dyscalculia in children may be related to functional analogs of these lesions (Kosc, 1974). Benton (1979) described a disturbance of body schema involving finger agnosia and right-left disorientation, but noted that the localization of the lesions in such syndromes was unclear. Gerstmann (1924, 1940) first described a syndrome involving finger agnosia, disorientation for right and left, agraphia, and acalculia. Kinsbourne and Warrington (1963) coined the term "developmental Gerstmann syndrome" to describe a number of youngsters who manifested a similar functional picture.

Infections of the central nervous system have been associated with nervous system impairment. The epidemic of Von Economo's encephalitis in 1918 tragically demonstrated the effect such an infection could have on subtle and complex functions such as behavior (Leahy and Sands, 1921). Survivors of herpes encephalitis have been found to have damage to the hippocampus and to have striking short-term memory impairments (Milner, 1970). Such an association implies that short-term memory may be mediated, in part, by the hippocampus. Shaywitz et al. (1982) reported a sibling-matched controlled study of the long-term consequences of Reye syndrome. They found that affected children under seven years of age had a significantly different IQ when compared with their siblings; the more severe the case, the more significant the difference in IQ and educational outcome. Thus, the sequelae of CNS infections such as encephalitis have helped show how focal lesions and more complex lesions may be related to learning and behavior and have lent some evidence to the argument that there may be continuum of effects on the central nervous system.

Geschwind (1965a) reviewed in great detail what he referred to as "disconnexion syndromes" in animals and humans. In his review of the literature on such clinical presentations, Geschwind discussed the concept of interruptions between intact primary sensory centers. For instance, alexia without agraphia was seen to correlate with a disconnection between the intact right occipital cortex and the intact left angular gyrus. Such a concept of neurologic disorder goes beyond the traditional idea of focal lesions corresponding neatly with specific clinical syndromes.

Geschwind and Fusillo (1966) discussed the case of a patient who could not match a color with its name, but could sort colors visually or discuss colors verbally. The patient also had alexia without agraphia. After the patient's death, pathologic examination of his brain revealed that there were infarcts in the splenium and the left calcarine cortex. It was hypothesized that the infarct in the splenium (which carries collosal fibers from the visual cortex) disconnected the still intact right visual cortex from the language centers on the left. Thus, the patient could not apply words (language) to colors (visual stimuli), but he could discuss the names of colors (exclusively language) or sort colors without language (exclusively visual).

Kimura (1967), using the dichotic listening test, demonstrated functional asymmetry in the brain. By simultaneously presenting different auditory stimuli to each ear he was able to determine which hemisphere of the brain was dominant for which type of auditory stimulus.

Thus, different words were presented to each ear in isolation simultaneously. The word presented to the right ear (processed by the left hemisphere) was preferentially heard. However, when melodies or sound patterns were presented simultaneously to the ears, those presented to the left ear (processed by the right hemisphere) were heard preferentially. Thus the pioneering work of Broca and Wernicke in establishing the dominance of the left hemisphere for language was further refined by Kimura's work, demonstrating differential hemispheric dominance for specific auditory stimuli.

Split-brain research with patients who have undergone division of the cerebral commissures has added to the concept of functional specialization of the hemispheres. Such work has suggested that commissural fibers are necessary for "discussion" (language) of tactile, auditory, or visual stimuli presented to the right hemisphere (Gazzaniga, 1970). In addition, individuals with auditory sophistication, such as musicians, appear to process melody more in the left hemisphere than unsophisticated listeners. Perhaps, the analysis of sound (in the left hemisphere) increases as an individual has particular experiences with sound, or perhaps it is a predisposition in such individuals, or both. In any event, such work has refined the concept of functional asymmetry.

More recently, Galaburda et al. (1978) demonstrated physical asymmetry between the hemispheres of the brain. Rosenberger and Hier (1979) showed that a discrepency between the right and left hemispheres (documented by computerized tomography) correlates significantly with differences between verbal and performance IQ. Hier et al. (1978) also described a reversed physical cerebral asymmetry in a subpopulation of patients with dyslexia. These patients had larger right hemispheres than left hemispheres as measured through computerized tomography and were all found to have a lower mean verbal IQ than the other dyslexic children. However, as Gould (1981), has pointed out many times, a straightforward assumption about the relationship between physical differences and functional disparity may be misleading. Functions such as language skills may not be localized to any specific physical part (or even hemisphere) of the brain.

Galaburda and Kemper (1979) performed pathologic examination of the brain of a patient who had had developmental dyslexia. They found mild cortical dysplasias in the limbic and primary and associative cortexes of the left hemisphere. In addition, they found polymicrogyria in the left temporal speech region. The abnormalities in cytoarchitecture may be a physical correlate to functional disordered wiring or disconnections in children with learning problems such as dyslexia. One possible explanation for disordered cytoarchitecture such as this may be seen in the work of Dorner and Straudt (1969), Raisman and Field (1973), and Gorski et al. (1980). These researchers have demonstrated the influence testosterone may have on neuronal migration. Also, Rakic (1972) has demonstrated that in the developing monkey neocortex such migration appears to be aligned by glial radial fibers. Disorders in this "roadmap" or of testosterone secretion could conceivably affect the final cytoarchitecture of the brain. The report by Geschwind and Behan (1982) of the association between left-handedness and autoimmune disease and possibly learning problems is intriguing because the findings may be related to the influence of testosterone. Geschwind and Behan hypothesized that a disorder of testosterone at crucial moments of fetal development could affect both thymic development and neuronal migration, leading to possible autoimmune disorders and left-handedness (and possibly learning problems) in adulthood. Clearly, this work raises intriguing possibilities but is still at the stage of speculation. Further work to understand the various influences on neural cytoarchitecture and its relationship to function is in order.

Duffy (1981) developed a method for analyzing electroencephalographic data so as to discern subtle but statistically significant findings by analyzing such data with the aid of a computer and a visual display, the so-called brain electrical activity mapping (BEAM). Dyslexic children have been found to have different electrical activity patterns than children in a control group, both at rest and when performing mental functions (Duffy et al., 1980a,b). Moreover the differences have been shown in both the right and left hemispheres. This implies that the neurologic differences between dyslexics and other children involve areas of both hemispheres and may not be confined to specific focal lesions. Other work using groups of dyslexic children compared to groups of other learning-disabled children have found differences in activation patterns but, again, no single locus of difference (Duffy, 1982). The work by Duffy and co-workers appears to bolster the concept of disordered wiring or disconnections as being of primary importance in learning problems.

Lassen, Ingvar, and Skinhoj (1978) have discussed the use of blood flow studies to analyze brain function. By using radioactively labeled glucose and a scintillator, they have been able to create a visual display of the areas of the brain that receive increased amounts of glucose (and presumably increased blood flow) during specific mental functions. Through this work, they have also demonstrated the synergistic interplay of many different parts of the brain during activities such as counting or saying single words repetitively. They have shown, for instance, that reading out loud or silently involves cooperation of several areas in both hemispheres, supporting the concept of interdependent wiring.

Toxins

A number of toxic agents have been associated with impairment of cognitive function and learning. David, Clark, and Voeller (1972) found an association between blood lead levels, postpenicillamine chelation urine lead levels, and hyperactivity in children. However, there was no control for socioeconomic variables. Needleman (1979, 1983), controlling for many variables including socioeconomic status, reported an association between elevated dentine lead levels and decreased performance on a variety of language assessments, decreased academic performance, and increased nonadaptive classroom behavior.

Ernhart, Landa, and Schell (1981) suggested that parental IQ may account for the impairments seen in children with increased lead levels. However, Bellinger and Needleman (1983) found that increased dentine lead was correlated with an increased discrepancy between maternal IQ and the IQ of offspring.

Yule et al. (1981) studied the association between previously obtained blood lead levels (all below 33 micrograms) and attainment on a variety of academic measures. A significant association was seen between lead level and attainment with reading, spelling, and intelligence. There was some control for social class but parental IQ was not included. Yule and co-workers properly caution that socioeconomic and family variables make interpretation somewhat difficult. Nevertheless, this work adds to the growing body of evidence that low elevation of lead levels may be a significant risk factor for learning difficulties.

Organic mercury compounds have been demonstrated to cause neurologic deficits. Berglund et al. (1971), studied the victims of a tragedy in Minimata Bay in Japan where an entire community was poisoned by fish contaminated with mercury. They found that the children exposed in utero to methyl-mercury developed paresthesias, ataxia, blindness, deafness, and cognitive impairment, among other neurologic manifestations.

Fowler et al. (1979) reported on infants who had been fed powdered milk contaminated with arsenic. Most of the infants died. Of the survivors, many were found to have learning disabilities and hearing deficits. Since arsenic is a by-product of smelting, subtler forms of poisoning for those children who live near smelters may constitute a risk factor for learning problems (Graef, 1983).

Polyhalogenated hydrocarbons are a group of chemicals that are becoming ubiquitous in the physical environment. One such compound, hexachlorophene, has been shown to cause severe neurologic pathology. In 1971, the use of baby powder contaminated with hexachlorophene led to the deaths of 36 infants. Of the 204 infants exposed, neurologic symptoms were seen in 25–37 percent (Martin-Bouyer, 1982). These symptoms included drowsiness, irritability, and coma. Seventeen percent had seizures. The long-term neurologic sequelae (such as learning problems) are still under study. Polyhalogenated biphenyls, such as polychlorinated and polybrominated biphenyls (PCBs and PBBs) have received much public attention recently because of their increasing occurance in soil, water, and food products. Tetrachlorodibenzodioxin (TCDD or dioxin) is also a widespread contaminant. Studies have been undertaken to determine the physical effects of these substances on adults. Many questions about children remain to be answered. Do children born to Vietnam veterans exposed to agent orange, (the principal ingredient of which is dioxin) have an increased incidence of birth defects and learning or cognitive impairments? Are children most susceptible? An awareness of these possible relationships and current lay concerns are important for pediatricians.

Biochemistry

A number of workers are currently examining the biochemistry of the biogenic amines. Shaywitz, Cohen, and Shaywitz (1978) have reviewed the metabolism of these amines and discussed the evidence for their role in behavior and learning. Along with Rapoport et al. (1980) and Wender (1976), they have all discussed the role of catecholamines in behavior. The evidence for the role of *dextro*-amphetamine and methylphenidate in neuronal catecholamine metabolism has been explored by these workers and others. In addition, much recent work has focused on the role of serotonin in mediating behavior and, possibly, learning. There has been much written in the psychiatric literature about the possible relationship between dopamine metabolism and thought disorders such as schizophrenia, and about the contribution of serotonin metabolism to affective disorders. Geller et al. (1982) and Ritvo et al. (1983) have reported on the effect of fenfluramine on the behavior of autistic children. Early results have found an association between the administration of fenfluramine and decreased blood serotonin levels. In addition, the children treated with this medication have improved in behavior and in verbal and performance scores on the WISC-R. Scores on various developmental inventories have also been noted to improve with the administration of fenfluramine. Of course, these results are preliminary since very small patient samples have been involved. However, in addition to the hope this work may hold for youngsters with autism, this research also adds to the body of evidence for the role of biogenic amines in behavior, development, and learning.

Yogman and Zeisel (1983) reported on the effects of altering tryptophan availability in the formulas fed to newborn infants. Those fed formulas with increased tryptophan availability (and presumably increased CNS serotonin levels) manifested a quicker onset of sleep. These and related studies are beginning to examine the complex biochemical contributions to arousal, behavior, and ultimately to learning readiness.

Feingold (1975) has hypothesized that food containing salicilates may play a significant role in behavior, especially with regard to hyperactive children. The Feingold diet was proposed as a means of controlling the activity level of such children. The restricted diets eliminated a vast array of foods and additives including food dyes, many fruits, and sugars. A number of researchers have attempted to ascertain whether any of these modifications in diet actually have an effect on behavior. In addition, some research has been done on the specific response to individual elements that have been restricted from diets (Thorley, 1983). Conners et al. (1976) found that the Feingold diet yielded no differences in a double-blind trial except that attention was improved on a continuous performance task. Swanson and Kinsbourne (1980) found that the use of high doses of certain food dyes led to impaired performance of hyperactive children in a learning task. Weiss et al. (1980) found that when a combination of seven food dyes was used as a challenge to twenty-two children on a restricted diet only one child demonstrated a dramatic behavioral response as observed by parents. Wender (1977) reviewed a number of the studies conducted on the various dietary restrictions and found little consistent proof that these dietary modifications lead to changes in behavior. In addition, a consensus conference (1982) at the National Institutes of Health concluded that there was not sufficient evidence to recommend the adoption of dietary restrictions, but, neither was there sufficient evidence to recommend against such restrictions. The conference recommended that if the physician and family involved in a particular case feel that such defined diets are helpful, then there would appear to be little reason not to continue them.

If dietary components cause behavioral changes in some children, why not in all? Are such children predisposed to such effects? If so, perhaps by studying diets we are asking the wrong question. The predisposition of such children may be the more proper focus of study. This may be analogous to the study of children with phenylketonuria; their diet is important, but the underlying contributing factors must be understood. Studies of the effects of specific components in defined diets are in order. If current hypotheses are correct, further work may well find a relationship between certain dietary components and disordered metabolism of biogenic amimes for some developmentally compromised children.

Clinical Phenomenology

School-age children with learning problems may manifest developmental dysfunction in one or a number of areas. Table 7–1 outlines a working taxonomy for these dysfunctions, each of which is discussed below in some detail.

Attention Deficit

Attention deficit is the neurodevelopmental dysfunction with which physicians are most familiar. Attention deficit has been identified by a variety of headings such as hyperkinetic syndrome, minimal brain dysfunction, and conduct disorder. The current use of the term attention deficit disorder (DSM-III) reflects our understanding that children with this disorder have a major dysfunction of attention and that the various behaviors seen are consequent to this.

Primary attention deficit is usually manifested by impulsivity, inattention to detail, impersistence with tasks, distractibility, insatiability, inconsistent performance, and physical overactivity. However, attention deficit in girls and older children is sometimes unaccompanied by physical overactivity. Some (but not all) children with primary attention deficit will have a history of problems in infancy including disturbances of temperament, sleep, or scheduling. The response of some children with primary attention problems to central nervous system stimulants such as methylphenidate and amphetamines has led to the postulate that attention deficit derives in part from dysfunction of the reticular activating system and catecholamine metabolism.

Secondary attention deficit is seen in many children who suffer from underlying perceptual difficulties that make different types of information confusing for them. Thus, a child who has difficulty processing visual stimuli may manifest inattention to visually presented information, becoming distractible, impersistent and fidgety. All the symptoms described for primary attention deficit may be seen with secondary attention deficit. The fact that symptoms of attention deficit are associated with certain activities (such as reading) but not seen with a variety of other activities may help in the differential diagnosis of primary and secondary attention deficit. For instance, the parents may report that the child can "draw for hours" but cannot sit still in class. Secondary attention deficit may also be seen in an anxious child.

Children with primary attention deficit may be helped by the use of nervous sytem stimulant medications such as Dextroamphetamine, Methxlphenidate, and Pemoline. However, such medications should only be used as part of a multifaceted treatment plan which also provides structure for the child and remediation and support for associated learning problems. Since recent work has shown that moderate doses may be more effective than higher doses, close clinical su-

Table 7–1
Neurodevelopmental Dysfunctions

Dysfunction	Academic Significance		Clinical Findings
	5–9	9–16	
Attention deficit			
Primary	+++	+++	Inattention to detail, impulsivity, impersistence, distractibility physical overactivity (not always seen), insatiability, inconsistent performance; history of tempermental sleep or scheduling difficulties, "colic" in infancy (not always seen).
Secondary			Same as with primary except: No history of difficulties in infancy; history reveals certain activities without symptoms ("he can draw for hours"); symptoms most pronounced in certain situations (e.g., reading); related to anxiety.
Language disorder			
Receptive	+++	+++	Requires frequent repetition of instructions. Delayed reading comprehension. Difficulty following directions.
Expressive	+	+++	Word-finding problems (dysnomia). Impaired verbal sentence formulation. Impaired written expression.
Memory impairment			
Automitization/ Rapid Retrieval Deficiencies	+	+++	Inability to retain "learned" information; inefficient output of work; poor handwriting (frequently slow), sight vocabulary, spelling; difficulties with multiplication tables, formulas; always rederiving formulas; child appears to understand concepts but cannot utilize them consistently or efficiently.
Active Memory	+	+++	Poor integration of skills, information simultaneously; Delayed written expression, sentence formulation, mental calculation; difficulty following verbal directions, difficulty resynthesizing information.
Secondary memory impairment			Seen with underlying difficulties such as attention deficit and visual processing problems. Initial exposure to information poorly imprinted.

Disorganization			
Temporal-sequential	+ +	+ + +	Cannot remember phone numbers, order of classes. Confused by months, days, time. Confuses beginnings and endings of stories.
Impaired integration	+	+ + +	Difficulty dealing with several sets of information at once; delayed reading comprehension.
Physical	+ +	+ +	Loses books, assignments, pencils; looks sloppy.
Secondary			Associated with attention deficit or other dysfunction making information confusing.
Fine motor dysfunction	+	+ + +	Agnosia, apraxia. Poor handwriting, drawing, eye-hand coordination.
Gross motor dysfunction	—	—	Apraxia. Poor performance with sports. Avoidance of physical activities. Clumsy demeanor.
Visual-spatial dysfunction	+ + +	+	Perceptual errors such as letter reversals. Delayed decoding, spelling. Poor drawings.
Cognitive impairment	+ + +	+ + +	May lead to any combination of symptoms described. Not a neurodevelopmental learning disability.

+ + + = very significant effect; + + = significant effect; + = some effect.

pervision and observation is necessary to obtain and maintain the optimum response.

Children with secondary attention deficit do not need medication. Rather, they require intervention for their underlying, primary problem (learning disorder, anxiety, depression for example). With proper intervention, the symptoms of attention deficit should lessen. If they do not, a reexamination of the situation is warranted.

Language

Language disorders may be both receptive and expressive and may be seen in all age groups. Children with receptive language disorders will frequently require repetition of instructions and may have difficulty following verbal directions. In addition, children with such disorders may have delayed reading comprehension because they are unable to grasp the language involved. Some children may have difficulty with auditory or language processing. Others may have difficulty with the structure of language itself. Thus, they may be able to process the sounds adequately, but their sense of grammar is insufficient to deal with the information.

Children with expressive language disorders may manifest dysnomia or word-finding problems (Denkla, 1972). In addition, they frequently have difficulty with verbal sentence formulation and written expression. Such difficulties are of great significance for children age nine and up. This is because the curriculum beginning in fourth grade requires a great deal of written work (book reports, projects, and so on). Difficulties with expressive language skills may not be apparent until middle childhood since the curriculum in the primary grades may not have required such work in sufficient amounts to elicit the output disorder (Levine, 1981).

Treatment of receptive language disorders may require work on auditory processing skills as well as the use of bypass strategies (such as using visual information). Difficulties with expressive language skills may require breaking down expressive language tasks into small components so that each component can be learned adequately. The overall structure of such tasks must be well learned by frequent repetition of this step-by-step method so that these children will eventually be able to perform expressive language tasks on their own.

Memory Impairment

Many children may manifest difficulties with memory. These difficulties may be described in two categories: (1) automization/rapid retrieval and (2) active memory/short-term memory. In addition secondary impairment of memory may be seen. LaBerge and Samuels (1974), Wilkinson, DeMarinis, and Riley (1983), Garnett and Fleischner (1983), and Eakin and Douglas (1971) established that automatization may be a crucial contributing factor toward success with a wide variety of tasks including reading, mathematics, and rapid remembering (or retrieval) in any area.

Deficiencies of automatization are usually noted in older children because the curriculum requires more rapid retrieval in the higher grades. Children with difficulties with rapid retrieval and automatization may appear to learn a particular skill for the moment, but they have great difficulty utilizing the skill at a later time. They appear to forget everything they have learned. For instance, such children may not be able to remember the multiplication tables or recall mathematical formulas because they have not become automatic for them. They will frequently be forced to derive the formula each time they are confronted with a particular type of problem. These children may have very poor spelling from dictation, with substantially less trouble choosing the proper spelling when given multiple choice stimuli. Because these children may have difficulties with the rapid retrieval of letter formation, they may be very inefficient with written tasks. Poor automatization of sight vocabulary may yield reading dysfluency.

Children with automatization and rapid retrieval difficulties may require frequent repetition of particular skills beyond the point of mastery. In other words, for such children it is not sufficient for them to simply learn a task and then to move on to other tasks. They must learn a task and then repeat it many times so that it will be adequately automatized. They then can move on to more difficult tasks that build upon the initial task or skill.

Many children appear to have difficulties with active memory (Brainerd, 1983). The concept of active memory refers to the simultaneous use of a variety of skills or information in the "mind's eye." For instance, children with active memory impairment may have difficulty formulating sentences in their mind. They may have difficulty with mental calculations and their written within expression may be impaired. Following verbal directions may be a problem for these children since retaining a direction in their mind while they act upon it may be a formidable assignment. Resynthesizing information (such as retelling a story) may also be difficult.

Some children will manifest secondary memory impairments. Such memory difficulties are due to underlying problems with processing (such as visual processing problems) or to attention deficit. For these children, the initial exposure to information is so poorly imprinted because of their inattention or difficulty processing that they have difficulty retrieving the information at a later time. Children with secondary memory impairments require intervention for their primary learning difficulties.

Disorganization

Many children suffer from difficulties with disorganization. These difficulties may be manifested in all age groups but are a particular problem for older children. Again, curricular demands place a special value on the ability to organize information.

Children with temporal-sequential disorganization may have difficulty remembering phone numbers or remembering the order of their classes. They may be confused by such automatic sequences such as the months of the year, the days of the week, or time. Such children may confuse the beginning and ending of a story. Children with temporal-sequential dysfunction may have difficulties with calculations in math and with spelling. Reading comprehension and following directions in class may also be impaired by such a dysfunction.

Children with impaired integration skills may have difficulty dealing with several sets of information at once. These children may manifest delayed reading comprehension. Other children may be physically disorganized. They may lose their homework or books or forget to bring an assignment home or to bring a completed assignment back to school. They may lose pencils and other articles and may appear sloppy. Some children may manifest disorganization secondary to other problems such as attention deficit. Other children may manifest such secondary disorganization because of a primary learning problem which makes certain types of information confusing for them.

Difficulties with disorganization may be dealt with by teaching organizational strategies. Thus, teaching a child how to break down tasks into their basic components may be helpful. For instance, the task of writing a paragraph might be broken down into a number of steps. First, the child can be asked to list several nouns and several verbs in separate columns. They can be asked to combine nouns and verbs that are appropriate for the topic into sentences. They can then be asked to add appropriate adjectives. The sentences can then be combined into appropriate paragraphs, and so on. Through such step-by-step methods children may learn how to approach a complex organizational task in an efficient and consistent manner. For children with physical disorganization the use of assignment books and checklists at home and at school may be helpful.

Fine Motor Dysfunction

Children may have considerable difficulties with fine motor skills. This may be due to problems with finger agnosia (impaired finger localization without visual monitoring) (Kinsbourne, 1963). Such children may have a great deal of difficulty receiving appropriate feedback from their fingertips when using a pencil and the product of their written work may be quite poor. Other children may manifest fine motor dyspraxia. These children have difficulty controlling their fingers and hands, and their written work may also be impaired.

In the school-age child difficulties with written expression may result from underlying fine motor dysfunction since the task of transforming thoughts into written letters may be so frustrating and overwhelming that the other aspects of writing may deteriorate. Thus, if handwriting itself is overwhelming, grammar, spelling, punctuation, and content may decline. Children with fine motor dysfunction may avoid writing or may write minimal amounts even though they have many complex ideas in their mind.

Gross Motor Dysfunction

Poor performance with sports may be due to gross motor difficulties. Children with such difficulties may be clumsy and may frequently avoid physical activities. Gross motor problems may involve impaired balance, apraxia, or eye-arm dyscoordination. Difficulties in any of these areas may make gross motor activities difficult for children. Of course, such difficulties do not play a significant role with regard to academics, but their effect on sports and physical activities may lead to social difficulties for such children.

Visual-Spatial Dysfunction

Many younger children may have difficulties with visual-spatial processing (Orton, 1937; Benton and Pearl, 1978; deHirsh, Jansky, and Langord, 1966). They may manifest perceptual errors such as letter reversals when they read. Decoding, spelling, and drawing may be quite difficult for such children. However, the relationship of visual-spatial difficulty and reading performance is obviously very complex and likely mediated by language (Vellutino, 1979) and other processes. The argument against a straightforward relationship has been augmented by the clinical findings that visual-spatial difficulties usually do not play as significant a role with older children as with younger ones and experimental work such as that of Stevenson et al. (1982) that indicates that the orthography of language has little or no relationship to the prevalence of reading disabilities.

Neuromaturation

Neuromaturational differences in children with and without learning problems continue to tease clinicians and investigators, keeping open the debate regarding a continuum of neurologic trauma or differential neurologic maturation. Clearly there is a higher incidence of neurologic soft signs such as difficulty with lateralization (Rosenberger, 1979), graphesthesia and dysdiadochokinesis (Adams, Kocsis, and Estes, 1974), the choreiform sign (Prechtl, 1962), and a higher number of these signs in children with clinical disabilities than in those without (Levine et al., 1983). How helpful these signs are and what relationship they have to actual performance remains an open debate (Adams et al., 1974; Levine et al. 1983).

Age Differences

Young children often are stymied by perceptual problems that may impair academic performance. Older children and adolescents are frequently plagued by a different set of learning problems, including impaired written output, disorganization, impaired rapid retrieval, and faulty active memory (Levine and Zallen, 1984). While the late onset of these problems may reflect the changes in the curriculum with increased demands for writing, automiatization, and so on, it is also possible that the different types of neurodevelopmental dysfunction actually have substantially different trajectories.

The work of Duke (1982) and Duke and Gross (1983) adds an interesting dimension to the question of developmental variation over time. In her study of adolescents with early-, mid-, and late-maturing patterns of physical and sexual development, late-maturing males were found to be delayed on intelligence and achievement tests when compared with early- and mid-maturing males over age thirteen through seventeen. Waber (1977) reported that late maturers performed better with visual-spatial tasks. Thus there may be a relationship between the time of onset of puberty and the type of learning problem.

Community Response

The Changing Environment

The growing recognition of the multiple needs of children with learning problems has led to an increasingly responsive and directed community approach. Three groups have been instrumental in orchestrating this community response: (1) parents, (2) schools, and (3) health care professionals.

Parents as Advocates

Parent advocacy for children with developmental disability arose in the 1960s in the context of the civil rights movement. Parents of moderately to severely retarded children began to ask why their children were being denied the right to an education guaranteed to all other children. The emphasis placed by the parents on "barriers" to education was consonant with the agenda of the larger handicapped movement, which was calling for a "barrier-free" environment. Parents brought suit against school systems throughout the nation. Two landmark cases, *P.A.R.C.* v. *Pennsylvania Board of Education* and *Mills* v. *Board of Education* fundamentally changed traditional assumptions when the courts found overwhelmingly in favor of the families. *Mills* v. *Board of Education* set a particularly important precedent by insisting that public schools must furnish education to disabled children even if the school system lacked the necessary funds.

Parents of children with milder learning problems such as speech impairments and learning disabilities had to make a conscious choice in requesting services for "handicapped" children. In a sense, the push for the inclusion of "learning disabilities" in the provisions for the handicapped created an unwritten premise that learning problems represent handicaps rather than variations from the norm. While this is a subtle point and of minor consequence in comparison to the major procedural advantages that have been gained for these children, the stigma of the handicapped label is real and may have psychological consequences for some children and families.

The Schools as Agents of Change

Once the courts had found in favor of the families, it was essential that new thinking take place with regard to the process and the content of educaton for children with disabilities. The procedural changes that emerged were codified in the federal statute, PL 94-142, and are as follows:

1. All handicapped children are guaranteed a free appropriate public education at no cost to their parents.
2. All handicapped children must be identified, located, and evaluated regardless of the severity of their disability.
3. Each handicapped child must be provided an individualized education plan (IEP).
4. Special education must be provided in the "least restrictive environment."
5. Procedural safeguards must be established to ensure parents due process in the identification, evaluation, and placement of their children.
6. Handicapped children placed in private schools by the state must be afforded the same rights as children in public educational placements.
7. States must establish in-service training for personnel in both general and special education and for staff providing support services.

The major and most basic result of the legislation was that all children, no matter how severe their handicap, were assured a free appropriate public education at no expense to their parents. To ensure this, the schools took on many nontraditional responsibilities, including specialized transportation and related services including occupational therapy, physical therapy, health evaluations, school health services, and counseling.

Beyond the procedural issues came the more fundamental question of a definition of education itself. Because PL 94-142 committed schools to educating children with developmental handicaps and to addressing the needs of the most severely affected first, "education" itself took on new meaning. No longer confined to the three R's, now education encompassed teaching activities of daily living (including eating, toileting, and dressing); for children with emotional disturbance, education was broadened to include the teaching of social cognition;

for children with learning disabilities, education was to include strategies necessary for children to conquer their disabilities or to bypass them. To provide such education, schools have had to expand their staffs, modify their buildings, and rethink their educational responsibilities.

Physicians and Developmental Dysfunction of School-Age Children

Pediatricians also have played a role in the expansion of services to children with learning problems. The Task Force on Pediatric Education has underscored the importance of this area for pediatricians by insisting that training programs in pediatrics integrate developmental and behavioral concepts into residency programs so that physicians in practice will be equipped to manage the care of children with school-related problems. Moreover, the major pediatric journals have devoted significant space to learning problems within the past few years. Finally, meetings such as the one at which this paper was presented brought researchers and practitioners together to examine jointly the important consequences of the so-called new morbidity.

Ongoing Issues

Such major community changes do not occur without considerable tensions, nor do they resolve all of the pressing educational, social, and medical issues that school-age children with developmental disabilities face. Three issues continue to be particularly pertinent: (1) diagnosis (evaluation), (2) placement, and (3) educational-pediatric interchange.

Diagnosis. A major impact of the new approach to children with learning problems has been the emphasis on diagnosis as a necessary prerequiste to services. Because evidence is mounting that school failure is the final common pathway for a large variety of basic problems, careful diagnostic work can allow a better understanding of a given child's strengths and weaknesses so that an individualized plan can be tailored to meet that child's needs. Recently, there has been considerable debate about the nature of that diagnosis.

For children with learning disabilities, traditional IQ testing can be unreliable or unrevealing because children will often have normal IQs or will respond in nontraditional and inconsistent ways to the testing (Levine, 1980; Meltzer, in press). For children with "mild mental retardation," traditional IQ tests have been faulted for cultural bias (Mercer, 1973) and for not being adequately sensitive to a child's functional and adaptive abilities. As a result, the past decade has witnessed a search for more meaningful diagnostic approaches which might allow greater insight into the child's learning style, attentional acuity, and coping mechanisms. Several approaches have been promising in this regard (Meltzer, in press).

In pediatrics and neurology, the current emphasis on neurodevelopmental profiles (Peters, 1975; Levine, 1983b; Levine et al., in press; Kinsbourne and Caplan, 1979) has allowed a more differentiated approach to the understanding of a given child's inherent strengths and weaknesses. In child psychology, the movement toward the notion of developmental conceptualization, first introduced by Piaget, has allowed adults to view the child's world as the child does. And finally in education, movement toward interactive assessment based on the model of Feuerstein is opening new awareness which may allow diagnostic data to truly inform intervention in an increasingly meaningful manner.

Neurodevelopmental Assessment. Neurodevelopmental assessment is predicated on the notion that outward manifestations or behaviors of a child can serve as a window for exploring central nervous system function if the tasks involved are designed to elicit a particular type of functioning. The observed delays are only the topography of the disorders. The goal of the differential diagnosis of such disorders is to discover some of the underlying, complex "geology." As a practical matter, this goal is rarely if ever, attained since behaviors (even the most straightforward) are almost always dictated centrally by complex, interactive loops. For example, when a child is directed to walk across the room, receptive language, active memory, propriokinesthesia, motor planning, gross motor ability, balance, and attention all must play some role. Obviously, the more complex the task the more involved the interaction. Nonetheless, if the examination is structured with enough observations, redundancies, and differentiations, it is possible to amass evidence to generate meaningful hypotheses about a given child's neurodevelopmental profile.

Understanding Children's Understanding. In child development, the past fifty years have witnessed a major exploration of children's psychological development as a result of the work of Jean Piaget. This work has transformed traditional thinking about intelligence and cognitive processing. Piaget has documented the stages of cognitive development through which children pass and has shown that a child's learning is an active and integrative function in which children must assimilate the facts they learn with the experiences they have already had and, with the newly incorporated facts, derive a new level of cognitive awareness. The major implication of this work that children process information from the world outside them quite differently from adults has challenged psychologists and others to undertake a fundamental redirection in the design of evaluation procedures.

Since Piaget showed that reasoning ability itself is measurable, (Piaget, 1952, 1964, 1969), assessment procedures based on his theoretical concepts have been introduced. While these procedures have been criticized as having little educational applicability (Reschly, 1984), they mark the beginning of an approach to entering the world of children in order to see more clearly through their eyes.

Interactive Educational Assessment. Another recent advance in diagnostic technology has been the incorporation into educational testing of the opportunity to assess children's strategies and when possible to try out a number of teaching approaches to see which ones work best with a given child. Meltzer (in press) is currently using an educational assessment model which incorporates descriptions of children's strategies including (1) impulsivity versus reflectivity, (2) trial and error versus systematic hypothesis testing, (3) fixation on detail versus generalization, and (4) erratic solutions versus consistent self-monitoring. These stylistic observations allow the diagnostician to make specific recommendations to teachers about the child's approach to learning. Understanding about a child's subtle learning impediments may help the teacher formulate rational interventions that help the child take more time to reason through a problem, build a systematic proposal to test, see the larger picture, and follow up leads that are already available.

Feuerstein, Miller, and Jensen (1981) suggested that diagnostic encounters for children should include practice teaching/learning segments so that the process of learning as well as the outcome can be examined. Feuerstein's techniques have come under attack for not being closely enough linked to classroom practice (Reshley, 1984), but clearly this type of approach has substantial potential for such a linkage.

Placement. School placement of children with special needs has been a topic of research interest as closer scrutiny has been placed on children with learning problems. A variety of potential school placements are available. A child may spend all school time within a regular classroom with the teacher using customized material. A child can spend the majority of time in the regular classroom with some resource room help up to half the time. When the child's problems are more pervasive or severe, he or she may spend most of the time in a special classroom within a regular school, joining children without learning problems for activities such as lunch, gym, music, and art. Finally, a child with significant learning problems may be placed in a special school with little or no integration with children who do not have learning problems.

In the early 1960s, the separate placement of children with learning difficulties was questioned on several fronts. First, there were concerns that the separate education the children were receiving was inferior to that of other children. Second, there was some concern about the social consequences of the isolated experience. Third, there were concerns that in many cases segregation of children with educational handicaps was de facto racial segregation (Heller, Holtzman, Messick, 1982). From these concerns, the notion of "least restrictive environment" was born and became a cornerstone of the Education of All Handicapped Children Act. The presumption of the least restrictive environment is that children ought to have as nearly normal a social experience as possible, as long as that socialization does not unnecessarily hamper educational growth or add additional burdens. While the notion of least restrictive environment does not per se suggest that every child will do best in the so-called mainstream, there is occasionally a confusion of the two terms.

Experience with the least restrictive environment over the past five years suggests that no consensus has yet been reached as to the best system for children with learning problems. From a practical standpoint, there is still extraordinarily diverse site-to-site variation in the way children with learning problems are placed. In the five sites studied for the collaborative project, one site places almost all children with learning problems in regular classes, another 75 percent, another 50 percent, and two others well under 50 percent (Walker et al., 1984). Madden and Slavin (1983) have made a systematic examination of all studies that have looked at placement to date. The results are far from conclusive but seem to favor regular placement if substantial special services are provided. Madden and Slavin join the authors of the National Research Council report (Heller, Holtzman, and Messick, 1982) in stating that placement is not the real issue. Rather, the central issues are the curricular material and the teaching methods used. They suggest that research in the next decade should focus on teaching approaches such as peer teaching and cooperative learning. Undoubtedly, the research literature over the next decade will include a number of experiments in these areas.

Educational-Pediatric Interchange. An area of promise whose time has not yet fully come is that of pediatric-educational interface. One major result of the changes of the 1970s and early 1980s has been more extensive communication between physicians and educators about their common constituency of school-age children. However, barriers between the two professions are still very high, and their interaction is far less than would be expected. In the collaborative study, less than 10 percent of children's doctors had communicated with school in the past year.

In order for complete service programs which include adequate preschool identification, fully articulated diagnosis, necessary family and child counseling, and the integration of health and sensory information to be accomplished, more planning is needed between educational and health leaders. Moreover, a meaningful dialogue is necessary so that educators know what to expect when they send children for physical evaluations and physicians know what is likely when they suggest educational modifications. Until this is developed there is the potential for a continuation of awkward and missed signals, with unrealized goals for children as a result.

Summary

This chapter focused on developmental issues with relevance to the health of school-age children. With school holding such a central position in the lives of children and with society placing so many of its hopes and aspirations on the next generation, the tasks of childhood are indeed ponderous. As a child moves through the school years, there are many potential risks including family distress, poor nurturance, environmental deprivation, hidden responsibilities, neurodevelopmental weaknesses, personality impairment, temperamental imbalance, illness, and insufficient coping. These risk factors contribute to a series of outcomes including poor academic performance, impaired affect, dissatisfaction, disordered social interaction, family dysfunction, poor physical or functional health, and further impairment of coping. Each of these outcomes works as a double-headed arrow causing a dynamic interplay with the child's environment or inherent makeup. A poor report card for a child under family stress with a long record of academic underachievement and shaky neurodevelopmental status may result in the child's leaving school, whereas that same report card for a child under more favorable circumstances may have only a transient negative effect. Likewise, an acute illness or accident may have very different outcomes in two different youngsters. A fully articulated, dynamic, and functional model is needed so that the concerns of the whole child can be addressed in the clinical setting.

In order to approach such a dynamic model, the new pediatrics requires the physician to incorporate many of the recent research ideas and findings into practice. Parents (and children) desire a clear idea about etiology. They want to know, Why has it happened to us? Are we guilty of something? Will it happen again? One reason parents turn to pediatricians rather than to other professionals for help with learning problems is that they want someone to take their questions about causation seriously. As a result, it is especially important for physicians to think through the differential diagnosis of known causes of developmental dysfunction with each case. While the yield of investigations is small, parents expect that their child will have as comprehensive an assessment as possible, and if the history is at all suggestive of a specific physiologic or anatomic etiology, it is worth the pursuit, if only for the positive value of parental reassurance.

Beyond the physical evaluation, an assessment of a child's inherent strengths and weaknesses allows the physician to avoid the trap of too quickly assigning a child to a homogeneous (and possibly meaningless) category. Moreover, looking at the child's range of abilities and disabilities allows a much more inflected response to the schools. While most pediatricians will find it difficult to perform extensive evaluations themselves, they can recommend that children in their practice have comprehensive evaluations and can read the reports with an eye toward their own generation of hypotheses.

Finally, with regard to assessment, pediatricians are in an ideal position to integrate material about associated situations and conditions. The school system may have a better notion of the child's academic skills and peer interactions, but pediatricians have more knowledge of other family members with similar learning problems. The pediatrician can help alleviate some family stresses while avoiding exposure of a family to the larger community.

With a notion of the interplay of educational problems with psychological and physiologic dysfunction, the pediatrician is in a position to question the possibility of underlying neurodevelopmental dysfunction when children present with depression, encopresis, or enuresis. Likewise, the pediatrician should try to elicit these issues when the primary problem is learning.

From the service point of view, the new pediatrician has a number of crucial roles to play. First, with the recognition that children are children and not categories, pediatricians can work with other child developmentalists and educators to develop a full understanding of the heterogeneous array of profiles that children exhibit. If possible, pediatricians can work for system approaches that avoid labels and provide children with functional rather than categorical services. Second, pediatricians can play an active role in the community as advocates for quality educational programs for specific patients and for children in general. And finally, pediatricians can provide important service to families and children by providing direct nonjudgmental developmental couseling addressing the specifics of the child's current functional problems and working toward their solution with parents and child.

The dynamic interplay of inherent and external factors, the importance of growth and change, and the dependence of children on the environment around them make work with school-age children with developmental symptoms intriguing and challenging. By consideration of all aspects of the cycles of childhood, a rich and rewarding approach can lead to improvement and success for many such children and can sustain others from falling behind. In many ways these are the goals of the new pediatrics.

References

Abramowicz, M., and Kass, E.: Pathogenesis and prognosis of prematurity. *N. Engl. J. Med.* 275:878–885; 938–943; 1001–1006; 1053–1059, 1966.

Adams, R.M., Kocsis, J.J., and Estes, R.E.: Soft neurological signs in learning-disabled children and controls. *Am. J. Dis. Child.* 128:614, 1974.

Alberman, E.D., and Goldstein, H.: The "at-risk" register: a statistical evaluation. *Br. J. Prev. Social Med.* 24:129–135, 1970.

Albert, M.L.: Alexia. In Heilman, K.M., and Valenstein, E. (eds.): *Clinical Neuropsychology.* New York: Oxford University Press, 1979.

Bellinger, D.C., and Needleman, H.L.: Lead and the relationship between maternal and child intelligence. *J. Pediatr.* 102:523, 1983.

Benson, D.F.: Aphasia. In Heilman, K.M., and Valenstien, E. (eds.): *Clinical Neuropsychology.* Oxford University Press, New York, 1979.

Benton, A.: Body schema disturbances: finger agnosia and right-left disorientation. In

Heilman, K.M., and Valenstein, E. (eds.): *Clinical Neuropsychology*. New York: Oxford University Press, 1979.

Benton, A.L., and Pearl, D.: *Dyslexia: An Appraisal of Current Knowledge*. New York, Oxford University Press, 1978.

Berglund, F., Berlin, M., Birke, G., et al.: Methylmercury in fish: a toxicologic-epidemiologic evaluation of risks. Report from an expert group. *Nord Hugien. TIDS*. Suppl. 4, 1971.

Bock, R.D., and Kolakowski, D.: Further evidence of sex-linked major-gene influence on human spatial visualizing ability. *Am. J. Hum. Genet. 25*:1, 1973.

Bouchard, T.J., and McGee, M.G.: Sex differences in human spatial ability: not an X-linked recessive gene effect. *Social Biol. 24*:332, 1977.

Brainerd, C.J.: Young children's mental arithmetic errors: a working memory analysis. *Child Dev. 54*:812, 1983.

Bronfenbrenner, U.: Is early education effective? In Leichter, H.J. (ed.): *The Family as Educator*. New York, Teachers College Press, Columbia University, 1975.

Broverman, D.M., and Klaiber, E.L., Negative relationships between abilities. *Psychometrika 34*:5, 1969.

Caldwell, B.M., Bradley, R.H., and Elardo R.: Early stimulation. In Wortis, J. (ed.): *Mental Retardation*, vol. 7. New York: Grune and Stratton, 1975.

Charles, D.C.: Ability and accomplishment of persons earlier judged mentally retarded. *Gen. Psychol. Monogr. 47*:3–71, 1953.

Cobb, H.V. *The Forecast of Fulfillment*. New York. Teachers College Press, 1972.

Conners, C.K., Goyette, C.H., Southwick, D.A., et al.: Food additives and hyperkinesis: a controlled double-blind experiment. *Pediatrics58*:154, 1976.

Consensus Conference: Defined diets and childhood hyperactivity. *JAMA 248*:290, 1982.

David, D., Clark, J., and Voeller, K.: Lead and hyperactivity. *Lancet 2*:(Oct. 28):900, 1972.

Davie, R., Butler, N., and Goldstein, H. *From Birth to Seven: The Second Report of the National Child Development Study*. London, Longman, 1972.

deHirsh, K., Jansky, J., and Langord, W.: *Predicting Reading Failure*. New York, Harper and Row, 1966.

Denckla, M.B.: Color-naming defects in dyslexic boys. *Cortex 8*:164, 1972.

Denckla, M.B., and Rudel, R.: Rapid "automatized" naming of pictured objects, colors, letters and numbers by normal children. *Cortex 10*:186, 1974.

Denckla, M.B., and Rudel, R.: Rapid "automatized" naming: dyslexia differentiated from other learning disabilities. *Neuropsychologia 14*:471, 1976.

Denhoff, E., Hainsworth, P.K., and Hainsworth, M.L. The child at risk for learning disorder. *Clin. Pediatr. 11*:164–170, 1972.

Dinwiddie, R., Mellor, D.H., Donaldson, S.H.C., Turnstall, M.E., and Russell, R.: Quality of survival after artficial ventilation of the newborn. *Arch. Dis. Child. 49*:703–710, 1974.

Dorner, G., and Straudt, J.: Perinatal structural sex differentiation of the hypothalmus in rats. *Neuroendocrinology 5*:103, 1969.

Drillien, C.M.: Aetiology and outcome in low birth weight infants. *Dev. Med. Child Neurol. 14*:563–574, 1972.

Duffy, F.H.: Brain electrical activity mapping (BEAM): computerized access to complex brain function. *Int. J. Neurosci. 13*:55–65, 1981.

Duffy, F.H.: Topographic display of evoked potentials: clinical applications of brain electrical activity mapping (BEAM). *Ann. N.Y. Acad. Sci. 388*:183–196, 1982.

Duffy, F.H., Denckla, M.B., Bartels, P.H. and Sanding: Dyslexia: regional differences in brain electrical activity by topographic mapping. *Ann. Neurol. 7*:412, 1980a.

Duffy, F.H., Denckla, M.B., Bartels, P.H. et al.: Dyslexia: automated diagnosis by computerized classification of brain electrical activity. *Ann. Neurol. 7*:421, 1980b.

Duke, P.M.: Educational correlates of early and late sexual maturation in adolescence. *J. Pediatr. 100*:633, 1982.

Duke, P.M., and Gross, R.T.: Effects of early versus late physical maturation on adolescent behavior. In Levine, M.D., Carey, W.B., Crocker, A.C., and Gross, R.T. (eds.). *Developmental-Behavioral Pediatrics.* Philadelphia, W.B. Saunders, 1983.

Eakin, S., and Douglas, V.: "Automatization" and oral reading problems in children. *J. Learn. Disabil. 4*:26, 1971.

Education for All Handicapped Children Act of 1975. P.L. 94-142; 20 U.S.C. 1401 et seg. *Fed. Reg. 42*(163):4274–42518, Aug. 22, 1977.

Eisenberg, L.: Definitions of dyslexia: their consequences for research and policy. In Benton, A.L., and Pearl, D. (eds.): *Dyslexia: An Appraisal of Current Knowledge.* New York, Oxford University Press, 1978.

Ernhart, C., Landa, B., and Schell, N.B.: Subclinical levels of lead and developmental deficit: a multivariate follow-up reassessment. *Pediatrics 67*:911, 1981.

Escalona, S.K.: Babies at double hazard: early development and social risk. *Pediatrics 70*:670, 1982.

Feingold, B.F.: *Why Your Child is Hyperactive.* New York, Random House, 1975.

Feuerstein, R., Miller, R., and Jensen, M.R.: Can evolving techniques better measure cognitive change? *J. Special Ed. 15*(2):201–270, 1981.

Fitzhardinge, P.M., and Steven, E.M.: The small-for-date infant. II. Neurological and intellectual sequelae. *Pediatrics 50*:50–57, 1972.

Fowler, B.A., Ishinishi, N., Tsuchiya, K., et al.: Arsenic. In Friberg, et al. (eds.): *Handbook on the Toxicology of Metals.* New York, Elsevier North-Holland, 1979.

Gaddes, W.: Learning disabilities: prevalence estimates and the need for definition. In Knights, R., and Bakker, D.J. (eds.): *The Neuropsychology of Learning Disorders: Theoretical Approaches.* Proceedings of NATO Conference. Baltimore, University Park Press, 1976.

Galaburda, A.M., Lemay, M., Kemper, T.L., and Gerschwind, N.: Right-left asymmetries in the brain. *Science 199*:852, 1978.

Galaburda, A.M., and Kemper, T.L.: Cytoarchitectonic abnormalities in developmental dyslexia: a case study. *Ann. Neurol. 6*:94, 1979.

Garnett, K., and Fleischner, J.E.: Automatization and basic fact performance of normal and learning disabled children. *Learning Disabil. Q. 6*:223, 1983.

Garron, D.C.: Sex-linked, recessive inheritance of spatial and numerical ability, and Turner's Syndrome. *Psychol. Rev. 77*:147, 1970.

Gazzaniga, M.S.: *The Bisected Brain.* New York, Appleton, 1970.

Geller, E., Ritvo, E.R., Freeman, B.J., and Yuwiler, A.: Preliminary observations on the effect of fenfluramine on blood serotonin and symptoms in three autistic boys. *N. Engl. J. Med. 307*:165, 1982.

Gerstmann, J.: Fingerangosie. Eine Umschriebene Storung Der Oreintierung Am Eigenen Korper. *Wien. Klin. Wochenschr. 37*:1010, 1924.

Gerstmann, J.: Syndrome of finger agnosia: disorientation for right and left, agraphia and acalculia. *Arch. Neurol. Psychiat. 44*:398, 1940.

Geschwind, N.: Disconnexion syndromes in animals and man. Part I. *Brain 88*:237–294, 1965a.

Geschwind, N.: Disconnexion syndromes in animals and man. Part II. *Brain 88:*585–644, 1965b.

Geschwind, N., and Behan, P.: Left-handedness: association with immune disease, migraine and developmental learning disorder. *Proc. Natl. Acad. Sci. 79*:5097–5100, 1982.

Geschwind, N., and Fusillo, M.: Color-naming defects in association with alexia. *Arch. Neurol. 15*:137, 1966.

Goodenough, D.R., et al.: A study of X chromosome linkage with field dependence and spatial visualization. *Behav. Genet. 7*:373, 1977.

Gorski, R.A., Harlan, R.E., Jacobson, C.D., et al.: Evidence for the existence of a sexually dimorphic nucleus in the preoptic area of the rat. *J. Comp. Neurol. 193*:529, 1980.

Gould, S.J.: *The Mismeasure of Man.* New York, W.W. Norton, 1981.

Graef, J.W.: Environmental toxins. In Levine, M.D., Carey, W.B., Crocker, A.C., and Gross, R.T. (eds.): *Developmental-Behavioral Pediatrics.* W.B. Saunders, Philadelphia, 1983.

Green, M.: A developmental approach to symptoms based on age groups. *Pediatr. Clin. North Am. 22*:571, 1975.

Hallahan, D., and Kauffman, J.: Labels, categories, behaviors: ED, LD and EMR reconsidered. *J. Special Ed. 11*:139–149, 1977.

Hamburg, B.A.: Chronic illness. In Levine, M.D., Carey, W.B., Crocker, A.C., and Gross, R.T. *Developmental-Behavioral Pediatrics.* Philadelphia, W.B. Saunders, 1983.

Hartlage, L.C.: Sex-linked inheritance of spatial ability. *Percept. Mot. Skills 31*:610, 1970.

Heller, K.A., Holtzman, W.H., and Messick, S. (eds.): *Placing Children in Special Education: A Strategy for Equity.* Washington, D.C., National Academy Press, 1982

Hier, D.B., LeMay, M., Rosenberger, P.B., and Perlo, V.P.: Developmental dyslexia: evidence for a subgroup with a reversal of cerebral asymmetry. *Arch. Neurol. 35*:90, 1978.

Hobbs, N.: *The Futures of Children.* San Francisco, Jossey-Bass, 1975.

Howard, R.B., and Cronk, C.: Nutrition and development. In Levine, M.D., Carey, W.B., Crocker, A.C., and Gross, R.T., (eds.): *Developmental-Behavioral Pediatrics.* Philadelphia, W.B. Saunders, 1983.

Huessey, H.R., and Cohen, A.L.: Hyperkinetic behaviors and learning disabilities followed over seven years. *Pediatrics 57*:4–10, 1976.

Johnson, D., and Myklebust, H.: *Learning Disabilities: Educational Principles and Practices.* New York, Grune and Stratton, 1967.

Karniski, W.M., Levine, M.D., Clarke, S., et al.: A study of neuro-developmental findings in early adolescent delinquents. *J. Adol. Health Care 3*:151–159, 1982.

Kennedy, R.J.R.: *A Connecticut Community Revisited.* Report on Project No. 655. Washington, D.C., Office of Vocational Rehabilitation, 1966.

Kimura, D.: Functional asymmetry of the brain in dichotic listening. *Cortex* 3:163, 1967.

Kinsbourne, M.: Developmental Gerstmann syndrome. *Ped. Clin. North Am.* 15:771, 1968.

Kinsbourne, M.: School problems. *Pediatrics* 52:697, 1973.

Kinsbourne, M., and Caplan, P.: *Children with Learning and Attention Problems.* Boston: Little, Brown, 1979.

Kinsbourne, M., and Warrington, E.K.: The developmental Gerstmann syndrome. *Arch. Neurol.* 8:40, 1963.

Klein, P.S., Forbes, G.B., and Nader, P.R.: Effects of starvation in infancy (pyloric stenosis) on subsequent learning abilities. *J. Pediatr.* 87:8, 1975.

Kosc, L.: Developmental dyscalculia. *J. Learn. Disabil.* 7:164–177, 1974.

LaBerge, D., and Samuels, S.J.: Toward a theory of automatic information processing in reading. *Cog. Psychol.* 6:293, 1974.

Lassen, N.A., Ingvar, D.H., and Skinhoj, E.: Brain function and blood flow. *Sci. Am.* 239(10):62, 1978.

Lazar, I.: *The Persistence of Preschool Effects.* DHEW Publ. No. (OHDS) 78-30130. Washington, D.C., Education Commission of the States, 1977.

Leahy, S., and Sands, I.: Mental disorders in children following epidemic encephalitis. *JAMA* 76:373, 1921.

Levin, H.S.: The acalculias. In Heilman, K.M., and Valenstein, E. (eds.): *Clinical Neuropsychology.* New York, Oxford University Press, 1979.

Levine, M.D.: Middle childhood. In Levine, M.D., Carey, W.B., Crocker, A.C., and Gross, R.T. (eds.): *Developmental-Behavioral Pediatrics.* Philadelphia, W.B. Saunders, 1983a.

Levine, M.D., Brooks, R., and Shonkoff, J.P.: *A Pediatric Approach to Learning Disorders.* New York, John Wiley and Sons, 1980.

Levine, M.D., Karniski, W.M., Palfrey, J.S., et al.: A study of risk factor complexes in early adolescent delinquency. *Am.J. Dis. Child.* (in press).

Levine, M.D.: Developmental variations and dysfunction in the school age child. In Levine, M.D., Carey, W.B., Crocker, A.C., and Gross, R.T. (eds.): *Developmental-Behavioral Pediatrics.* Philadelphia, W.B. Saunders, 1983b.

Levine, M.D.: *The School Function Program: Profile of a General Pediatrics Consultative Service Model.* Boston, Children's Hospital, 1979.

Levine, M.D., Meltzer, L.J., Busch, B., et al.: The pediatric early elementary examination: studies of a neurodevelopmental examination for 7 to 9 year-old children. *Pediatrics* 71:894, 1983.

Levine, M.D., Oberklaid, F., and Meltzer, L.: Developmental output failure: a study of low productivity in school age children. *Pediatrics* 67:18, 1981.

Levine, M.D., and Satz, P. (eds.): *Middle Childhood: Developmental Variation and Dysfunction From 6–14.* Baltimore, University Park Press, 1984.

Levine, M.D., and Zallen, B.G.: The learning disorders of adolescence. *Pediatr. Clin. North Am.* 31:345, 1984.

Lewis, D.O., Shanock, S.S., Pincus, J.H., et al.: Violent juvenile delinquents: psychiatric, neurological, psychological, and abuse factors. *J. Am. Acad. Child Psychiatr.* 18(2):307–319, 1979.

Lilienfeld, A.M., and Pasamanick, B. The association of maternal and fetal factors with the development of mental deficiency. II. Relationship to maternal age, birth order, previous reporductive loss, and degree of mental deficiency. *Am. J. Men. Defic.* 60:557–569, 1955.

Luria, A.R.: *Higher Cortical Functions in Man* (2nd ed.). New York, Basic Books, 1980.

MaCoby, E.E., and Jacklin, C.N.: *The Psychology of Sex Differences.* Stanford, Stanford University Press, 1974.

Madden, N.A., and Slavin, R.E.: Mainstreaming students with mild handicaps: academic and social outcomes. *Rev. Ed. Res.* 53(4):519, 1983.

Marcie, P., and Hecaen, H.: Agraphia: writing disorders associated with unilateral cortical lesions. In Heilman, K.M., and Valenstein, E. (eds.): *Clinical Neuropsychology.* New York, Oxford University Press, 1979.

Martin-Bouyer, G., Lebreton, R., Toga, M., et al.: Outbreak of accidental hexachlorophene poisoning in France. *Lancet 1*:91, 1982.

Masica, D.N., Money, J., Ehrhardt, A.A., et al.: Fetal sex hormones and cognitive patterns: studies in the testicular feminizing syndrome and androgen insensitivity. *Johns Hopkins Med. J.* 124:34, 1969.

Meltzer, L.J.: Cognitive assessment and diagnosis of learning problems. In Levine, M.D., and Satz, P. (eds.): *Middle Childhood: Developmental Variation and Dysfunction between Six and Fourteen Years.* Baltimore, University Park Press, 1984.

Mercer, J.: *Labeling the Mentally Retarded: Clinical and Social System Perspective on Mental Retardation.* Berkeley, University of California Press, 1973.

Milich, R., and Loney, J.: The role of hyperactive and aggressive symptomatology in predicting adolescent outcomes among hyperactive children. *J. Pediatr. Psychol.* 4:93–112, 1979.

Milner, B.: Memory and the medial temporal regions of the brain. In Pribram, K.H., and Broadbent, D.E. (eds.): *Biology of Memory.* New York, Academic Press, 1970.

Money, J., and Granoff, D.: I.Q. and the somatic stigmata of Turner's syndrome. *Am. J. Ment. Defic.* 70:69, 1965.

Natelson, S.E., and Sayers, M.P.: The fate of children sustaining severe head trauma during birth. *Pediatrics 51*:169–174, 1973.

Needleman, H.L.: Lead at Low Dose and the Behavior of Children. *Acta Psychiat. Scand.* Suppl. 303:26, 1983.

Needleman, H.L., Gunnoe, C., and Leviton, A. et al.: Deficits in psychologic and classroom performance of children with elevated dentine lead levels. *N. Engl. J. Med.* 300:689–695, 1979.

Niwander, K.R., Friedmna, E.A., Hoover, D.B., Pietrowski, H., and Westphal, M.C.: Fetal morbidity following potentially anoxgenic obstetric condition. I. Abruptio placentae. II. Placenta prevai. III. Prolapse of the umbilica cord. *Am. J. Obstet. Gynecol.* 95:838–859, 1966.

Orton, S.T.: *Reading, Writing, and Speech Problems in Children.* New York, W. W. Norton, 1937.

Oski, F.A., and Honig, A.S.: The effects of therapy on the developmental scores of iron-deficient infants. *J. Pediatr.* 92:21, 1978.

Oski, F.A., Honig, A.S., Helu, B., and Howanitz, P.: Effect of iron therapy on behavior performance in nonanemic, iron-deficient infants. *Pediatrics 71*:877–880, 1983.

Palfrey, J.S., Levine, M.D., and Pierson, D.E.: The antecedents of middle childhood functioning. In Levine, M.D., and Staz, P. (eds.): *Middle Childhood: Developmental Vari-*

ation and Dysfunction between Six and Fourteen Years. Baltimore, University Park Press, 1984.

Palfrey, J.S., Mervis, R., and Butler, J.A.: New directions in the evaluation of children with handicaps. *N. Engl. J. Med. 298*:819, 1978.

Peters, J.E., Ramine, J.S., and Dykman, R.A.: A special neurological examination of children with learning disabilities. *Dev. Med. Child Neurol. 17*:63, 1975.

Piaget, J.: *The Child's Conception of Number.* London, Routledge and Kegan Paul, 1952.

Piaget, J.: *Six Psychological Studies.* London, University of London Press, 1964.

Piaget, J.: *The Mechanism of Perception.* London, Routledge and Kegan Paul, 1969.

Pierson, D.E., and Bronson, M.: The impact of early education: measured by classroom observations and teacher ratings of children in kindergarten. *Eval. Rev. 7*:191–216, 1983.

Pless, I.B., and Zvzgulis, I. The health of children with special needs. In Klerman, L.V. (ed.): *Research Priorities in Maternal and Child Health.* Washington, D.C.: Office for Maternal and Child Health, U.S. Department of Health and Human Services, 1981.

Pollitt, E., Greenfield, D., and Leibel, R.: Significance of Bayley score changes following iron therapy. *J. Pediatr. 92*:177, 1978.

Prechtl, H.F.: The choreiform syndrome in children. *Dev. Med. Child Neurol. 4*:119, 1962.

Raisman, G., and Field, P.M.: Sexual dimorphism in the neuropil of the preoptic area of the rat and its dependence on neonatal androgen. *Brain Res. 54*:1, 1973.

Rakic, P.: Mode of cell migration to the superficial layers of fetal monkey neocortex. *J. Comp. Neurol. 145*:61, 1972.

Rapoport, E.L., Buchsbaum, M.S., Weingartner, H. et al.: Dextroamphetamine: its cognitive and behavioral effects in normal and hyperactive boys and normal men. *Arch. Gen. Psychiatry 37*:933, 1980.

Reschly, D.J.: Beyond IQ test bias: The National Academy panel's analysis of minority EMR overrepresentation. *Ed. Res. 13*:15–19, 1984.

Richmond, J.B.: Communities in action: a report on Project Head Start, *Reading Teacher 19*:323–331, 1966.

Ritvo, E.R., Freeman, B.J., Geller, E., and Yuwiler, A.: Effects of Fenfluramine on 14 Outpatients with the Syndrome of Autism. *J. Am. Acad. Child Psychiatry 22*:6:549, 1983.

Rosenberger, P.B., and Hier, D.B.: Cerebral asymmetry and verbal intellectual deficits. *Neurology 19*:544, 1979.

Rutter, M.: Raised lead levels and impaired cognitive/behavioral functioning: a review of the evidence. *Dev. Med. Child Neurol 22*(Suppl. 42), 1980.

Rutter, M.: School effects on pupil progress: research findings and policy implications. *Child Dev. 54*:1, 1983.

Saenger, G.: *The Adjustment of Severely Retarded Adults in the Community.* Albany, N.Y., Interdepartmental Health Resources Board, 1957.

Sameroff, A.J., and Chandler, M.J.: Reproductive risk and the continuum of caretaking casualty. In Florowitz, F., and Hetherington, E. (eds.): *Review of Child Development Research*, Vol. 4. 1975.

Satterfield, J.H., Hoppe, C.M., and Schell, A.M.: A prospective study of delinquency in

110 adolescent boys with attention deficit disorder and 88 normal adolescent boys. *Am. J. Psychiatry* 139:795–798, 1982.

Schonhaut, S., and Satz, P.: Prognosis of the learning disabled child: a review of the follow-up studies. In Rutter, M. (ed.): *Behavioral Syndromes of Brain Dysfunction in Childhood*. New York, Guilford Press, 1983.

Shaywitz, S.E., Cohen, D.J., and Shaywitz, B.A.: The biochemical basis of minimal brain dysfunction. *J. Pediatr.* 92:179, 1978.

Shaywitz, S.E., Cohen, P.M., and Cohen, D.J. et al.: Long-term consequences of Reye syndrome: a sibling-matched, controlled study of neurologic, cognitive, academic, and psychiatric function. *J. Pediatr.* 100:41, 1982.

Shonkoff, J.: Biological and social factors contributing to mild mental retardation. In Heller, K.A., Holtzman, W.H., and Messick, S. (eds.): *Placing Children in Special Education: A Strategy for Equity*. Washington, D.C., National Academy Press, 1982.

Smith, A.C., Flick, G.L., Ferriss, G.S., and Sellman, A.H.: Prediction of developmental outcome at seven years from prenatal, perinatal and postnatal events. *Child Dev.* 43:495–507, 1972.

Smith, C.A.: The effect of wartime starvation in Holland upon pregnancy and its product. *Am. J. Obstet. Gynecol.* 53:599, 1947.

SRI International, Inc.: *Longitudinal Study of the Impact of PL 94-142 on a Select Number of Local Education Agencies*. Palo Alto, 1979.

Stanfield, J.S.: Graduation: what happens to the retarded child when he grows up? *Except. Child.* 39:548–552, 1973.

Stevenson, H.W., et al.: Reading disabilities: the case of Chinese, Japanese, and English. *Child Dev.* 53:1164, 1982.

Swanson, J.M., and Kinsbourne, J.: Food dyes impair performance of hyperactive children on a laboratory learning test. *Science* 207:1485, 1980.

Thorley, G.: Childhood hyperactivity and food additives *Dev. Med. Child Neurol.* 25:527, 1983.

Turner, G. Brookwell, R., Daniel, A., et al.: Heterozygous expression of X-linked mental retardation and the marker X: fra(x) (927). *N. Engl. J. Med.* 303:662, 1980.

U.S. Department of Health, Education and Welfare. *Progress Toward a Free Appropriate Public Education*. HEW Publication. No. (DE)79-05003. Washington, D.C., 1979.

Vellutino, F.: *Dyslexia: Theory and Research*. Cambridge, MIT Press, 1979.

Waber, D. Sex differences in mental abilities, hemispheric lateralization and, rate of physical growth in adolescents. *Dev. Psychol.* 13:29, 1977.

Walker, D.K., Butler, J.A., Palfrey, J.S., and Singer, J.D.: State and federal policy implications of selected findings from the collaborative study of children with special needs. Paper presented at the annual meeting of the American Educational Research Association, New Orleans, April 1984.

Webb, T.E., and Oski, F.A.: Iron deficiency anemia and scholastic achievement in young adolescents. *J. Pediatr.* 82:827, 1973.

Weiss, B., et al.: Behavioral responses to artificial food colors. *Science* 207:1497, 1980.

Weiss, G., Hechtman, L., Perlman, T., et al.: Hyperactivities as young adults: a controlled prospective 10 year follow-up of 75 children. *Gen. Psychiatr.* 36:657, 1979.

Wender, E.: Food additives and hyperkinesis. *Am. J. Child* 131:1204, 1977.

Wender, P.H.: Hypothesis for a possible biochemical basis of minimal brain dysfunction. In Knights, R.M., and Bakker, D.J. (eds.): *The Neuropsychology of Learning Disorders Theoretical Approaches,* Baltimore, University Park Press, 1976.

Werner, E., Bierman, J., and French, F.: *The Children of Kauai: A Longitudinal Study From the Prenatal Period to Age Ten.* Honolulu, University of Hawaii, 1971.

Werner, E., and Smith, R.: *Kauai's Children Come of Age.* Honolulu, University Press of Hawaii, 1977.

Wiener, G. The relationship of birth weight and length of gestation to intellectual development at ages 8 to 10 years. *J. Pediatr.* 76:694–699, 1970.

Wilkinson, A.C., DeMarinis, M., and Riley, S.J.: Developmental and Individual Differences in Rapid Remembering. *Child Dev.* 54:898, 1983.

Winick, M.: *Malnutrition and Brain Development.*New York, Oxford University Press, 1976.

Yogman, M.W., and Zeisel, S.H.: Diet and sleep patterns in newborn infants. *N. Engl. J. Med.* 309:1147–1149, 1983.

Yule, W., Lansdown, R., Millar, I.B., et al.: The relationship between blood lead concentrations, intelligence and attainment in a school population: a pilot study. *Dev. Med. Child Neurol.* 23:567, 1981.

8

Psychosocial Factors in the Somatic Symptoms of Children and Adolescents

Stanford B. Friedman

Somatic symptoms have traditionally been divided into those with an organic, or physical, cause and those with a psychologic etiology. This dichotomy has been the customary approach to diagnosis and clinical management, but it frequently limits our understanding of the symptomatology in a given patient and interferes with the correct diagnosis. In turn, less than optimal or inappropriate management may follow.

The problem is that those diseases and symptoms labeled as "physical" may be significantly influenced by psychological or social factors. Such psychosocial factors may interact with genetic and other biologic attributes in the patient in a manner that leads to illness or symptoms or, at a minimum, affects how the patient will respond to his illness or symptoms. Likewise, psychological and emotional causes of symptoms do not exert their influences in isolation, but rather act upon the patient so as to effect his biologic and physiologic status. In essence, this interaction of the biologic and psychosocial is the basic element of the biopsychosocial model of disease described by Engel (1977).

The relevance of Engel's biopsychosocial model to prevention has received little attention. It is obvious that consideration of psychosocial issues has not led to the virtual elimination of such diseases as diphtheria and measles, nor has psychological understanding of patient and family been responsible for the marked reduction of infantile diarrhea and childhood malnutrition. However, now that common devastating acute diseases of childhood have been mostly eliminated, pediatricians can turn their attention to the quality of life of their patients. Thus, the psychosocial aspects of pediatric practice assume new importance; psychosocial, developmental, and learning problems compromising quality of life constitute, in part, the new morbidity of pediatrics (Haggerty, Roughmann, and Pless, 1975). Prevention of such problems and illnesses demands an approach consistent with the biopsychosocial model. By the early identification of psychological and emotional events in patients and the related development of symptoms or problem behaviors, the pediatrician or other health professional has the potential to prevent the more severe problems that characterize this new morbidity.

In summary, psychological factors may (1) be of etiologic importance in the development of disease or symptoms usually considered to be physical or organic in nature, (2) significantly influence the adaptation of the patient and family to an illness or symptom no matter what etiologic factors are of clinical importance, or (3) play a primary role in the development of a somatic symptom. It should be noted that these three general influences attributed to psychological factors, as related to symptom development, are not mutually exclusive and all three may be seen in any given patient. This chapter briefly discusses psychological factors as they relate to disease and symptoms under three headings: psychomatic medicine, response to symptoms and disease, and psychogenic symptoms.

Psychosomatic Medicine

Concepts

Folklore, as well as ancient medicine, have frequently incorporated the notion that psychological factors are associated with the development of physical illness. However, it was Alexander, French, and Pollack (1968) who introduced to modern medicine the concept that specific psychological conflicts were related to seven specific disease entities (bronchial asthma, rheumatoid arthritis, ulcerative colitis, essential hypertension, neurodermatitis, thyrotoxicosis, and duodenal peptic ulcer). These diseases came to be regarded as the "holy seven" illnesses of psychosomatic medicine. Modifications of this concept were forthcoming, and especially influencial were the writings of Dunbar (1943). She proposed that personality types were of etiologic importance, rather than the nature of psychological conflict, and identified personality profiles that predisposed to specific diseases. Common to psychosomatic theories of this sort was the assumption that identifiable psychological problems or traits could be linked to specific diseases—hence, the evolution of the theory of specificity.

The theory of specificity has been questioned on a number of grounds. Not the least of these has been the repeated observation that not all individuals with a particular psychological conflict or personality profile develop the anticipated disease, nor do all individuals with a given "psychosomatic" disease have the expected psychological characteristics. Furthermore, psychotherapy judged successful in resolving the psychological problem or conflict thought to be associated with a physical symptom or disease, frequently did not result in improvement of the organic symptomatology. It also became increasingly obvious to many clinicians that the natural history of a number of diseases not considered to be psychosomatic in nature were influenced by psychosocial factors, for example, diabetes mellitus.

A psychological condition or situation leading to a specific disease was an overly simplistic psychosomatic model, as was the concept that one could divide diseases into those that were psychosomatic and those that were not. Investigators and clinicians began to appreciate the complexity of the causation of disease, and interactive models of the etiology of disease were proposed. However, it was not until Engel introduced the "multifactorial etiology" concept of disease in 1954 that a new model was generally available to explain the relationship between psychological phenomena and physical symptoms and disease. Inherent in his model, which later evolved into the biopsychosocial approach to disease (Engel, 1977), is the concept that psychological factors do not cause disease, but rather modify susceptibility to disease in the individual. Other factors, including the biologic and environmental, have obvious etiologic importance. Psychosocial factors, therefore, have the potential to influence other determinants of disease, and their influence varies markedly in any given patient or disease (Plaut and Friedman, 1981).

The degree to which a psychosocial factor, or stressor, influences the development or clinical course of disease is dependent upon a number of considerations. First is the particular disease in question. As mentioned, all disease processes have the potential to be influenced by psychosocial factors. However, it is useful to view susceptibility to such influence as a continuum, with such diseases as asthma and ulcerative colitis strongly influenced, in terms of their clinical course, by the psychosocial environment of the patient. At the other extreme, there is no evidence that brain tumors in children are affected by psychosocial factors; however, this may be due to insufficient study of this possibility. It is interesting to note that fifteen years ago the relationship between psychologic stress and lymphoma was little appreciated, yet such an association would currently appear to be accepted by most physicians.

Second, the nature and intensity of the psychological event or stimulus must be considered, and again, susceptibility to the effects of such events is best conceptualized as a continuum. It is assumed that some events, such as the loss of a parent, represent a major psychologic distress to all children, but children vary greatly in their ability to adapt or cope with such a loss. Furthermore, the presence or absence of support systems have a marked influence on an individual's success or failure to cope. On the other hand, events appearing to be relatively minor in importance, such as a child arriving late to school because of a delayed bus, may be extremely distressing to a child who is under strong parental pressure to be perfect in performance or who has developed obsessive-compulsive traits.

Third, there are major individual differences in susceptibility to psychosocial factors, even given the same disease process. These differences relate to the biologic and psychological status of the individual, which in turn, is based on genetic and experiential (acquired) determinants. Thus, one child with asthma, due to strong biologic predispositions to this disease, will develop wheezing no matter how stable his or her psychological life whereas another child, also asthmatic, will develop wheezing only under psychological stress.

Fourth, there are temporal and developmental factors which may be of importance in altering the role of psychological factors in the disease process. Again, using asthma as an example, a child or young adolescent may develop wheezing in situations of family conflict, but as this same individual matures similar conflicts with family do not result in symptomatology. This change may be due to the increased psychological independence of the older adolescent or young adult or to biologic factors related to age. These four continuums, discussed as components of the biopsychosocial model of disease developed by Engel (1977), are as follows:

1. nature of disease
2. nature and intensity of psychological factors
3. individual susceptibility
   biologic
     genetic
     acquired
   psychologic
     biologic
     experimental
   social and cultural
4. temporal and developmental factors

Clinical Implications

The argument presented is that psychosocial factors may potentially influence the development and clinical course of all diseases. However, the enumeration of some practical limitations are in order. First, the state of the art of psychosomatic medicine is such that preventing specified physical symptoms or disease is not possible. Undoubtedly, anticipatory guidance and family counseling, by promoting optimal child rearing and family functioning, may reduce susceptibilities to somatic complaints and perhaps even physical diseases in one's practice, but the results of these preventive measures can neither be delineated or validated at this time. Yet, prevention remains the most exciting aspect of psychosomatic medicine within the field of pediatrics. For instance, there are data from animal experimentation to suggest that hypertension may have its anlage in the early life of the individual (Henry, Meehan, and Stephens, 1967). If such findings in animals are found to apply also to humans, future preventive intervention in infants and children might have impact on a number of major public health problems.

Second, even though theory and experimental findings may support a relationship between psychological events and disease, in a given disease process for a particular patient such an association may not be of practical use to the clinician. As an example, it has been repeatedly observed that high scores on recent life event questionnaires (Petrich and Homes, 1977) are associated with an increased risk of illness. However, the risk of disease is nonspecific and the correlations, though of statistical significance, are of a low order of magnitude and do not account for more than 10 to 15 percent of the variance. Thus, though of importance to the conceptualization of psychomatic processes and to issues related to the overall delivery of health care, having children evaluated by scores on recent life event questionnaires is not helpful to the practicing health professional.

Last, the previous discussion of the biopsychosocial model noted significant variability in the actual influence psychosocial factors may have in a given patient. The appropriate task of the pediatrician is to determine whether or not the psychological life of the patient has significant clinical importance in the natural course of the patient's disease and response to medical management.

This assessment should focus on the psychological and social functioning in the child's major spheres of activity; namely (1) role and relationships within the *family,* (2) relationships with peers, and (3) social and academic functioning in the school setting. Psychological, social, and academic problems and conflicts thus identified can then be related to exacerbations of disease. Then intervention can be instituted to reduce pressures and conflicts experienced by the child, and to increase the child's ability to cope with life experiences. Thus, in a child with ulcerative colitis with symptoms judged to be related to the parents' high, and unrealistic, expectations of academic achievement, the pediatrician might intervene by counseling the parents and helping the child develop alternate coping strategies for responding to parental and school pressure to perform beyond his or her ability. Such an approach would acknowledge the importance of psychological influences in *this patient's illness,* without abandoning the role of biologic determinants of etiology of disease.

Response to Symptoms and Disease

The etiologic importance of psychological factors has been discussed. To be differentiated from the psychosocial contribution to the causation of disease is the influence psychological and social factors have upon an individual's response to illness, no matter what factors are of etiologic importance. Illness is always imposed on a patient who has an individual history, lives in a family and social environment, and is part of a culture (Pless and Pinkerton, 1975). Some children have learned to ignore illness and thus report few symptoms. For other children, their illness and accompanying symptoms represent the major vehicle for gaining attention in an otherwise nonresponsive family. Still other children discover the manipulative value of somatic complaints; for example, the teenage son with ulcerative colitis who threatens to bleed if his parents do not abide by his wishes. A child with learning problems may attempt to avoid school by exaggerating symptoms secondary to a mild upper respiratory infection.

The disease itself may significantly alter the psychological status of a child, and that alteration may inappropriately be considered to be of etiologic importance. For instance, there is a body of literature that claimed that overdependency in children is of etiologic importance in the development of asthma. This dependency fostered anger in the child, and the wheezing in asthmatic children was said to be the "suppressed cry" expressing this anger. Later studies did not support this theory that overdependency bears linear causality to asthma. Rather, having asthma, especially the experience of "air-hunger," probably contributes to the dependency traits observed in many children with this disease. This is an example of the inadequacy of linear causality in relation to somatic symptoms and the important place of feedback and circular causality.

The issues reviewed in this and the previous section suggest three questions that the clinician should always consider:

1. What are the psychological and social issues related to the etiology of physical symptoms and disease?
2. How do the psychological, social, and cultural attributes of the patient and family influence the patient's experiencing and reporting of symptoms?
3. How does the disease affect the psychological status of the patient and family?

Psychogenic Symptoms

The term *psychogenic* denotes that the symptom is due primarily to an intrapsychic or psychological process. This section focuses upon conversion reactions, which are a common explanation of pain symptoms in later childhood and adolescence (Friedman, 1973). Mention is also made of malingering, hypochrondriasis, and psychophysiologic mechanisms as explanations of pain symptoms. In adults, these disorders appear, in general, to be relatively discreet entities; however, this may not be nearly as true for children and adolescents.

The unconcscious process, thought to be crucial to the definition of conversion reaction, may be less relevent in many children and adolescents. The child complaining of a headache or abdominal pain prior to an important examination at school may not have an underlying unconscious psychological conflict, and the symptom may depend on mechanisms that are largely psychophysiologic or merely semiotic, for example, everyday sensations ordinarily ignored but now communicated as pain because of their demonstrated capacity to influence the behavior of others. Thus, the impending examination, representing a psychological stressor, results in visceral changes that in turn produce the abdominal pain, and therefore is similar to the psychosomatic processes discussed earlier. Furthermore, the child may be fully aware that the complaint is related to academic pressure, and if the symptom allows the child to avoid attending school, he or she may exaggerate the discomfort being experienced. This process borders on being a hypochondriacal complaint, which reflects preoccupation and overconcern with normal bodily functions. In some children with somatic complaints, at any given point in time, the pain may be feigned for purposes of avoiding a threatening situation or gaining attention, and thus may be similar to malingering. The clinician also has to consider the uncommon occurrence of bizarre somatic complaints reflecting delusional thinking in a psychotic patient.

Recurrent abdominal pain has received much recent attention (Apley, 1975; Green, 1967; Barr and Feuerstein, 1983). Whether in the majority of instances this disorder represents a conversion reaction, a view previously proposed by Friedman (1973), is unknown. Barr and Feuerstein (1983) have suggested that conversion symptoms are a psychogenic disorder and occur in psychopathologic conditions of children and adolescents and that relatively few children with recurrent abdominal pain should be thus diagnosed. Rather, they suggest, the majority of patients with recurrent abominal pain should be classified as *dysfunctional*, a term that is ill-defined but assumes a lack of psychopathology in the child or adolescent. These investigators have hypothesized that recurrent abdominal pain, as a dysfunctional disorder, may be associated with altered autonomic nervous system functioning in response to environmental stress, suggesting that this clinical entity belongs in the category of psychophysiologic disorders. However, I believe there is no reason to postulate psychopathology in the majority of adolescents with conversion symptoms; indeed, for many the symptom may represent a relatively benign resolution to a transient developmental problem.

Conversion Reactions

Conversion (hysterical) reactions are mediated by a psychic mechanism "whereby an idea, fantasy, or wish is expressed in bodily terms rather than in words and is experienced by the patient as a physical rather than a mental symptom" (Engel, 1983). Implied in this definition is that the direct expression of the wish is unacceptable, and if acknowledged, would result in anxiety and guilt. The conversion to bodily representation or symptomatology is an unconscious process, and the patient cannot initially convey to the physician the unconscious link between the unacceptable wish and the somatic symptom. The symptom results, however, in a reduction in anxiety or guilt, which traditionally has been viewed as the primary gain for the patient. Restated, the primary gain to the patient represents the psychodynamic explanation for the existence of conversion symptoms.

The conversion symptom also, however, serves the patient in another major way; namely, by providing secondary gains. Thus, a teenager with fainting spells gains great attention from parents and peers, which in turn tends to sustain the symptomatology. Fainting also may serve to avoid a threatening situation, such as sexual advances from one's peers.

Conversion symptoms are thought to be common in adolescents (Friedman, 1973), and in my experience in two medically oriented adolescent clinics they were one of the most common diagnoses. This perhaps should not be surprising, as adolescents are frequently in conflict about sexuality and other developmental issues. Unacceptable aspects of this and other tasks of adolescence may lead to avoidance of anxiety (primary gain) and increased ability to gain attention or to cope with a threatening environment (secondary gain) by the development of conversion symptoms. Among the more frequently seen conversion symptoms in adolescents and older children are abdominal and chest pain, dizziness and fainting spells, headaches, and hyperventilation. Less frequently seen in adolescents, but apparently more common in adults, are limb paralyses, hysterical blindness, complaints of nausea, and paresthesias. Conversion symptoms are not due to structural or pathophysiologic changes, though such symptoms may secondarily produce biochemical or structural abnormalities. Thus, hyperventilation may cause derangement of the blood gases, even resulting in tetany, and limb paralysis may result in muscle atrophy. These are best conceptualized as the complications of conversion reactions (Engel, 1983).

In making the diagnosis of conversion symptoms, it is of critical importance to obtain substantiating data. As mentioned, secondary gains may be obvious and frequently impress the physician with their role in the maintenance of the symptom. On the other hand, the exact nature of the unacceptable wish or fantasy may not be obvious; evidence does suggest, however, that such existing psychic mechanisms can be ascertained through skillful interviewing. The adolescent is often aware that a symptom is "emotional" and may even be able to identify the general area of conflict. Thus, conversion process may not be entirely unconscious, and this phenomenon may be more characteristic of adolescents with conversion reactions than adults. The following case illustrates the typically unconscious etiology of conversion reactions in a girl who, it was eventually learned, had fears about her own sexual identity.

Jane, a fourteen-year old girl, was reported to have had three episodes of hyperventilation followed by fainting while in school. The symptom occurred twice in the hallways during change of classes, and once on the school steps while the girl was awaiting a ride from her mother. Jane denied being upset at these times. It was later determined from the patient that on each occasion she had just been greeted by her counselor, a middle-aged woman, though the girl did not attach any importance to this "coincidence." The meaning of what appeared to be a casual meeting of the girl and the counselor was revealed only when the school principal was contacted. It was then learned that this counselor had allegedly made homosexual advances toward several girls, and that these advances were never made during scheduled interviews with students, but rather when she met them informally.

This case also illustrates the relationship between an environmental stressor, in this instance, encounters with the counselor, and the precipitation of the symptom. Though the occurrence of symptoms are probably never random, the precipitating factor may be intrapsychic (for example, during day dreaming), and relating all episodes to environmental stresses thus may not be possible.

The symptom, according to traditional psychoanalytic thinking, has symbolic meaning. For example, an adolescent with severe shaking of the hands, may have conflict over masturbation. In children and adolescents, the symbolic meaning may not be obvious, and indeed the selection of a given symptom may not always involve a symbolic thought process.

It is generally believed that conversion reactions are more common in females than males. Also, individuals with hysterical personality traits—such as the use of nonverbal communication, seductive behavior, and dramatization of life events—are more likely than others to develop conversion symptoms; however, such symptoms are seen in individuals lacking hysterical features. Characteristically, though, a teenager with a conversion reaction will report the symptom in a vivid, dramatic, sometimes nearly bizarre manner; typical of such reports was a boy's complaint of "a hot knife twisting through my chest." Nevertheless, there is characteristically a lack of true concern about the symptoms ("la belle indifference"). This may be an unreliable criterion for diagnosing conversion symptoms, however, as adolescents may also appear unconcerned when experiencing symptoms secondary to organic disease, due to the need to deny a threatening illness.

The symptom is often modeled after a similar complaint in an individual psychologically significant to the patient, such as a parent or sibling, or the patient may use symptomatology associated with a previous physical ailment as a model. This can present a most difficult diagnostic problem, such as the teenager with epilepsy who develops conversion symptoms modeled after a perception of seizures. It should be noted that the symptom may be a distortion of the model, based on what the patient has been told about a symptom occurring in a relative or friend.

There have been few systematic studies of the families of children and adolescents with conversion symptoms. It appears, however, that such children are often overprotected and also have a history of past unexplained illnesses. Family members may frequently use health issues and symptoms in family communication; for instance, a father might say, "We will go on our picnic tomorrow if your mother doesn't have a headache."

Last, the symptom is frequently consistent with anatomic and pathophysiologic reality, as illustrated by the "glove anesthesia" that is at variance with anatomic nerve distribution. However, if the conversion reaction is modeled after the patient's own past physical symptoms, the conversion symptom may closely mimic one having an organic basis. In summary, the criteria for diagnosis of conversion symptoms in children and adolescents are as follows:

Symptom reduces anxiety (primary gain).

Symptom helps adolescents cope with environment (secondary gain).

Symptoms occurs at times of stress.

Symptom has symbolic meaning.

Symptom is more common in individuals with hysterical personality.

Symptom is reported characteristic style.

Patient has apparent lack of concern about symptoms.

Patient has a model for the symptom.

Parents are often overprotective.

There is frequently a medical history of past unexplained symptoms.

Family frequently uses health issues and symptoms in communication.

There is a history and complaints not consistent with anatomic or pathophysiologic concepts.

In-Care Issues

Of primary importance in the assessment of unexplained somatic symptoms is to include early consideration of psychological, as well as physical, factors and to communicate this consideration to patient and parents. Relegating psychosocial evaluation to the end of a comprehensive medical workup conveys to patient and parents that such a focus is a last resort and comes only after the failure to discover anything physically wrong. This promotes rejection by the family of the diagnostic relevance of psychological or emotional problems. Such rejection can usually be avoided by the simultaneous evaluation of possible physical and psychological factors.

Another point worthy of mention is the frequent lack of appreciation of the role of secondary gain. It is tempting to view secondary gain as inappropriate and as representing the child's "taking advantage" of the environment, rather than the child's attempt to cope with problematic issues. Although sound medical care acknowledges the fact that secondary gain may indeed promote the persistence of symptoms and suggests minimizing such reinforcement as part of any intervention (Green, 1984), the pediatrician can gain valuable information about the psychosocial life of the child and family by a thoughtful analysis of the secondary gains accruing to a particular patient. Increased attention from parents in a child with abdominal pain, for instance, may indicate a realistic deficiency in the time the parents are spending with their child. In a similar manner, malingering and hypochondriacal complaints can reflect psychological or frank psychiatric problems in a troubled child, and not behaviors to be eliminated without an understanding of etiology.

Finally, it should be noted that in some dysfunctional families, children's symptoms may offer secondary gains to the entire family system, and the child's symptomatic behavior can be viewed as altruistic within this context. For example, the identified patient's symptoms may so consume the parent's attention and energy that they are diverted from overt marital conflict.

The care of children with psychogenic symptoms, including conversion reactions, is an appropriate role for the pediatrician. Complete understanding of the psychodynamic processes underlying the symptom is not necessary for counseling in a majority of cases, and focusing on the nonsymptom aspects of the child's life may be the basis for successful intervention. However, referral to a mental health professional always should be considered if the child continues to be dysfunctional, or if, over time, issues arise that are beyond the expertise of the pediatrician (Phillips, Sarles, and Friedman, 1980).

Concluding Remarks

Psychosocial factors clearly can contribute to the etiology of somatic symptoms and physical disease in children and adolescents, though their etiologic importance in any given patient can vary greatly. Furthermore, the distinctions among psychosomatic symptoms, psychophysiologic disorders, conversion reactions, and hypochondriasis are often blurred. Nevertheless, there are common denominators, in that all demand optimal assessment and management, an understanding of the interactions between psychosocial and physical factors, and the ability to comprehensively evaluate the child in the context of his family and total environment.

References

Alexander, F., French, T.M., and Pollack, G.H.: *Psychosomatic Specificity: Experimental Study and Results.* Chicago, University of Chicago Press, 1968.

Apley, J.: *The Child with Abdominal Pain.* London, Blackwell, 1975.

Barr, R.G., and Feuerstein, M.: Recurrent abdominal pain syndrome: how appropriate are own basic clinical assumptions? In McGrath, P.J., and Firestone, P. (eds.): *Pediatric and Adolescent Behavioral Medicine.* New York: Springer, 1983.

Dunbar, H.F.: *Psychomatic Diagnosis.* New York, Harper (Hoeber), 1943.

Engel, G.L.: Conversion symptoms. In MacBryde, C.M., and Blacklow, R.S. (eds.): *Signs and Symptoms* (6th ed.). Philadelphia, J.B. Lippincott, 1983.

Engel, G.L.: Selection of clinical material in psychosomatic medicine. *Psychosom. Med.* 16:368, 1954.

Engel, G.L.: The need for a new medical model: a challenge for biomedicine. *Science* 196:129, 1977.

Friedman, S.B.: Conversion symptoms in adolescents. *Pediatr. Clin. N. Am.* 20:873, 1973.

Green, M.: Diagnosis and treatment: psychogenic, recurrent abdominal pain. *Pediatrics* 40:84, 1967.

Green, M.: Psychogenic pain disorders. In Green, M., and Haggerty, R.J. (eds.): *Ambulatory Pediatrics,* Philadelphia, W.B. Saunders Company, 1984.

Haggerty, R.J., Roughmann, K.J., and Pless, I.B.: *Child Health and the Community.* New York, Wiley InterScience Series, 1975.

Henry, J.P., Meehan, J.P., and Stephens, R.M.: The use of psychosocial stimuli to induce prolonged systolic hypertension in mice. *Psychosom. Med.* 29:408, 1967.

Petrich, J., and Holmes, T.H.: Life change and onset of illness. *Med. Clin. N. Am.* 61:825, 1977.

Phillips, S., Sarles, R.M., and Friedman, S.B.: Consultation and referral: when, why, and how. *Ped. Ann.* 9:269, 1980.

Plaut, S.M., and Friedman, S.B.: Psychosocial factors in infectious disease. In Ader, R. (ed.): *Psychoneuroimmunology.* New York, Academic Press, 1981.

Pless, I.B., and Pinkerton, P.: *Chronic Childhood Disorder: Promoting Patterns of Adjustment.* London, Henry Kimpton Publishers, 1975.

9
Eating Disorders in the Young: A New Plague

George D. Comerci

T he eating disorder syndromes of food avoidance and self-starvation, binge eating, and purging are classic examples of biopsychosocial disorders. Each condition has strong biologic, psychological, and sociocultural determinants. Abundant evidence supports the hypothesis that the genesis of eating disorders is primarily sociocultural, familial, and psychiatric. Nevertheless, one cannot discount the significance of biologic influences in the development of these problems and especially their perpetuation once established.

Sociocultural Dilemmas

Fasting and purging have long been part of man's spiritual quest for purity, virtue, and holiness. Through self-sacrifice and denial, the weak become strong, the faint-hearted become brave, and the immoral are cleansed and forgiven. Thus, the powerless gain power and by self-control approach a state of godliness and veneration. The majority of religions and philosophies extol fortitude and embrace some form of fasting and suffering as a means of atonement and forgiveness. Similar feelings and attitudes are verbalized by persons with eating disorders. In Western society, thinness connotes asceticism, and fatness suggests slovenliness and lack of self-discipline and control. In the West, one must search long and hard to find an obese saint or martyr, but in the East, Buddha, the incarnation of selflesness, virtue, and wisdom, is portrayed as quite substantial, a kind and benevolent parent figure. It may be no accident then, that anorexia nervosa and bulimia are primarily encountered in Western societies. Although affluence and an abundance of food seem to be critical environmental factors

I wish to thank Dr. Vincent Fulginiti for his editorial comments and suggestions, especially with regard to organization of the manuscript. Alice "Dede" Carroll, M.S.W., was most helpful in pointing out ambiguities in content and style. Thanks to Susan Hunt, my secretary, who makes all things possible.

enhancing the occurence of eating disorders, strong religious and cultural forces affect their prevalence as well.

It is against this backdrop of fasting, purging, and self-denial as a reciprocal of goodness and worthiness that we must consider our particular culture's perception of beauty or what we feel constitutes an aesthetically and sexually appealing human form. There is an association between what a society values philosophically and spiritually, and how that society defines physical beauty. Changes in desired and acceptable body forms vary with the ebb and flow of a society's attitudes, value systems, and perceptions of reality.

Art reveals much about societal mores during a particular time. Concepts of beauty have changed throughout history and vary from culture to culture. Tribal women are maimed and endure pain in order to achieve status and beauty, which is not unlike the patterns of food restriction and excessive exercise employed by modern men and women in their struggle to obtain and maintain socially acceptable body forms. Renaissance and Baroque artists' portrayal of the female form would be viewed as corpulent by modern standards. In general, this concept of beauty in women persisted through the turn of the last century. The early twentieth century was a time of ferment, turmoil, and significant social change. We emerged from the Victorian age amid the aftershocks of the Industrial Revolution. The surface calm and stability was shattered by World War I, the first global confrontation. The 1920s was a decade of changing behaviors among women culminating in part from previously evolving revolutionary attitudes about women's rights, sexual freedom, and political roles. Interestingly, women strived to flatten their chests and hide their curves in an attempt to achieve the "flapper" look. Parenthetically, in the 1970s and 1980s during a second thrust of feminist activism and dramatic change in attitudes and behaviors toward the feminine role, we again saw women's fashions and appearance moving more in the direction of thinness. During and shortly following the Great Depression there was a return to an appreciation of a larger woman, especially during the 1940s and early 1950s. It was during the second half of the twentieth century that an exceedingly thin fashion model named Twiggy replaced Elizabeth Taylor as the most popular figure in London's Wax Museum. Subsequently, we have witnessed, mostly at the behest of male fashion czars, the emergence of a modern sex symbol typified by an athletic body .orm and youthful, almost prepubertal appearance. The present cultural emphasis on extreme thinness, a youthful tubular form, and androgenous appearance very likely increases the vulnerability of women at risk for developing an eating disorder.

The incidence of eating disorders in Western cultures during the 1970s and 1980s has increased dramatically and now is believed to have reached epidemic proportions (Willi and Grossman, 1983; Crisp, Palmer, and Kalucy, 1976; Szmukler, 1983). Although in the past considered a rare condition, the occurrence of anorexia nervosa is now one per year for every 200 to 250 middle or upper class adolescent girls. The prevalence of the bulimia syndromes is not known, al-

Table 9–1
Diagnostic Criteria for Anorexia Nervosa and Bulimia

Anorexia Nervosa	*Bulimia*
Refusal to maintain minimal normal body weight.	Recurrent episodes of binge eating.
Weight loss of at least 25% of original body weight.	At least three of the following:
	1. Consumption of high-calorie, easily ingested food during binge
Disturbance of body image.	2. Termination of binge with abdominal pain, sleep, or self-induced vomiting.
Intense fear of becoming obese.	
No known physical illness that would account for the weight loss.	3. Inconspicuous eating during binge
	4. Repeated attempts to lose weight by fasting, or using laxatives or diuretics
	5. Frequent weight fluctuations of greater than 4.5 kg
	Awareness of abnormal eating pattern with fear of not being able to stop eating voluntarily.
	Depressed mood after binge.
	Not due to any physical disorder.

Source: *Diagnostic and Statistical Manual of Mental Disorders* (3rd ed.). Washington, D.C., American Psychiatric Association, 1980.

though among college women it is estimated to be as high as 20 percent (Johnson et al., 1983; Halmi, Falck, and Schwartz, 1981; Pyle et al., 1983). Bulimia, with and without associated purging behaviors (laxative and diuretic abuse, self-induced vomiting, self-administered enemas), is believed to account for the bulk of the increase in eating disorders. Bulimia, more commonly known as binge eating or binging, is the rapid ingestion of large amounts of food in a relatively short time period. Bulimia is closely related to and may complicate classic anorexia nervosa, but is considered to be a distinct category of eating disorders (table 9–1). Binging may represent a discharge of anxiety related to environmental stress. It may also be an act of desperation or an attempt to deal with dysphoric feelings and depression. Bulimia may reflect poor impulse control. The associated purging behavior at once relieves guilt related to the binge but also satisfies the bulimic's intense desire for control, not only of body weight but of those in the environment (Gandour, 1984). Other cultures undoubtedly have sanctioned gorging and even postprandial vomiting, but such activities were likely more hedonistic and devoid of the underlying psychological conflicts and issues peculiar to persons with anorexia nervosa and bulimia.

The incidence of eating disorders, other than obesity, rises with socioeconomic status and is highest in affluent communities in which there is an abundance of food. Where food is not in short supply, its symbolic meanings tend to override its importance as a life-sustaining substance. There are "good foods" which are low in caloric density and "bad foods" such as red meats, carbohydrates, and fats. To eat is to be bad, but to diet is to be good. To break one's diet is a sign of weakness, but to refuse food is a sign of strength and character. The sense of nurturing and love in the act of offering and accepting food has somehow diminished in modern Western society.

There is little question that environmental and social factors have contributed to the recent increase in persons suffering from these eating maladies (Berger et al., 1977; Crisp, 1980; Garner and Garfinkle, 1980; Casper, 1983; Schwartz, Thompson, and Johnson, 1982).

Psychological Determinants

Support for a primary psychiatric etiology of eating disorders is strong. Bruch (1973) has emphasized the finding that food intake and body size are manipulated by the young person "in a futile effort to solve or camouflage inner stress or adjustment difficulties." The eating disorder patient has often been overprotected, overcontrolled, and overvalued resulting in a feeling of inadequacy and a sense that his or her destiny is in the hands of others. After a lifetime of "performing" for parents, relatives, teachers, and others, the young person is poorly prepared to cope with the demands of adolescence for autonomy and independence. Familial expectations of achievement, socioeconomic status, and individual temperament combine in the vulnerable youngster to create a climate for developing an eating disorder (Bruch, 1976, 1977). The observation that at least one-quarter of anorectic patients develop amenorrhea before significant weight loss occurs also lends support to a primary psychiatric etiology; the cessation of menstrual periods is felt to be stress related (Vande Wille, 1977). In patients with bulimia as well as in those with anorexia nervosa, one is impressed by the findings of low self-esteem, depression, interpersonal sensitivity, and lack of assertiveness. These characteristics in the anorexia nervosa patient sometimes are well hidden under a cloak of pseudomaturity, confidence, and overachievement, while constant physical and mental hyperactivity holds depression at bay (Eckert et al., 1982; Carlson and Cantwell, 1979).

Pubertal females have probably always had concern and anxiety about their bodies, especially about early breast development and the acquisition of body fat. For some young women, growth and sexual development intensify their concerns about "growing up" with all its implications of need for autonomy, control, and independent decision making (Casper et al., 1981). These concerns are exaggerated in the person denied during childhood the experience of independent functioning and autonomy, as is the case in patients at risk for developing an eating disorder. The competitive nature of a relationship with a very thin (or even anorectic) parent, or the fear of becoming like an overweight or matronly middle-aged parent, often is operative in the family dynamics of eating disorders. Although concern and anxiety about pubertal body changes is universal, studies now show that Western girls increasingly are dieting and periodically fasting in order to change their bodies to a form more acceptable to themselves and one thinner than that of their girlfriends. For most young women, dieting and food avoidance merely reflect a conscious desire to be thin and fashionable. For some, however, the "relentless pursuit of thinness" has less to do with fashion and more to do with self-sacrifice, self-restraint, impulse control, and a desire to achieve a feeling of uniqueness and specialness in their search for identity. In a society characterized by dramatic and rapid change, but lacking universal behavioral guidelines and codes of conduct, it is not surprising that a young person should seek his or her own internal controls and restraints through manipulation of eating and body weight (Maloney and Klykylo, 1983; Wilbur and Colligan, 1981; Bruch, 1977; Nylander, 1971; Schleimer, 1983).

The absence of consistent and well-established social and cultural standards of behavior has made parenting a difficult and confusing task. Adolescents no longer can rely on their parents for guidelines and direction. They find little help from insecure, uncertain, and confused parents who, without clear and absolute societal mandates, falter in their child-rearing efforts. As a function of their own uncertainty, parents often become overinvolved and overprotective, but at the same time, partly due to their insecurity, oversubmissive. Denied a comfortable, traditional, and authoritarian role possible only in a more static society, many parents become hopelessly trapped in the lives of their children.

In a sexually liberal society a young woman, more so than her male counterpart, has an increasing need to control her burgeoning sexuality and instinctual genital-sexual drive. Since societal and familial controls are lacking, the anorectic person finds this need for sexual control and mastery satisfied or replaced by an absolute control over eating—the most basic of all instinctual drives. The anorectic unconsciously reasons, "If I can control my eating and the growth of my body, I certainly should be able to control the other feelings I'm experiencing . . . and furthermore, if I stop growing I won't have to deal at all with these problems of growing up." Young women receive conflicting messages from parents and society. On the one hand, they spend a lifetime learning to conform to familial and societal codes of acceptable "little girl" behavior; on the other, they are expected to accomplish the tasks of adolescence (autonomy, sexuality, career) in an assertive, strong, and deliberate manner.

Family Considerations in Management

A major determinant of success in the management of eating disorders is the degree of healthy as opposed to pathologic family functioning (Selvini-Palazzoli, 1974; Minuchin et al., 1978; Bruch, 1971). The significance of the level of family competence must be appreciated. An understanding of the family, its dynamics and level of functioning, is essential in the treatment of the young person still living at home (Morgan and Russell, 1975). Also important, albeit less critical, is an understanding of the family of the young adult who may already have separated physically (but not psychologically) from parents and siblings. The degree of family dysfunction has been found to be a rather accurate prognostic indicator (Crisp et al., 1977).

Lewis (1978) suggests that family competence should be viewed on a continuum rather than in terms of the identified patient's presenting symptomatology. The basis for family evaluation and therapy rests on the major tasks of the family: (1) economic and physical survival; (2) stabilization and growth of the parents' personalities; and (3) the production of autonomous children. A systems approach to the evaluation of the family's level of functioning probably is more relevant and clinically useful than describing a family on the basis of the family member's diagnosis, such as the typical family of the delinquent, the schizophrenic family, or the family of the person with an eating disorder (Haley, 1970).

Lewis (1978) describes four parts of a continuum of family competence: (1) the optimal family; (2) the competent family; (3) the midrange dysfunctional family; and (4) the severely dysfunctional family. Family structure can be viewed as a system. The system involves the interaction of various biopsychosocial factors, and the patient's problem is a symptom of system malfunction. The organizational structure can range from the optimal one of flexibility through rigidity to frank chaos. The structure is revealed by the ways in which power, or interpersonal influence, is distributed within the system. Families of patients with anorexia nervosa and most families of bulimics fall in the midrange dysfunctional or rigidly competent range; a minority of bulimic patients with significant character problems and some patients with "bulimarexia" (food restriction associated with bulimia and purging) are from families that are severely dysfunctional and chaotic.

Familial Determinants

There is a strong relationship between the sociocultural and individual psychological determinants of eating disorders and the familial characteristics and backgrounds of eating disorder patients. In classic anorexia nervosa and in the majority of bulimic syndromes, the family is close and intact, members deny conflict, and on the surface the family appears to interact positively and to function smoothly and competently. More in-depth evaluation frequently reveals considerable family pathology with: (1) enmeshment of parents and children, particularly mother and anorectic daughter; (2) rigidity of family structure and interpersonal interactions; (3) poor communication within the family; (4) avoidance of conflict; (5) denial of anger; and (6) lack of conflict resolution. An analyses of family structure shows closeness but with poorly defined individual boundaries.

There is often great emotional distance between family members. Parents, especially the mother, tend toward overprotectiveness and overindulgence associated with too great an investment in and control over all the children, but especially the anorectic daughter (or more rarely son). The overcontrolled anorectic child becomes more concerned with pleasing parents and others than with pleasing herself. Mothers, and less often fathers, seem to sacrifice their own pleasure and happiness for their children; the mothers are often chronically depressed, and the family displays a tone of politeness (less often hostility), depression, and sometimes cynicism. Mothers seem to seek nurturance from their daughters in a kind of role reversal and often the daughter assumes the role of caretaker for her parents and siblings. A pathologic anorectic daughter-mother dyad and the disturbed father-mother dyad are crucial elements in the psychodynamics of anorexia nervosa and other eating disorders. The anorectic daughter rigidly restricts her usual activities and interpersonal relationships in an attempt to establish autonomy and psychological distance, while engaging in increased and compulsive motor activity and bizarre and abnormal eating and feeding behaviors as a means of manipulating her environment, diminishing her body, and thus escaping confrontation with the demands of growing up. Underlying much of the family pathology is a disturbed mother-father relationship that leads the mother to seek emotional gratification and fulfillment from her children and the father from his work.

An accurate description of the classic anorectic family was recently offered by Yager (1982):

> Superficially, this is a healthy family concerned with external appearances and with avoiding social shame, diligent about putting up a congenial facade. Certain unaddressed conflicts between the parents lurk below the surface." . . . The family communicates along narrow lines and rigidly denies or minimizes that anyone is angry toward anyone else. Parental stresses and concerns are channelled and deflected toward the children so mother becomes excessively involved with them. . . . Parents are somewhat fearful of their children's adolescent psychosexual development and impending separation.
>
> This parental overinvestment and overdirectiveness leads to a situation in which a vulnerable daughter becomes more concerned with parental approval than her own internal satisfaction." Her poor sense of self and accompanying sense of ineffectiveness are ignored by the parents. . . . At a point of family disequilibrium during her adolescence, anorexia begins.

A minority of bulimics and some with bulimia complicating anorexia nervosa (especially those manifesting purging behaviors) have severe character disorders (Hudson, Pope, and Jonas, 1983). In contrast to many who seem to function very well in almost all other aspects of their life, this small but definite subgroup of bulimics manifests impulsive behavior. Their more hedonistic orientation makes it difficult for them to delay gratification. They frequently abuse drugs and alcohol, sometimes exhibit increased sexual activity with multiple partners; and less often engage in delinquent behavior such as shoplifting (Mitchell and Pyle, 1982). Families of these bulimics, whose dietary intake is often as chaotic as their lives, are clearly dysfunctional with frequent parental separations and divorce and alcohol and drug abuse. Often but not always these families are from a lower socioeconomic group as compared to the less dysfunctional families of other persons with eating disorders. The structure of families of bulimics with severe character disorders is usually typified by: (1) a chaotic structure with little or no parental leadership or equalization of power (no stable dominant-submissive parental pattern, let alone an egalitarian sharing of power; (2) individual boundaries that are blurred and amorphous and impair family communications; (3) strong parent-child coalitions and weak parental coalitions; (4) much interpersonal conflict with little empathy; and (5) a mood of anger, cynicism, and sometimes hoplessness (Schwartz, Thompson, and Johnson, 1982).

Of the many techniques used by parents in their struggle to resolve issues related to psychological separation from daughters and sons, at least three can be identified as pathologic; (1) a binding technique in which the parent refuses to allow the child to develop autonomy; (2) a delegating technique in which the parent seeks vicarious reward by sending the child out as a delegate, reflecting a need to complete parental ambitions through the child; (3) an expelling or rejecting technique in which the dependent child is prematurely moved out of the family thus acquiescing to or relieving themselves of parental responsibilities. In general, in families of persons with eating disorders, the parents vear in the direction of binding or delegating. In the minority of families in which the bulimic or bulimarexic member manifests characteristics of a severe character disorder, the parents are more apt to be expelling or rejecting and the families dysfunctional and chaotic. An understanding of the parental orientation in this regard is crucial in both family and individual therapy of eating disorders.

Successful intervention is positively related to the level of family competence, with the poorest prognosis and most difficult management occurring in those patients from severely dysfunctional families. However, until further research is accomplished, it should not be assumed that the essential determinants in the development of eating disorders are exclusively psychosocial and familial. Other factors—genetic, anatomic, biochemical, pathophysiologic, and developmental—may play vital roles in the onset and perpetuation of eating disorders and cannot be ignored.

Biologic Determinants

Although there is overwhelming evidence that there are psychosocial determinants of eating disorders and there has been strong documentation of many pathophysiologic and anatomic changes in established anorectic and bulimic conditions, it is not known to what extent persons who develop eating disorders may be biologically vulnerable and predisposed to these conditions. The possibility exists that, under a given set of stresses and environmental influences, persons with a biologic deficit, such as a hypothalamic dysfunction, will succumb to an eating disorder; whereas those with similar personalities and in like situations without this deficit will not. It is as yet not known whether subtle changes or modifications in the production or metabolism of certain central nervous system or gastrointestinal neurotransmitters or other hormones play a primary role in the initiation and perpetuation of these disorders or whether these changes themselves are secondary to the primary psychopathology or to the weight loss, vomiting, and resultant metabolic aberrations (Keesey, 1983; Mrosovsky, 1983; Garfinkel, 1974).

The physical, metabolic, and endocrine changes of anorexia nervosa are, with rare exceptions (carotene levels, vomiting, cardiac murmurs), the same as those described in states of involuntary starvation (Vande Wille, 1977; Silverman, 1974; Warren and Vande Wille, 1973; Halmi and Falk, 1981; Kanis et al 1974). Many of the psychological and behavioral manifestations of anorexia nervosa are also described in involuntary starvation such as in those persons studied by Keys et al (1950) during and after World War II. As patients with anorexia nervosa gain weight, their clarity of thinking improves and they are less obsessional about food, food preparation, and eating. A major difference between the victim of voluntary versus involuntary starvation is the marked fear of fatness and the intense desire to lose increasing amounts of weight characteristic of eating disorder patients. In both groups, there is a disturbed perception of body size which in some studies has been found to worsen with weight loss and to improve as weight is regained (Slade and Russell, 1973). The bizarre attitudes and behaviors about food, food preparation, eating, overactivity, and sleep observed in eating disorder patients are likely to be related to severe malnutrition and may not accurately reflect the mental state of the patient. On the other hand, persons with anorexia nervosa who are severely debilitated from voluntary self-starvation stubbornly deny that they are ill. This is certainly not the case in involuntary starvation and debilitation from other causes. Is this refusal to acknowledge illness, fatigue, or hunger primarily psychologically derived or organically mediated (Cabanac, 1971; Schielle and Brozek, 1948)?

Indirect evidence of biologic factors affecting the development of an eating disorder includes the familial occurrence of anorexia nervosa and, to a lesser extent, bulimia and purging behaviors. There is a greater likelihood that a sister of a patient with an eating disorder will develop a similar disorder than a sister of a nonaffected person. There is also an increased percentage of parents of anorexia nervosa patients with a history of significant weight loss or weight phobia during adolescence. There is a higher incidence of parents of eating disorder patients including bulimics who themselves have chronic eating disorders. The twin sister of a patient with anorexia nervosa has an increased chance of developing the same or similar eating disorder (Holland et al., 1983). A more frequent occurrence of anorexia nervosa has been reported in persons with short stature, Turner's syndrome, and congential genitourinary abnormalities (Pitts and Guze, 1963; Halmi and Rigas, 1973). These observations strongly suggest that there are considerable biologic influences on the occurrence of anorexia nervosa and bulimia. Distinguishing psychological, social, and environmental from genetic and other biologic factors is a formidable if not impossible task!

Teleologic Considerations

The search for an animal model of anorexia nervosa has highlighted some fascinating information. Bilateral lesions of the lateral hypothalamus in rats, cats, and monkeys have produced a syndrome of severe aphagia, thereby leading to the concept of a hypothalamic "feeding center" (Mrosovsky and Sherry, 1980). These lesion-induced syndromes may also occur naturally. Nesting behaviors of birds, in which little or nothing is eaten even though food is readily and easily available, is one example. Another example is the hibernating behavior of mammals that literally sleep on top of their food but refrain from eating while progressively losing weight. In the migratory patterns of sea mammals such as the whale, the animal travels thousands of miles without food and does not deviate from its instinctually determined route—another example of a natural state of aphagia or anorexia. What is the relationship between these naturally occurring phenomena and eating disorders? There is a difference between hunger, appetite, and food-seeking and collecting behaviors. Animals may show intense food-seeking and collecting behavior in preparation for hibernation or other circumstances, but not show evidence of hunger or appetite (Anand, Dua, and Schoenberg, 1955). The exaggerated food-seeking behavior of animals severely deprived of food and the motor hyperactivity, peculiar food handling, and hoarding of anorectics may have common pathways. We know that bulimic patients insist that they eat excessively but are not hungry. Do observations such as these reflect specific and precise areas of central nervous system dysfunction that may determine subtle differences in the behavior of patients with eating disorders? Does the food preparation and the feeding of others by anorectics somehow relate to the animal model's need to care for others (that is, the temperature control of eggs, nesting, and mating)?

There is increasing speculation that neuroendocrine dysfunction may be responsible for a number of primary psychiatric conditions, most notably depression. It is also clear that patients with primary endocrine disease manifest psychiatric symptoms probably secondary to hormonal effects on the central nervous system. It has long been apparent to clinicians that emotional upheaval and stress seem to precipitate such conditions as diabetes or hyperthyroidism. It is obvious that stress causes widespread responses in the nervous and endocrine systems.

Remaining obscure are the specific brain centers, biochemical pathways, neuro-transmitters, hormones, peptides, and central nervous system receptors respon-sible for effecting the changes observed in anorexia nervosa and bulimia.

A relationship between eating disorders and certain causative neuroendo-crine events has not been established. The relationship between eating disorders, neuroendocrine aberrations, and normal primitive eating behaviors in animals remains a challenging mystery. Studies conducted on animal models probably will not define the etiology of eating disorders. They probably will not further define the eating disorders as pathophysiologic (that is, organic) disorders of feeding or explain these conditions as derangements of the physiologic regulation of body weight. It is possible, however, that the study of animal models and neu-roendocrine events associated with eating disorders may provide new insight into the course if not the cause of eating disorders and may lead to the development of alternative, perhaps pharmacologic, treatment modalities.

References

Anand, B.K., Dua, S., and Schoenberg, K.: Hypothalamic control of food intake in cats and monkeys. *J. Physiol.* 127:143, 1955.

Berger, J., et al.: *Ways of Seeing.* New York, British Broadcasting Corporation and Pen-guin Books, 1977.

Bruch, H.: *Eating Disorders.* New York, Basic Books, 1973.

Bruch, H.: Family transactions in eating disorders. *Compr. Psychiatry* 12:238–248, 1971.

Bruch, H.: Psychological antecedents of anorexia nervosa. In Vigersky, R.A. (ed.): *An-orexia Nervosa.* New York, Raven Press, 1977.

Bruch, H.: The treatment of eating disorders. *Mayo Clin. Proc.* 51:269, 1976.

Cabanac, M.: Physiological role of pleasure. *Science* 173:1103, 1971.

Carlson, G.A., and Cantwell, D.P.: A survey of depressive symptoms in a child and ado-lescent population. *J. Am. Acad. Child Psychiatry* 18:587, 1979.

Casper, R.C., Offer, D., and Ostrov, E.: The self-image of adolescents with acute anorexia nervosa. *J. Pediatr.* 98:656, 1981.

Casper, R.C.: On the emergence of bulimia nervosa as a syndrome: a historical view. *Int. J. Eat. Dis.* 2(Spring):3–16, 1983.

Crisp, A.H.: Existential aspects of maturation. In *Anorexia Nervosa: Let Me Be.* New York, Grune and Stratton, 1980.

Crisp, A.H., Kalucy, R.S., Lacey, J.H., and Hardin, B.: The long-term prognosis in an-orexia nervosa: some factors predictive of outcome. In Vigersky, R.A. (ed.): *Anorexia Nervosa.* New York, Raven Press, 1977.

Crisp, A.H., Palmer, R.L., and Kalucy, R.S.: How common is anorexia nervosa? A preva-lence study. *Br. J. Psychiatry* 128:549, 1976.

Eckert, E.D., Goldberg, S.C., Halmi, K.A., Casper, R.C., and Davis, J.M.: Depression in anorexia nervosa. *Psychol. Med.* 12:115, 1982.

Gandour, M.J.: Bulimia: clinical description, assessment, etiology, and treatment. *Int. J. Eat. Dis.* 3(Spring):12, 1984.

Garfinkel, P.E.: Perception of hunger and satiety in anorexia nervosa. *Psychol. Med.* 4:309, 1974.

Garner, D.M., and Garfinkle, P.E.: Socio-cultural factors in the development of anorexia nervosa. *Psycho. Med. 10*:647, 1980.

Haley, J.: *Leaving Home: The Therapy of Disturbed Young People.* New York, McGraw-Hill, 1970.

Halmi, K.A., and Falk, J.R.: Common physiological changes in anorexia nervosa. *Int. J. Eat. Dis. 1*:16, 1981.

Halmi, K.A., Falk, J.R., and Schwartz, E.: Binge-eating and vomiting: a survey of a college population. *Psychol. Med. 11*:697, 1981.

Halmi, K.A., and Rigas, C.: Urogenital malformations associated with anorexia nervosa. *Br. J. Psychiatry 122*:79, 1973.

Holland, A.J., Hall, A., Murray, R.M., Russell, G.F.M., and Crisp, A.H.: Anorexia is more likely to affect both twins in monozygotic pair. *Pediatric News 17*:15, 1983.

Hudson, J.I., Pope, H.G., and Jonas, J.M.: Treatment of bulimia with antidepressants: theoretical considerations and clinical findings. *Psychiatr. Ann. 13*:965, 1983.

Johnson, C.L., Lewis, C., Love, S., et al.: A descriptive survey of dieting and bulimic behavior in a female high school population. In *Understanding Anorexia Nervosa and Bulimia.* Report of the Fourth Ross Conference on Medical Research. Columbus, Ohio, Ross Laboratories, 1983.

Kanis, L.A., Brown, P., Fitzpatrick, K., et al.: Anorexia nervosa: a clinical, psychiatric, and laboratory study. *Q.J. Med. N. S. 43*:321, 1974.

Keesey, R.E.: A hypothalamic syndrome of body-weight regulation at reduced levels. In *Understanding Anorexia Nervosa and Bulimia.* Report of the Fourth Ross Conference on Medical Research. Columbus, Ohio. Ross Laboratories, 1983.

Keys, A., Brozek, J., Henschel, A., et al.: *The Biology of Human Starvation.* Minneapolis, University of Minnesota Press, 1950.

Lewis, Jerry M.: The adolescent and the healthy family. In Feinstein and Giovacchini (eds.): *Adolescent Psychiatry,* Vol. 6. Chicago, University of Chicago Press, 1978.

Maloney, M.J., and Klykylo, W.M.: An overview of anorexia nervosa, bulimia, and obesity in children and adolescents. *J. Am. Acad. Child Psychiatry 22*:99, 1983.

Minuchin, S., Rosman, B.L., Baker, L. et al.: *Psychomatic Families: Anorexia Nervosa in Context.* Cambridge, Harvard University Press, 1978.

Mitchell, J.E., and Pyle, R.L.: The bulimic syndrome in normal weight individuals: a review. *Int. J. Eat. Dis. 1*(Winter):64, 1982.

Morgan, J.G., and Russell, J.F.M.: Value of family background and clinical features as predictors of long-term outcome in anorexia nervosa: four year follow-up of 41 patients. *Psychol. Med. 5*:355, 1975.

Mrosovsky, N., and Sherry, D.F.: Animal anorexias. *Science 207*:837, 1980.

Mrosovsky, N.: Animal models of anorexia nervosa. In *Understanding Anorexia Nervosa and Bulimia.* Report of the Fourth Ross Conference on Medical Research. Columbus, Ohio. Ross Laboratories, 1983.

Nylander, I.: The feeling of being fat and dieting in a school girl population: an epidemiologic interview investigation. *Scand. J. Soc. Med. 3*:17, 1971.

Pitts, F.N., and Guze, S.B.: Anorexia nervosa and gonadolydysgenesis (Turner's syndrome). *Am. J. Psychiatry 119*:1100, 1963.

Pyle, R.L., Mitchell, J.E., Eckert, E.D., et al.: The incidence of bulimia in freshmen college students. *Int. J. Eat. Dis.* 2:75, 1983.

Schielle, B.C., and Brozek, J.: "Experimental neurosis" resulting from semistarvation in man. *Psychosom. Med.* 10:31, 1948.

Schleimer, K.: Dieting in teenage schoolgirls: a longitudinal prospective study. *Acta. Pediatr. Scand. Suppl. 312*, 1983.

Schwartz, D.M., Thompson, M.G., and Johnson, C.F.: Anorexia nervosa and bulimia: the socio-cultural context. *Int. J. Eat. Dis.* 1(Spring):20, 1982.

Schwartz, R.C.: Bulimia and family therapy: a case study. *Int. J. Eat. Dis.* 2(Autumn):75–82, 1982.

Selvini-Palazzoli, M.: *Self-Starvation.* London, Chaucer Publishing Co., 1974.

Silverman, J.A.: Anorexia nervosa: clinical observations in successful treatment plan. *J. Pediatr.* 8468, 1974.

Slade, P.D., and Russell, G.F.M.: Awareness of body dimensions in anorexia nervosa: cross-sectional and longitudinal studies. *Psychol. Med.* 3:188, 1973.

Vande Wille, R.L.: Anorexia nervosa and the hypothalamus. *Hosp. Pract.* 12(Dec.):45–51, 1977.

Szmukler, G.I.: Weight and food preoccupation in a population of English school girls. In *Understanding Anorexia Nervosa and Bulimia.* Report of the Fourth Ross Conference on Medical Research. Columbus, Ohio, Ross Laboratories, 1983.

Warren, M.P., and Vande Wille, R.I.: Clinical and metabolic features of anorexia nervosa. *Am. J. Obstet. Gynecol.* 117:435, 1973.

Wilbur, C.J., and Colligan, R.C.: Psychologic and behavioral correlates of anorexia nervosa. *JDBP* 2:89, 1981.

Willi, J., and Grossman, S.: Epidemiology of anorexia nervosa in a defined region of Switzerland. *Am. J. Psychiatry* 140:564, 1983.

Yager, J.: Family issues in the pathogenesis of anorexia nervosa. *Psychosom. Med.* 44:43, 1982.

10
Developmental Tasks of Adolescence: Conflicts with Contemporary Society

Donald P. Orr

A dolescents have always maintained a unique niche in society. The degree of complexity period of maturation between childhood and adulthood varies with elements of the particular society and its culture, past historical events, and the extent to which these factors are congruent with the biologic and developmental maturation of youth. It is important that adolescents are understood in the context of their environment, culture, history, and society, because the relationship between youth and their environment is a reciprocal one. Adolescents are affected by their surroundings, and they, in turn, affect them.

Derived from the Latin *adolescere*, which means to grow into maturity, adolescence encompasses the biologic, social, and psychological processes that a child undergoes to become a functional member of adult society. Biologic, social, and psychological maturation of course occur simultaneously. This chapter focuses on adolescent growth and development, the tasks a child must accomplish to become a competent member of American society, and some of the conflicts or impediments that exist between these developmental tasks and society. This review of adolescent development does not deal with all conflicts; it is not limited to American society and does not deal with those aspects of our culture that support youth's progression to adulthood.

Adolescence may be divided into early, middle, and late stages (Adelson and Doehrman, 1980). In each stage, biologic, psychological, and social maturation proceed along their own axes (figure 10–1). If maturation is viewed in three dimensions along hypothetical X, Y, and Z axes, representing biologic, psychological, and social, the overall maturation of the individual young person can be viewed as the resultant vector of all forces. Each axis not only affects the overall maturation but also influences all others. A particular stage may be dominated more by one force; for example, in early adolescence the biologic changes appear most influential (figure 10–2). Moreover, a condition which alters one axis has the potential to alter the overall maturation of the adolescent. Social issues such as poverty, psychological conditions such as psychiatric delay of development, and biologic problems such as chronic illness have an impact on maturation.

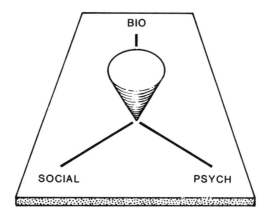

Figure 10–1. Adolescent Developmental Framework

On the average, growth along each axis proceeds in a more or less orderly fashion. Adolescents in the same stage tend to share similar biologic, psychological and social characteristics; however, maturation may not be synchronous along each axis, so an individual young person may be more mature in one as compared to the other two areas. While we speak of early, middle, and late adolescent stages as if they were separate periods, their boundaries are indistinct and they merge into each other.

Several older misconceptions or myths about adolescent development are no longer tenable (Rutter et al., 1976). The biologic imperative suggests that adolescence is dominated by biologic forces; thus behavior and development are entirely a result of biologic pressures. Somewhat analogous is the view that instinctual drives are so strong (at a time when psychological defenses are weak), leaving the organism extremely unpredictable and labile. As a result, any behavior may be considered normal and expected. Behaviors which would cause an adult to be labeled psychiatrically disturbed could be considered as normal in adolescents. As a period of "transient insanity," one is able to define neither normal nor abnormal. The implications for behavioral expectations and treatment are obvious.

Biologic

Biologic maturation, characterized by rapid increase in physical growth and appearance of secondary sex characteristics, is discussed first and separately because it probably initiates the process of adolescence. The biologic basis for the

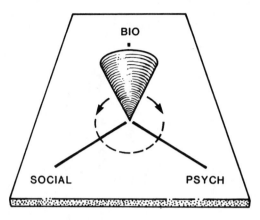

Figure 10–2. Early Adolescent Development Showing Influence of Biologic Axis

onset of puberty is only partially understood. It appears that changes in the neurohormonal sensing mechanisms of the hypothalamus cause increased production of releasing factors (Grumback et al., 1974). These releasing factors signal the anterior pituitary to produce more gonadatropic hormones, which, in turn, cause a greater production of sex hormones and growth of the ovaries and testes.

The age of onset of puberty is influenced by heredity, nutrition, and the physical environment. Tanner provided the first evidence that biologic growth proceeds in a defined, orderly sequence (Tanner, 1962). He also established that normative ages for these events exist (Marshall and Tanner, 1969, 1970; Marshall, 1975). As a result, the Tanner stages in pubertal growth now describe the observable physical changes in pubic hair, genital, and breast development. The range of normal ages for each stage so identified is the basis for evaluating physical growth in all youngsters.

It is important to remember that there is great dispersion around the mean for each stage and that a wide range in the ages may be considered normal. Boys and girls are discussed separately (figure 10–3). In girls the sign observed during puberty is usually breast budding or, occasionally, growth of pubic hair. Whereas the average age for these events is 11.1 years, the normal range is from 8 to 13 years (Marshall and Tanner, 1969). In contrast to boys, rapid physical growth occurs early in the sequence for girls, giving rise to the misconception that boys are two years behind girls in pubertal development. In the United States, the mean age of menarche, an event late in the sequence of puberty, is 12.75 years (MacMahon, 1973). Black girls tend to mature earlier than their white counterparts. During the past 100 years, the age of menarche has gradually declined from about 17 years (Marshall, 1975). This secular trend appears to have pla-

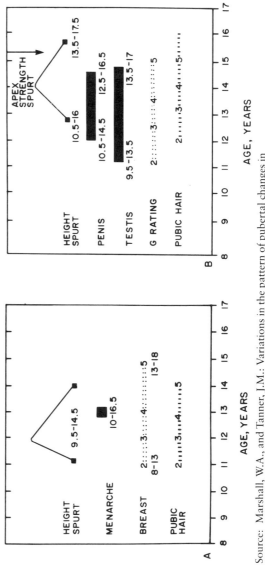

Figure 10–3. **Sequence of Events at Puberty in Girls and Boys**

Source: Marshall, W.A., and Tanner, J.M.: Variations in the pattern of pubertal changes in boys. *Arch. Dis. Child.* 45:13, 1970, with permission.

teaued, and no measurable decrease in the age of menarche has occurred over the last several decades.

For boys, the mean age of puberty is 11.6 years ($\pm$ 1.07), an average of only six months later than girls. Puberty may begin as early as 9.5 or as late as 13.5 years and still be normal (Marshall and Tanner, 1970). The first physical indication is an increase in the size of the testes. Peak physical growth and the ability to produce spermatozoa occur at about 14 years of age (Katchadourian, 1980). A secular trend among boys has probably also occurred, although confirmatory data are not available.

Whereas normal biologic maturation progresses in an orderly sequence, for individual adolescents, the wide range of normal for boys and girls means that at any given chronological age one may expect prepubertal, mid-pubertal, and late pubertal adolescents to be represented. Because of this variation in biologic maturation at similar chronological ages, it is helpful to speak of maturational (Tanner stages) rather than chronological age. This physiologic disparity in physical development coupled with normal bodily concerns among youth sets the stage for considerable anxiety as individuals compare their growth with that of their peers.

Early Adolescence

Biologic growth can be integrated with psychological and social by characterizing the stages as early, middle, and late adolescence. Chronological age boundaries for these stages are only approximate. Early adolescence, which may begin as early as ten years of age and lasts until about thirteen years is characterized by the rapid growth of secondary sex characteristics. Physical growth and the changes in secondary sex characteristics predominate. Young adolescents are preoccupied with their changing bodies. These dramatic, physical changes force young persons to restructure their body images. Self-esteem and self-concept fluctuate (Adelson and Doehrman, 1980). Since it is no longer a child's body, the individual begins to look at himself or herself in a new way. New bodies require new roles. Adult and societal attitudes toward puberty are very important in either facilitating or hindering the young person's acceptance of an adaptation to puberty (Peterson and Taylor, 1980). If society portrays puberty in a negative fashion or ignores the event, the youngster may have increased difficulty in maintaining high self-esteem. Psychologically and socially, family ties are loosened. Allegiance to parents and their values decreases and shifts to peers. In fact, the affiliation with the peer culture is instrumental in loosening the dependence on the family. Although there is a beginning substitution of peers for family, this remains largely a quiet time for families and adolescents. Cognitive maturation progresses slowly (Keating, 1980). At this stage, most young persons remain concrete in their thought processes, they are unable to project into the future or plan ahead, and they have little ability to think abstractly.

Mid-Adolescence

Mid-adolescence, which begins around age fourteen and ends at approximately age seventeen, is the most conflictual period for adolescents and their families. Biologic growth has diminished. By fifteen years of age, 49.8 percent of boys (Harlan, et al., 1979) and 51 percent of girls (Harlan, Harlan and Grillo, 1980) are physically mature (Tanner stage 5). Less disparity exits among individuals and, thus, les anxiety about physical normality. Thus mid-adolescents tend to be less preoccupied with their bodies. By age seventeen over 95 percent are capable of reproduction. Girls have achieved menarche, and most are menstruating regularly. Boys are capable of producing spermatozoa. Sexuality becomes increasingly important and physical and acquires more adult characteristics (Zelnik and Kantner, 1980). Psychologically and socially the shift from family to peers is in full swing. Peers, in fact, set the standards for behavior thought, and dress. They fulfill emotional needs for stimulation, empathy, and loyalty. Furthermore, they provide the opportunity for role playing, identification, sharing of guilt and anxiety, and feelings of safety and identification during the difficult struggle for autonomy. Autonomy may be considered along three lines (Havighurst, 1951):

1. *Emotional Autonomy.* There is a relaxation of ties to the family, and the individual emotionally unfolds to establish bonds elsewhere.
2. *Behavioral Autonomy.* The adolescent acquires the skills and the courage to decide what to do and what not to do.
3. *Ideational Autonomy.* The adolescent thinks and struggles through basic ideas and establishes convictions.

The family must support the adolescent in the struggle for autonomy. This is a problematic period since control becomes an issue for both. Independence and autonomy can prevent a frightening process for both adolescents and parents. In an attempt to minimize anxiety, the adolescent may use rebellion, acting out, and other techniques because family ties are strong. For parents this difficult time forces them to look at themselves, their age, and their sexuality. Parental expectations for themselves and their adolescents must be confronted; although overreaction is understandable, both must master the process of independence.

Self-image undergoes further definition and consolidation. The physical changes are now nearly complete, and sexuality increases in importance. This is a time of trying out social behaviors, some of which are culturally determined. Masturbation is almost universal. Increasing numbers of young people are sexually active. By age seventeen, 48.5 percent of American females and 55.7 percent of males have had intercourse (Zelnik and Kantner, 1980). Sex fulfills both physical and psychologic needs; however, relationships usually tend to be one-sided and narcissistic but monogamous.

Cognitively, the mid-adolescent's thought process becomes less concrete. Increasing numbers are capable of abstract thought, planning ahead, and anticipating the consequences of behaviors and actions.

Late Adolescence

Late adolescence, from about seventeen to twenty-one years of age, is a quieter period. Biologic growth is nearly complete. Youth are reproductively mature toward the end of this period. Psychologically, the adolescent progresses toward total emancipation. Self-image is more stable. Value systems are consolidated and tend to be similar to those of parents.

Cognitively the late adolescent is mature. Most now have reached the state of formal operations in which they are able to think abstractly. They are now able to plan ahead, and their future should contain specific plans and actions for jobs and careers.

Social relationships have shifted from the peer group to the individual. Relationships are more physically and psychologically intimate, longer lasting, more stable, and characterized by mutual sharing and reciprocity. By age nineteen, over 70 percent of young adults have had intercourse, and many have made plans for marriage.

Developmental Tasks

In the context of the life span from child to adult, the individual progresses from early to mid through late adolescence and matures along biologic, psychological, and social axies. This maturational process may also be viewed as a series of developmental tasks which require completion. First described by Havighurst (1951), these have been modified many times. Although the age and time sequence have not been defined, this schema is a useful way to view development. The tasks include:

1. acceptance of body changes and the sex roles which will accompany them
2. establishment of new peer relationships of increasing intensity
3. separation from the family—physical, psychological, social
4. preparation for an occupation and intellectual growth which includes the ability to plan ahead and think more complexly and abstractly
5. the development of socially responsible behaviors
6. the ability to make the transitions into adult sexuality and sexual roles
7. the development and stabilization of an identity and self-concept consonant with the individual's reality

Mastering these developmental tasks requires a balance between the individual and families' inherent strengths, weaknesses, and vulnerabilities and the extent to which a society and its culture support or hinder each of these factors. Certain conditions exist (and to an extent have always existed) which may conflict with the process of adolescence.

Technological/Urban Growth

Probably the single greatest historical influence on adolescence is the urban/technological transformation, a process which to a large extent has shaped adolescence as we know it. Improved nutrition, by resulting in earlier biologic maturation at a time when the expression of sexual maturation is expected to be delayed, widens the gap between biologic and social adulthood. Technology's need for super specialization accentuates the discontinuity and isolation of social positions and increases the training and educational requirements.

Technological societies tend to view pubescence in negative cultural terms. "American culture turns pubescence into an adolescent reinforcing event by making the young feel that they must go through a stage which should not be mentioned or discussed" (Sebald, 1977), while at the same time glamourizing adolescent sexuality. American youth are largely left unprepared for puberty. Parents have great difficulty discussing sexuality with their children. The information offered at school or church is usually too little and too late. Basic information about the physical and emotional changes that will occur during puberty is particularly important because youth's adjustment to these biologic changes is influenced by their acceptance or rejection by society. If society views pubescence in a negative fashion, the youth are more likely to have difficulty accepting it. Less-developed countries have had rites of passage and puberty rights that inform the individual, publicly announce the event, and set the stage for emotionally anchoring the new role. The lack of puberty rights and initiation activities reduces the awareness of and clarity of one's status and creates a potential for maladjustment.

Cultural Expectations

Potential for additional conflict exists when this negative view of puberty is combined with the mixed expectations that society holds for youth. These mixed expectations have defined a culture for youth. Culture in the simplest terms may be defined as a blueprint for behavior which is maintained by both formal and informal sanctions. Society then must share some responsibility for adolescents behavior since they have helped define the culture.

Media Affluence

One manifestation of the mixed expectations is the culture defined by the media as they represent youth in advertisement, radio, television, movies, and music. In an attempt to manipulate consumer buying patterns, the media have defined a culture of violence, unreality, sexuality, immaturity, and materialism as ideal, and the way to instantaneous success. Youth become involved directly when they are the primary consumers and indirectly when adults are the target population. As an indirect target the adult product is presented as conferring special properties upon the consumers such as youth, sexuality, masculinity, feminity. This presents youth with what appears to be socially desirable behaviors necessary to become adults—drinking, smoking, and sexual activity.

As direct targets, American adolescents are eagerly sought after. Thirteen to twenty year olds have an estimated fifteen billion dollars to spend freely (U.S. News and World Report, 1972).

In this competitive market, American business exploit youth in an attempt to alter their buying patterns. Since peer groups are so important, the media rewards youth for conforming to peer norms and behavior styles. Popularity and prestige in peer groups are the rewards, and material goods are often made to seem a necessity. The result is reinforcement of stereotypical adolescent behaviors. It is claimed that the affluence of twentieth century youth promotes the spread and survival of the collective expression of adolescents—the teen subculture (Sebald, 1977). Perhaps most importantly, the item for sale is not always the most important product. Subliminal information about behavior is always present. Sexuality is a frequent by-product. Clothing, alcohol, tobacco, soft drinks, and even shoes are sold with adolescent sexuality. In doing so, however, we present youth with serious inconsistencies. While selling sex and drugs, we insist on abstinence. For those adolescents who attempt to behave in a sexually responsible manner, we refuse access to care for these sensitive problems. Contraceptive services are often unavailable without parental permission or are very limited. While lamenting the serious drug problem of youth, we refuse to fund drug prevention and drug treatment programs. Some commentators have called this the schismatic conflict of American values.

Family

This direct attack on youth is occurring at a time when the American family has significantly changed (Sebald, 1977). The modern American family is now smaller, more isolated, and unclear. The numbers of dual-career families, single-parent families, and divorced parents has increased. Increased mobility has resulted in less interaction with the community and fewer ties to it. Fewer adult family role models are available, and there is an increase in nonfamily peer groups. Compulsory education has become to a large extent custodial and, in fact, adolescent-inducing by reinforcing peer relationships over which the family has little control.

Part-Time Work/Health Care

Two more examples of conflicts between values of society and youth involve part-time work and health and technology. Part-time work for young people has been promoted as supporting self-reliance and strengthening self-respect, and as a time for rehearsing and practicing sexually responsible behaviors, in addition to encouraging economic independence. However, Steinberg et al. (1982) suggest that part-time work may have negative consequences. In a longitudinal study of a large number of southern California youth, they found that while personal responsibility was facilitated for females it declined for males. There was no effect on social responsibility. Autonomy was enhanced more for females than males. Family relationships were reduced for these females but improved for males. Peer relationships were altered. While there was no effect on the time spent with peers, there was a decreased emotional closeness among those youth who worked. Attitudes toward work became more cynical, and adolescents were more likely to tolerate unethical work practices. Finally, while economic independence and spending power were promoted, drug use among youth including cigarettes and marijuana increased.

Lastly, we have presented youth with another dilemma. Medical advances have increased the life expectancy of many children with chronic disorders. It is now estimated that nearly one-fifth of youth twelve to seventeen years old have a chronic medical problem (U.S. Series, 1973). There is increasing evidence that adolescents with illnesses which impair the activities of daily living are at greater risk for psychosocial problems (Orr et al., 1984). They have increasing difficulty with psychological adjustment; their independence is hindered, and they report less satisfaction with family activities. These youth are less likely to remain in school, and they have fewer plans for their future. While medical technology has advanced, parallel programs have not been implemented to assist these young people to develop into competent adults. Those same institutions and funding agencies which promote medical technology fail to support, fund, or even recognize those programs which can provide psychological counseling for chronically ill children and adolescents.

Summary

It is possible to look at each developmental task and note potential conflicts between that task and contemporary society (table 10–1). The acceptance of physical changes may be hindered by negative cultural interpretations of puberty, current social norms, and pubertal asynchrony. Adopting adult sex roles may conflict with the disparity between the attainment of sexual and social maturity, ambiguity of adult roles, sexism, and the media. Independence from the parental family may be hindered by an unclear role status of youth in the United States, the need for prolonged education, part-time work, and chronic illness. Career choice and preparation for economic independence may come into conflict with part-time jobs, high unemployment for minorities, disenchantment with college education, and chronic illness. The need to establish new peer relationships can be hindered by educational systems that are unresponsive to the needs of youth and increased family mobility. Ability to develop socially responsible behaviors may conflict with the schism of all American values. The discontinuity between

Table 10–1
Developmental Tasks and Conflicts

Tasks	*Conflicts*
Accept physical changes	Negative cultural interpretation Social norms Pubertal asynchrony
Establish new peer Relationships	Educational system Family mobility
Independence from parental family	Unclear role status Prolonged education Part-time work Chronic illness
Career choice and preparation	Part-time work Labor force status Disenchantment with college education Chronic illness
Develop socially responsible behaviors	Schismatic all-american values Adult-Child role discontinuity American cultural expectations
Accept and adapt to sex roles	Sexual-social maturity disparity Ambiguity of adult roles—sexism Media messages
Identity stabilization	Culture as adolescence-reinforcing Chronic illness Family changes

adult and child roles and American cultural expectations of the behavior may promote irresponsible behaviors more than is realized. Identity stabilization may be difficult when the culture is adolescent reinforcing. This is particularly true when the media promotes adolescents in an overall supercilious and negative manner. Chronic illness and changes in the American family may again conflict with this task.

In summary, adolescence as a process has always existed and will continue to exist as a transition period between childhood and adulthood. "Its variation reflects the degrees to which roles are assigned on the basis of age criteria, the prevelance of groups based on age, and certain demographic and economic conditions" (Eisenstadt, 1956). We must remain alert to the culture we have helped create and the manner in which it supports or fails to support our youth. It is our task as professionals and parents working together to find creative solutions to meet the challenges that arise when society and developmental tasks come into conflict.

This presentation has raised several issues. A few suggestions are in order. All children, adolescents, and parents should have access to appropriate information to help prepare them for puberty and adolescence. For most, it may be family based and largely educational. Depending on the particular circumstances and needs of the family, several coexisting models should be available. It is clear, however, that most families need help in this area.

In a health-care-based model, health providers would include appropriate anticipatory guidance about puberty for parents and child. This probably occurs in some practices; however, most physicians and nurses would require additional training to provide this service. It has the advantage that the patient and family are already well known to the physician or nurse, but this argument is inefficient.

A community-based model would utilize existing religious, school (parent teacher organizations), or other community agencies to provide voluntary services to interested families. Private and public health providers would be involved in a collaborative effort.

But some adolescents and families will not be served by these models. Many adolescents have no regular source of medical care, and some families will not elect this anticipatory information as a priority. I suggest that school-based preparation, in cooperation with families, adolescents, and health providers, is an alternative model. By enlisting the support of the participants, most may be served.

In this fashion it may be possible to create informal rites of initiation or passage that are educationally based and that will acknowledge pubescence in a positive fashion supportive of healthy adjustment. I suggest that these "new rites of initiation" may be sufficiently strong and supportive to withstand the culture created by others such as the media. It is also possible that as consumers, parents and others may use economic pressure to change media practices.

Health professionals also have another responsibility—namely, health care whether office or clinic based. Youth must have access to appropriate services that are developed to meet their health and developmental needs. Second, health professionals must be assured that the psychological support services for chronically ill and their families keep pace with the technological advances.

These support services should be integral to the care of the chronically ill. They require the personal effort of health providers and also a political effort. Policies must be changed at local, state, and national levels. Funding and third-party payment providers must be reached.

It is our task, as profesionals working together with parents, to find creative solutions to meet the challenges that arise when society and adolescent development tasks conflict. The new pediatrics must include advocacy.

References

Adelson, J., and Doehrman, M.: The psychodynamic approach to adolescence. In Adelson, J. (ed.): *Handbook of Adolescent Psychology*. New York, Wiley & Sons, 1980.

Eisenstadt, S.N.: *From Generation to Generation*. Glencoe, Free Press, 1956.

Grumback, M., Roth, J., Kaplan, S., and Kelch, R.: Hypothalamic-pituitary regulation of puberty: evidence and concept derived from clinical research. In Grumback, M.M., Grade, G.D., and Mayer, F.E. (eds.): *Control of the Onset of Puberty.* New York, Wiley & Sons, 1974.

Harlan, W., Grillo, G., Cornoni-Huntley, J., and Leaverton, P.: Secondary sex characteristics of boys 12 to 17 years of age: the U.S. Health Examination Survey. *J. Pediatr. 95*:293, 1979.

Harlan, W., Harlan, E., and Grillo, G.: Secondary sex characteristics of girls 12 to 17 years of age: the U.S. Health Examination Survey. *J. Pediatr. 96*:1074, 1980.

Havighurst, R.J.:*Developmental Tasks and Education.* New York, Longmanc, Green, 1951.

Katchadourian, H.: Adolescent sexuality. *Pediatr. Clin. N. Am. 27*:17, 1980.

Keating, B.: Thinking processes in adolescence. In Adelson, J. (ed.): *Handbook of Adolescent Psychology.* New York, Wiley & Sons, 1980.

MacMahon, B.: *National Health Examination Survey: Age at Menarche.* DHEW, Publ. 74-1615, Series 11, No. 133, 1973.

Marshall, W.A.: Growth and sexual maturation in normal puberty. *Clin. Endocrinol. Metab 4*:3, 1975.

Marshall, W., and Tanner, J.: Variations in the patterns of pubertal changes in girls. *Arch. Dis. Child. 44*:291, 1969.

Marshall, W., Tanner, J.: Variations in the patterns of pubertal changes in boys. *Arch. Dis. Child 45*:13, 1970.

Orr, D., Weller, S., Satterwhite, B., and Pless, I. Psychosocial implications of chronic illness in adolescence. *J. Pediatr. 104*:152, 1984.

Peterson, A., and Taylor, B.: The biological approach to adolescence: biological change and psychological adaptation. In Adelson, J. (ed.): *Handbook of Adolescent Psychology.* New York, Wiley & Sons, 1980.

Rutter, M., Graham, R., Chadwick, O., et al.: Adolescent turmoil: fact or fiction? *J. Child. Psychol. Psychiatr. 17*:35, 1976.

Sebald, H.: *Adolescence: A Social Psychological Analysis.* Englewood Cliffs, N.J., Prentice-Hall, 1977.

Steinberg, L., Greenberger, E., Gardupue, L., et al.: Effects of working on adolescent development. *Dev. Psychol. 18*:385, 1982.

Tanner, J.: *Growth at Adolescence.* Oxford, Blackwell Scientific, 1962.

U.S. News and World Report: Millions of young adults: a new wave of buyers. *72*:16, 1972.

U.S. Series. *Examination and Health History Findings among Children and Youth 6–17 Years.* 11(129), Rockville, Md., 1973.

Zelnik, M., and Kantner, J.: Sexual activity, contraceptive use and pregnancy among metropolitan-area teenagers: 1971–1979. *Fam. Plan. Persp. 12*:230, 1980.

11
Adolescent Sexuality

Iris F. Litt

A dolescence is not a synonym for sex, yet pediatricians who discourage children from continuing as patients after they reach puberty often do so because of their own disinclination to deal with issues of sexuality. Sexuality is not the exclusive domain of adolescence, but rather a process that begins at the time of conception and continues throughout the life cycle. In fact, the determinants of adolescent sexuality are largely to be found in earlier childhood development and represent an amalgram of gender role, gender identity, physical characteristics, hormonal effects, societal expectations, and peer and parental influences: cognitive, moral, and psychological development superimposed on actual experience. Viewed in this way, "sexually active" refers to all children and adolescents, not solely those who have had sexual intercourse.

Gender identity is the first building block in the process of the child's sexual development. It is initiated by announcement of the biologic sex of the baby at birth or earlier with amniocentesis and leads to a complex set of reactions in the minds of parents. Their reaction to the child's genital sex, determined by personal and cultural expectations, will contribute significantly to the newborn's emerging development of gender identity. This is reinforced throughout the first year of life through assignment of name, choice of toys, and clothing. By eighteen months of age, a child has a firm sense of gender identity and regards self as male or female. Even at this young age there is evidence of differences in gender identity between males who later become either homosexual or heterosexual. For example, early behaviors such as cross dressing, preference for dolls, female playmates, and female roles in the doll house are more common among homosexual males. Interestingly, the presence or absence of rough-and-tumble play did not distinguish the groups (Green, 1979).

In addition to genital sex, other biologic realities contribute to developing sexuality during childhood, including the potential for erection and orgasm. Spontaneous erection has been observed from the time of birth, in association with various forms of arousal (such as crying and elimination), as well as during sleep, leading to the belief that erections are reflexive. Nonetheless, direct stimulation of the genitalia of three to four month olds may elicit erections, often accompanied by smiles and cooing sounds suggesting that this initially reflexive response may early become endowed with pleasurable potential. The discovery of the pleasurable potential of genital contact during the process of random self-exploration in the first year of life leads to more purposive genital self-stimulation, commonly referred to as masturbation. Orgasm without ejaculation is known to occur as early as six months of age. Kinsey's estimate was that more than half of all males could achieve orgasm by three to four years of age and that almost all could do so three to five years before puberty is reached (Kinsey, Pomeroy, and Martin, 1948). The psychological implications of early masturbation and its relationship to this seemingly similar behavior in later adolescence have been debated in the literature over the past half-century. The Freudian view, on one hand, argues for masturbation as an important cause of neurosis if it occurs beyond three years of age at which time oedipal fantasies presumably become linked to it, resulting in guilt and fear of punishment. Spitz, Kinsey, and more recently Kleeman deny a connection between masturbation and later sexuality or pathology, the presently accepted position. The absence of data has not, however, prevented the dissemination of advice to parents on this subject by pediatricians. Shackling arms or legs and other behavioral deterrents were widely recommended in the 1930s and 1940s.

It is likely that the parental response to observation of erectile and masturbatory activity is more important to the development of sexuality than is the behavior itself. To the extent parents respond to these, as well as other, clinging and searching movements of the infant with warmth and consistency, the child will learn to be comfortable with his or her own body and find it a source of pleasure. To the extent that the parental response is cruel or inconsistent, the child's ability to receive or give sexual pleasure in the future may be impaired. Pediatricians may impact positively on this process by including a discussion about normality of masturbation before it occurs. Verbal as well as physical sanctions may have a negative effect on the child's developing sexuality. Gagnon (1965) has described parents as exercising three main types of information control concerning sexual matters: (1) unambiguous labeling of certain behaviors as being negative without explanation as to why this is so (for example, "Don't touch that—it's naughty"); (2) nonlabeling by responding to a child's interest in a sexual matter with distraction; and (3) mislabeling by condemning a sexual activity for a spurious reason (for example, "Don't touch your penis, you will get germs"). When punishment is associated with mislabeling, as is often the case, it may result in creating a generalized anxiety about the behavior without necessarily inhibiting it. As a result, Conn and Kanner (1947) reported that during the ages of four to twelve years the average child asks only two questions about sex. The actual questions may vary, but there are usually only two. "Since parents seem willing to answer other sorts of questions, sex often stands out for young children as a peculiar topic, leading to heightened curiosity" (Conn and Kanner, 1947). The pediatrician would do well to provide anticipatory guidance to the parent of the young child to prepare them for that first question so that more might follow. Parents need reassurance that they are capable of doing so and assistance in responding, perhaps by role playing.

Nowhere can the impact of parental reaction on developing sexuality be better appreciated than in the context of the child's actual viewing of parental intercourse, the so-called primal scene. Aaron Esman (1973) has reviewed the early literature on this subject, including the important works of Freud who was of the opinion that children witnessing sexual intercourse of parents may "adopt what may be called a sadistic view of coition," something the stronger was inflicting on the weaker. Esman concludes that most reports of psychopathology resulting from primal scene exposure were most likely due to threats of actual brutalization which occurred in association with children having come upon the scene, rather than the viewing of intercourse per se. According to Gary May (1977):

> It is still good preventive mental health for parents in our culture to put a simple lock on the bedroom door, to be discreet in their lovemaking and, if they are seen or heard, to react with some compassion and descretion to assure the child that love is good and fun, not harmful. The parents should be prepared to deal with the child by talking about feelings and ask questions. This is a great deal to expect of many parents in our culture—a few will be able to manage that kind of positive response. Therefore, it is better to lock the door and be discreet. Above all, the potential trauma of primal scene observation should not be turned into the absolute trauma of true physical and verbal child abuse.

Although accidental viewing of sexual intercourse of parents will surely impact on the child in some way, Gagnon (1972) believes that an even stronger influence than what goes on in the bedroom is what happens in the living room. In other words, parents who serve as role models for trust, intimacy, and nonexploitation between the sexes will surely exert the most significant effect on their child's developing sense of sexual adequacy.

Up until this point, we have focused on biologic development of the infant and child and the role of parents as socializing agents in the process of developing sexuality. Another important aspect of this process is the youngster's developing ability to process the information received about sex. The processing of sexual information undergoes transformation during childhood. In a study by Bernstein and Cowan (1975), it was found that from the ages of two to twelve the individual passes through six levels of processing of sexual information, roughly paralleling those of Piaget. This developmental sequence was observed in responses to the question, "Where do babies come from?" (table 11–1).

By the age of twelve years, most youngsters have had exposure to all the factual information they could ever need in order to understand reproduction, and most from sources other than their parents. It is important for parents to know that the majority of adolescents would like to be able to ask parents ques-

Table 11–1
The Six Levels of a Child's Sexual Information Processing

	Age (years)	Child's Response to the Question: "Where Do Babies Come From?"
Level I	3–4	*Geography:* Children at this stage believe that a baby who now exists has always existed, and their question is, "Where was this baby before it was born?"
Level II	4–7	*Manufacturing:* These children believe that a baby did not always exist; it had to be made. Their view of creation of the baby is, however, akin to that of an assembly line.
Level III	7–10	*Transitional:* These children are in transition from level II to level IV.
Level IV	8–12	*Concrete physiology:* Children at this stage know that you need male and female contribution to the developing baby.
Level V	8–12	*Preformation:* In these children's minds a miniature baby exists preformed within either sperm or egg. It needs material from the opposite sex to unite and release it.
Level VI	8–12	*Physical causality:* By the time the subjects were twelve years of age they had reached the highest level, physical causality, and could give a physiologic explanation of reproduction, the idea that the embryo begins its biologic existence at the moment of conception and that it is a product of genetic materials from both parents. These twelve year olds were also aware of moral and social aspects of reproduction and recognize that marriage is not necessary for conception.

Source: Adapted from Bernstein and Cowan (1975).

tions about sex, but are afraid of repercussions according (Sorensen, 1973). Parents in most surveys would conversely like to be sex educators of their children, but often feel inadequate to the task. Again, the pediatrician is in an ideal position to assist parents in becoming the sort of resource person their offspring needs.

The stage of cognitive development during adolescence also contributes to developing sexuality. When individuals enter the highest stage, that of formal operations, they are able to reason from hypothetical constructs. The possibility of becoming pregnant as a result of engaging in sexual intercourse is one sort of abstraction which is difficult for a child at an earlier stage of development to comprehend fully. From a somewhat different perspective, that of Kohlberg (1972), the development of formal operations

"leads . . . to a new view of the external and the physical. The external and the physical are only one set of many possibilities of a subjective experience. . . . It seems that for all adolescence the discovery of the subjective is a condition for aesthetic feeling in the adult sense, for the experience of nature as a contemplative experience and for religiosity of a mystical variety. It is probably the condition for adolescent romantic love as well. This whole constellation of experiences is called romantic because it is centered on a celebration of the self's experience as the self enters into union with the self's counterpart outside.

Kohlberg's description of moral development also bears on a discussion of sexual development. While the behavior of four to ten year olds at the preconventional level is manifested against a background of cultural labels of good and bad, those at the conventional level (preadolescents) are concerned with behaving in accordance with familial standards, as well as with justifying the validity of these standards. In adolescence, the postconventional level is reached. At this stage, right or wrong is determined by peer group consensus, as well as personal values and opinion, guided by abstract and ethical principles. Although Kohlberg (1972) believes that these stages "represent an invariant developmental sequence," recent work by Gilligan (1982) showing differences between the sexes in their moral development suggests that some variability exists in this as in other developmental processes.

In addition to cognitive and moral development, adolescence is characterized by development of secondary sex characteristics and acceleration of physical growth, collectively referred to as puberty. Puberty results from the effect of augmented secretion of growth-promoting hormones by the pituitary (lutenizing hormone, follicle-stimulating hormone, and growth hormone) on their respective target organs, and the resulting effects of their hormonal secretions. As a result, boys grow tall, muscular, and hirsute, experience growth of their external genitalia, and develop the capacity for ejaculation, while girls grow taller and fatter, develop breasts, pubic hair, experience menarche, and become capable of reproduction.

Although it has always been assumed that increased levels of gonadally derived hormones are responsible for stimulating sexual desire and influencing adolescent behavior, actual data to support this assumption is lacking. In fact, in one study of onset of adolescent dating, Dornbusch et al. (1981) demonstrated better correlation with grade in school than stage of sexual development. Similarily, in other studies no correlation between sexual activity and serum testosterone level in adult males could be found.

With the advent of these physical changes in puberty and new ways of thinking about familiar things in formal operations, the previously established equilibrium is disrupted, forcing confrontation with the crucial question: "Who am I?" Implicit in this question is the question: "Am I normal?" Deviation from the peer group pattern of sexual development seriously impacts on the young person's perception of self. Their readiness to interpret any such deviation as an abnormality renders teenagers vulnerable to feelings of diminished self-worth. Duke et al. (1982) have shown that males who mature later than their peer group have a poor self-image, as well as diminished school performance and lower expectations for their future educational advancement. Earlier longitudinal studies by Jones et al. (1971) have suggested that early-maturing females are at a social disadvantage when compared to their later maturing peer group. Simmons et al. (1979) have explored this issue in a more recent longitudinal sample and conclude that developing self-image is multidetermined. They found, for example, that early maturation in females is associated with poor self-image when coupled with certain environmental factors, such as movement from an elementary to a junior high school setting. Regardless of its etiology, poor self-image during adolescence has far-reaching consequences. In the specific context of sexuality, for example, it has been demonstrated by our group and others to be associated with earlier onset of intercourse activity, as well as nonuse of contraception, both risk factors for early pregnancy.

Just when the young adolescent is asking the question, "Who am I?" society responds to the physical signs of maturity by asking not only "Who are you?" but "Who are you going to be?" The adolescent is thus challenged to find a role to which he or she may become committed and, in so doing, to achieve an identity. The adolescent must integrate, at once, these exciting, sometimes perplexing changes in body habitus and feelings with cognitive information, on the one hand, and societal expectations, on the other.

Resolution of the identity crisis, in Erikson's view (1950), will allow the individual to move to the next stage, characterized by developing the capacity for intimacy. Once there is a self to give, so to speak, the individual is capable of giving of self. Although Erikson's sequences are probably not universal, and clear evidence that mastery over one stage is necessary for progression to the next is lacking, it provides one system for integrating physical, psychological, and social factors.

To turn from the implications of physical development for the adolescent's personality development to that of its social significance, the emergence of signs of sexual development serves as a signal to adults that their youngster is now reproductively capable, a phenomenon which often elicits ambivalence and fear, particularly when the offspring is female. The resultant imposition of curfews, rules, and advice about dress and makeup often precipitates a change in the earlier familial homeostasis. Adolescents are thus often stifled by increasing restrictions at a time when they need to develop autonomy and independence. Overt rebellion, occasionally coupled by sexually provocative dress or behavior, may result when lack of trust is implied through imposition of arbitrary and stricter rules. The teenager's need for privacy or alternatively the parents' discomfort at physical displays of affection may be misinterpreted by either as rejection. Alternatively, a previous incestuous relationship may come to light under these stresses. Anticipatory guidance can help parents prepare for the predictable pressures of adolescence, as well as a general strategy for responding to the many which are unpredictable.

Just as adolescents need leeway in order to be able to try on potential educational and vocational roles, they also need to be able to explore their own potential for becoming a sexual being. Contrary to popular opinion, early sexual exploration rarely includes intercourse but is accomplished through observation of genitalia of peers or through mutual masturbation. Although the latter is often alarming to adults who may discover it and assume it to be a manifestation of homosexuality, there is ample evidence that this behavior is usually narcissistic and assists in the process of self-discovery in the service of future heterosexual relationships. The next stage of sexual experimentation during adolescence consists of social gatherings among both sexes with "kissing" and sometimes "feeling" games tentatively introduced. Pairing off and involvement with petting is next on the hierarchy of experimentation, and probably the most important of all. According to Katchadourian (in press), it provides the bridge to alter adult heterosexual relationships by teaching adolescents about each other's bodies, their own emotional and sexual responses, and those of the opposite sex, as well as teaching and testing social rules and customs of sexual behavior. Sexual intercourse is experienced by less than 50 percent of adolescent females.

Gagnon (1972) points out major differences between males and females with regard to the organizing experience of sexuality at puberty which he feels to be directly linked to earlier gender role socialization. For males, the fantasy which accompanies any heterosexual act suggests needs of achievement, mastery, omnipotence, and aggression; for females such fantasies emphasize love, marriage, and social attachment. For males, there develops a commitment to sexual acts and the gratification they produce; for females, sexual activity of any kind during early adolescence represents a commitment to affect-laden relationships and to the rhetoric of romantic love.

In conclusion, every stage of development of childhood and adolescence is thus equally important in the development of sexuality (figure 11–1). At each, biologic, psychological, and social factors exist in equilibrium. Disruption in any part of the system will cause reverberations in others.

> Parents, as the major agents of socialization, may contribute most significantly to this process by teaching modesty, by serving as role models for mutual respect and nonexploitation between sexes, and by providing factual information and a yardstick against which children and adolescents may measure their own behavior. Peers undoubtedly contribute heavily during adolescence by providing the most information about sex, as well as an arena for sexual experimentation (Litt and Martin, 1983).

The pediatrician has perhaps the greatest role to play in assisting in the development of sexuality by (1) providing parents with the information they need in order to respond comfortably to their youngsters earliest two questions about sex and (2) later by preparing preadolescents for the tremendous range of normal development of secondary sex characteristics they may experience and (3) still later by creating an atmosphere of comfort and trust conducive to helping teen-

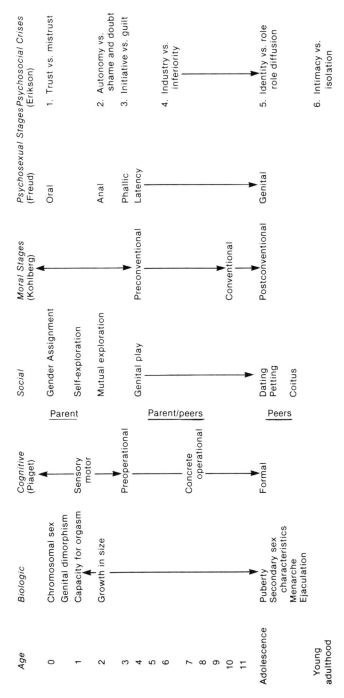

Figure 11–1. Development of Sexuality

agers make responsible and growth-promoting decisions about their sexual activity.

References

Bernstein, A.C., and Cowan, P.A.: Children's concepts of how people get babies. *Child Dev.* 46:77–91, 1975.

Conn, J.H., and Kanner, L.: Children's awareness of sex differences. *J. Child Psychiatry* 1:3–57, 1947.

Dornbusch, S.H., Carlsmith, J.M., and Gross, R.T. et al.: Sexual development, age and dating: a comparison of biologic and social influences upon one set of behaviors. *Child Dev.* 52:179–185, 1981.

Duke, P.M., Carlsmith, J.M., and Jennings, S.D. et al.: Educational correlates of early and late sexual maturation in adolescence. *J. Pediatr.* 100:633, 1982.

Erikson, G.H.: *Childhood and Society.* New York, W.W. Norton, 1950.

Esman, A.H.: The primal scene: a review and reconsideration. In *The Psychoanalytic Study of the Child,* Vol. 28. New York, International University Press, 1973.

Gagnon, J.H.: Sexuality and sexual learning in the child. *Psychiatry* 28:212–228, 1965.

Gagnon, J.H.: The creation of the sexual in early adolescence. In Kagan and Coles (eds.): *12 to 16: Early Adolescence.* New York, W.W. Norton, 1972.

Gilligan, C.: *In a Different Voice: Psychological Theory and Women's Development.* Cambridge, Harvard University Press, 1982.

Green, R.: Childhood cross-gender behavior and subsequent sexual preference. *Am. J. Psychiatry* 136:106–108, 1979.

Jones, M., Bayley, N., MacFarlane, J., et al. (eds.): *The Course of Human Development.* Toronto, John Wiley and Sons, 1971.

Katchadourian, H.A.: *Fundamentals of Human Sexuality* (4th ed.). New York, Holt, Rinehart and Winston (in press).

Kinsey, A.C., Pomeroy, W.B., and Martin, C.E.: *Sexual Behavior in the Human Male.* Philadelphia, W.B. Saunders, 1948.

Kohlberg, L.: The adolescent as a philosopher. In Kagan and Coles (eds.): *12 to 16: Early Adolescence.* New York, W.W. Norton, 1972.

Litt, I.F., and Martin, J.A.: Development of sexuality and its problems. In Levine, M.D., Carey, W.B., Crocker, A.C., and Gross, R.T. (eds.): *Developmental-Behavioral Pediatrics.* Philadelphia, W.B. Saunders, 1983.

May, J.G.: Sexual abuse: the undercover problem. *Curr. Prob. Pediatr.* 7:12–16, 1977.

Simmons, R., et al.: Entry into early adolescence: the impact of school structure, puberty and early dating on self-esteem. *Am. Sociol Rev.* 44:948–67, 1979.

Sorenson, R.C.: *Adolescent Sexuality in Contemporary America.* Mountain View, Calif., World Publications, 1973.

12

High-Risk Youth: Changing Problems into Solutions

Richard G. MacKenzie

From whatever theoretical vantage point one views that period of the life cycle called adolescence, the concept of *change* is central. Adolescence, as used here, refers to that psychosocial process of change occurring concomitant to and as a consequence of the biologic changes of puberty. This transition is a dynamic and kinetic state, sometimes purposeful and other times exploratory and testing. It is within this exploration, this seeking out of new experiences, that teenagers become "at risk" and will by chance or by influence take a direction not in their best interests in the sense that continued participation or involvement in such activity would be unhealthy biologically and psychologically.

Adolescence by definition has inherent risk that increases the susceptibility of any teenager to behaviors that will lead to problems for that individual. These behaviors may be a product of disturbances in the psychological development of the individual over time or in the social environment at any given point in time. In other words, the teenager is not an end product with definite shape governed by previous life experience and influenced by environmental and ecologic factors at any given point. In reality, teenagers are in a continual state of dynamic interaction with previous life experiences, present socioecosystems, and future aspirations and fantasies influencing their perception. Adolescents negotiate their way through the maze of daily experiences and developmental influences and determine their behavior on the basis of their personal histories. They have variable levels of awareness of immediate influences on them. Choices made through thought or impulsivity are not simply choices in time but expressions of complex interactional forces generated by an earlier script and influenced by the present situation.

There is no need to review the generally accepted developmental concepts of adolescence as proposed by Havighurst and others. The general goal of individuation and autonomy motivate the teenager to venture into experiences and respond to impulses at a frequency which is not to be repeated again in the life cycle. These adventures into yet unexplored or inexperienced parts of the human mind or anatomy are at times filled with excitement and challenge, and at other times with fear and insecurity. As a consequence of their nature and nurture, so to speak, teenagers, in the springtime of their lives, continue to be shaped not only by their beliefs and values, but also by three major social institutions: the family, the school, and the peer group.

Within the concept of the psychobiologic developmental model there is a sense of the individual as a victim of earlier childhood experience and influence. But within the context of adolescence choices emerge. This awareness of choices is one of the prime characteristics of a mentally healthy adolescent. Emphasis is on the word *awareness*, for in reality many of the decisions have already been made by society. For instance, privileges are differentially granted to minors and adults, options for education are limited, and employment essentially non-existent. But even in the presence of these limited options, choices are still possible: school dropout, truancy, unemployment, or deviant employment. However, the majority of teenagers, as shown by Dan Offer in his study, "From Teenager to Young Manhood," follow the socially determined path, responding to the nurture and nature of their earlier developmental years, and focusing their energy on the traditional values and goals of society. There is, on the other hand, a yet undetermined number of teenagers, who have a variation of this experience. These individuals are more likely to be at higher risk than their peers who have followed the more common path of individuation through education and traditional employment. These high-risk adolescents travel a path that, for a variety of reasons increases their susceptibility to develop behaviors, occupations, and lifestyles which are deviant from the norms of the dominant culture. These individuals, in a sense, have a different way of accomplishing the developmental challenge or task of the teenage years. These individuals are the high-risk youth who run away or who are thrown away, who use or sell drugs or alcohol, who enter into lifestyles characterized by day-to-day survival and night-to-night casual sex, who are at risk for violent behaviors toward themselves and others. These are the young people who are at risk for repeated confrontation with law enforcement. These are also the youth who are at risk for a variety of medical problems.

What begins as a biopsychosocial expression of a normative developmental period, becomes for these high-risk young people, a series of disasters and victimizations. These adolescents who by choice or impulse, deviate from the traditional to gain freedom paradoxically become the victims. Although their behaviors, their dysfunctions, and their diseases may be promoted by their peers, they are fueled by the adult culture. In most instances, it is the adult culture again which determines their direction, their education, and their employment. These young people ranging in age from ten to twenty-five years are educated to the deviant occupations of the street—hustling, prostitution, drug dealing, pornography, violence, and burglary. In a developmental sense, they become society's high-risk deviant scholars.

It becomes clear that in creating a clinical model for intervention or prevention, a variety of factors must be considered. This is not to say that models of care cannot be developed which address only singular or isolated needs of this high-risk population, for example, drug abuse and sexually transmitted diseases (STDs). But in so doing, a valuable opportunity is lost with these young people. Physicians occupy a unique position on the health care team. Their knowledge and skills are focused on the physical function and dysfunction of the body. Physical illness or symptom is a legitimate reason to seek out help. Inasmuch as this physical complaint is a "ticket of entry" into the health care team via the physician, it permits an opportunity to develop an integrated biopsychosocial evaluation and intervention for that individual. What is necessary for this to occur is that the physician have an integrated knowledge of adolescent physical, psychological, and social development. The initial biopsychosocial integration will not involve the complexity of personalities and theoretical models of the multidisciplinary team. The team issues often undermine the outcome for the client/patient/adolescent. The biopsychosocial integrative model is best demonstrated diagrammatically in what I refer to as the "daisy model" (figure 12–1).

In this model, there is a body of core knowledge (1) which is common to all those individuals who primarily work with adolescents. Inasmuch as the common focus is the adolescent, there always occurs an overlap of knowledge and skills by various members of the team. This overlap knowledge is represented by shade area 2. There are those professionals who have an indepth knowledge (3) and who, as part of the team, are available for consultation or referral. Area 4 represents the necessity for communication, common language, and resolution of team-centered issues. The physician, with training, can develop the skills and knowledge in 1 and 3 for initial assessment and, at times, intervention. The physician must also be a team player and be aware of those issues represented by 4.

An ancillary yet important advantage of utilizing the integrated approach is to provide an opportunity to raise the issue not only of disease but also of prevention or health maintenance. The teenager may ask questions, but in most instances the prevention and maintenance issues must be introduced into the clinical interaction by the physician or health professional. In the general adolescent and young adult population, and occasionally in the high-risk group, the issue of health promotion may be introduced. During the clinical interaction, the physician may motivate or educate the teenager not only to maintain health but even to feel better. High-risk youth more commonly focus on disease. It then becomes important to probe below the surface of disease to identify the developmental contributions to the problem. It is this development, "psychosocial biopsy," which calls upon the unique skills and knowledge of the professional trained in adolescent medicine. This biopsy also identifies the deeper causes of the present complaint.

It becomes apparent that developing a risk profile for an adolescent is a complex issue. This is not to infer that developing a risk profile for an adult is a simple matter. But risk profiles that primarily focus on physical contributions to disease tend to be less complex than those that also define psychological and

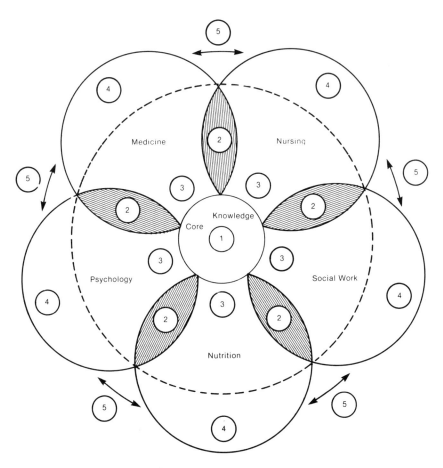

Figure 12–1. The Daisy Model

human socioecologic contributions. The Framingham study, for instance, was able to develop a risk profile for coronary artery disease. The risk factors were defined by measurable, quantifiable, physical parameters such as serum cholesterol, diet, body weight, blood pressure, blood sugar, cigarette habit, and heredity. In using the term *high-risk youth,* we infer that we know what we are talking about. We do not have what can be described as a risk profile for young people. Most of us would intuitively know a high-risk youth when we saw one. Our intuition would be based upon the interplay of a number of factors in the high-risk profile. There is yet to be developed an instrument which can, with any clinical reliability, cull from our adolescent population those who are at greater risk for either biologic, psychological, or social morbidity.

An examination of the morbidity and mortality data for the adolescent and young adult population demonstrates the complexity of the risk profile only too well. Motor vehicle accidents are the most common documented cause of death in adolescents. One does not need to pry too deep below the surface of a motor vehicle accident to find multiple premorbid contributions such as drugs, alcohol, suicidal ideation, "showing off" as a ritual to accomplish a developmental task, some underlying medical illness such as seizure disorder, or undiagnosed myopia. Morbidity, on the other hand, is less frequently documented for a variety of reasons. First of all, teenagers obtain their medical care from a number of sources because of a fear of breach of confidentiality with parents. Interestingly, teenagers will go to their pediatricians for general medical care, but to a family planning, free, or county clinic, for birth control and STDs. In addition, statistics are collected not recognizing the usually accepted boundaries of adolescence and young adult. That is, the National Center for Health Statistics collects data from five to fourteen years of age and fifteen to twenty-four years of age. No data has been collected that correlates either prospectively or retrospectively with a multifactorial risk profile for adolescents and young adults. A preliminary attempt is being made to do this in our High-Risk Youth Project in Los Angeles. At least we need to identify the problems which bring high-risk teenagers to the health care professionals and what turns up on the "psychosocial biopsy." Their "chief complaint" is the ticket of entry into the health care system for most high-risk adolecents. The four most common diagnoses for this group of adolescents is sexually transmitted disease, depression, family planning, and substance abuse. Interestingly, one can abstract from this data that there is a certain risk at least on physical reproductive health with initiation of sexual activity. It is our impression, yet to be substantiated, that there is a considerable risk to an individual's psychological and social health. But even this statement is an oversimplification. After two years of working with high-risk youth in Los Angeles, we are just beginning to formulate the questions that need to be addressed.

In formulating our questions about high-risk youth, we "framed" and "reframed" the issues in a way which led to asking different kinds of questions. For instance, in medicine we tend to assume that what people bring to us are problems seeking solutions—that an individual who has chest pain has a definable problem and is requesting evaluation for alleviation and resolution. But in the high-risk teenager, the deviant scholar, the individual who is somewhat encapsulated by the options allowed by the dominant culture, what we see as problems may actually in fact be their solutions! In other words, there is a limit to their problem-solving options, and it is their solutions that actually create the problems for them. It is these problems that are a bonafide ticket of entry into the health care system without need to declare psychological or social morbidity. Seen from this vantage point, one may raise the question, "What is the real problem?" In light of this, the importance of developing a practical model of assessment and intervention that considers these psychosocial contributants becomes

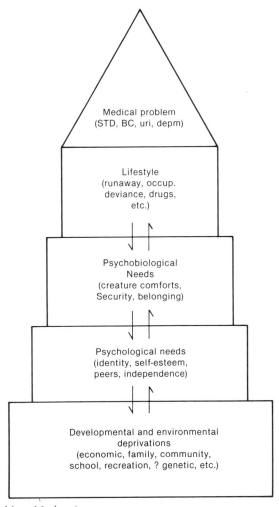

Source: Adapted from Mackenzie.

Figure 12–2. Medical Model of Integrated Health Care for High-Risk Youth

obvious. This we have termed the hierarchical model of biopsychosocial assessment and intervention. Although I primarily refer to the use of this model with high-risk youth, it is essentially a model which has application to all medicine.

In figure 12–2, the ticket of entry is in the top triangle. This is the medical problem, the presenting complaint, or for many the solution. It may be a physical disorder, such as a sexually transmitted disease. Lying underneath this problem within every individual, of course, is a number of levels which we have labeled lifestyle, psychobiological need, and psychosocial environmental deprivations. This model then becomes the guiding paradigm in several different ways. First, the presenting complaint is merely a ticket to entry, a solution to a larger problem which is usually not apparent to the unskilled clinician. Assessment of this presenting complaint needs to include an exploration, a documentation of other levels of this young person's functioning. Second, in some individuals, all aspects of each level may or may not be accessible. Certain aspects may be ignored, but it is important not to skip a level. And third, intervention and management plans must address sequentially these various levels. It would be foolish to have an individual present with a venereal disease as the chief complaint, ignore that problem, and begin to do a childhood developmental assessment and provide psychotherapeutic intervention for the identified dysfunction. Although this would seem ridiculous to some, it is not uncommon that a teenager will present with the "problem" of substance abuse, suicide, or runaway behavior, and after a history and mental status exam, traditional intervention will be initiated at the level of developmental and environmental deprivations. The physician should need to provide whatever symptomatic or definitive therapy there is for the presenting problem, intervention for the psychobiological needs, and intervention at the other levels and should not jump into the all-too-often mode of providing counseling and therapy for deep-rooted issues.

Although the hierarchical model is simplistic, its application requires a broad base of knowledge not only in human biology and pathology, but also in the psychological, developmental issues that are characteristic of this age group. The social or ecological issues that form the environment in which this young person functions can be as definable as the family and school or as amorphous as the message of music and media (socioecology). Brought together, all these factors create what is commonly referred to as the youth culture. Although not having replicability nationally, there is some consistency of shape. Youth in all parts of the United States tend to respond in their unique ways to the fairly consistent social ecology despite the variations in specific influences. One subculture of the youth culture are the runaways, the throwaways, and the walkaways. These young people, usually for family reasons, leave home, and although they are no longer bound by the rules or customs of the dominant culture, they have their options restricted by the dominant culture. They become victims of that very philosophy which was developed to protect them. This population points out quite clearly how problems are really solutions and how below these solutions lies many of the real problems. Time does not permit me to do justice to all that we have learned about this population. We know that it is of significant proportions and is made up of sons and daughters from all socioeconomic strata. We also know that these young people are not the bad, the recalcitrant, the delinquent, or the promiscuous sons and daughters. Their high-risk destiny has been a product of limited choices, and their options are the options of the street subculture.

Jennifer James in Seattle uses the anthropological concept of acculturation, particularly in reference to her work with teenage prostitutes. A teenager becomes assimilated into new subcultures at pretty much established time frames. Variable markers indicate the degree of assimilation, and degree of assimilation defines the probability of being able to change and leave the subculture.

Although the model has been primarily used to understand the population of young people, it does have its application generically to all youth subcultures. Its concepts can be applied to the young person who changes neighborhood, school, or peer group, or who moves away to college or gains employment. The difference with high risk youth is that acculturation focuses on negative attributes. With increasing acculturation, change becomes increasingly difficult. Interventions then must be based more in reality. Initial attempts must be more successful. Community support systems must be focused on the needs of these indigenous youth and must understand the sociopsychopathology of the particular youth subculture.

In developing a network of support services for our High-Risk Youth Project in Los Angeles it became apparent to us that many of the traditional helping institutions spent more of their time validating the administrative procedures of the institution rather than addressing the needs of their target service population. These traditional institutions were and are much more difficult to network, access, and develop working relationships with, owing to complex policies and procedures. Indigenous services have become a much more valuable part of the network inasmuch as they are individual centered, more flexible in their administrative structure, and more grounded in their approaches to young people. They tend to focus on first-, second-, and third-level needs. On the other hand, the indigenous services often do not have the regard of the traditional services and are viewed as transient agencies. The staff often lack the necessary credentials, which the traditional services view as necessary to working with a particular target population. However, we have found that it is important to develop a network of services for young people made up of both traditional services, such as the United Way agencies, YMCAs, churches, schools, public and social services agencies, and indigenous agencies such as free clinics, gay and lesbian services, and street drug programs.

How does one, within a framework of limited facility and time, operationalize this hierarchical model of assessment and intervention? This is best done within the medical model by what we call the psychosocial biopsy. This is a clinical instrument which is readily learned by convergent-thinking physicians and guides them in assessing and evaluating the often divergent issues of psychosocial background and functioning. This instrument was developed under the leadership of Eric Cohen, the physician-preceptor of our High-Risk Youth Project. We use the mnemonic HEADS. This becomes as much a part of the clinical evaluation of a patient as is the history, physical examination, and review of systems. The mnemonic stands for:

H: home

E: education

A: activities and affect

D: drugs

S: sex

This information, taken on every individual, helps to define the risk profile. At the same time, it assesses the individual, defines the problem, and perhaps even in some instances, justifies the young person's solution (which may have been the presenting problem).

It is also apparent to us that the degree to which intervention is possible, or change probable, must be defined in the management plan. We would all like to create miracles, and totally rehabilitate every individual with whom we have a therapeutic contact. Unfortunately, this is not usually possible, especially when dealing with the complex biopsychosocial issues of adolescence and specifically when dealing with a high-risk youth population. But again, these problems in high-risk youth and perhaps in all young people must be approached on a logical, hierarchical basis, interventions must be well defined and practical, and energies of the helping network must be adolescent and not institution focused.

There is a concept in adolescent psychology which is termed the universal myth of adolescence. This concept suggests that there are times, especially during the early teenage years, when teenagers feel that the whole world is focused on them and that every mistake they make quickly becomes a subject of social intercourse. In relation to high-risk youth I would like to suggest an unfortunate variation on that theme. Many of these young people are watched, but the focus of attention is often use and abuse. And those that abuse, often through sexual intercourse, are not the identified perpetrator. It is the adolescent as the victim who becomes the villain!

13
Psychosocial Impact of Chronic Illness in Childhood

Barbara M. Korsch

I t has been documented consistently that the psychosocial impact of chronic illness on child and family is determined in large measure by factors not intrinsic to any particular diagnostic category. Funding for health care is frequently allocated on a categorical basis, and many clinical services are so organized, based on technologic considerations and mostly for the physician's convenience. However, the evidence accumulates that there are more commonalities between the attributes of chronically ill children across diagnostic categories than within any one diagnosis (Pless and Pinkerton, 1975; Richardson et al., 1961) and that the determinants for ultimate function are in a large degree demographic, psychosocial, and developmental and are as follows (Korsch et al., 1973):

age

development

family

personality

community

practical

These considerations are relevant to program planning, especially in treatment centers where there is not the critical mass of patients present that would be required to justify adequate psychosocial support systems within any one diagnostic category. In these centers a support team could be provided if chronically ill children were considered as a group noncategorically and treated on the basis of their common needs.

In pediatric medicine the chronologic age and the developmental stage of the sick child as he or she experiences illness and treatment are two uniquely important considerations. The developmental tasks characteristic for a specific time in the child's life span will be the ones most vulnerable to the stress of the illness. In the first year of life, separation from the mother or caretaker will be one of the most stressful experiences. Also, the feeding experience for the mother and infant may be so altered as to influence the child's attitude about food as well as the mother's self-esteem for a long time to come.

In the second year of life, inadequate outlet for development of autonomy and limitation of the opportunity for big muscle activities such as walking, running, and climbing constitutes a major deprivation. Also in the second year, habit training and the achievement of sphincter control are a central task for mother and child that is uniquely distorted, for instance, in children with major anomalies of the genitourinary tract. During the preschool years, socialization within the family, progressive identification with the parent of the same sex, learning the roles within the family, socialization outside the family, and development of increasing independence may all be prejudiced by the need for repeated hospitalization and by periods of enforced inactivity and malaise.

An exhaustive inventory of stage-specific developmental tasks and their distortion by illness and treatment is beyond the scope of this discussion. However, there are a few other generalizations worthy of mention in this context. Education and acculturation, the main accomplishments of the school-age child, are especially important for the child with physical illness who may later have to substitute brains for brawn. Clearly, sick children are at a great disadvantage in this respect. Not only may physical limitations, hospital visits, and treatment interfere with school attendance and study, but unfortunately the school system is not sufficiently educated, prepared, or funded to deal appropriately with these children's needs. In many cultures competitive sports are an important feature of the educational experience. The sick child's inadequacies in this respect may also greatly depress an already vulnerable self-esteem and socialization.

Separate emphasis needs to be devoted to the many sources of special anguish for the adolescent patient suffering from a physical illness. Maturing physically, rebelling against childhood dependency and family control, developing an adult sexual role, and planning a career are difficult even for adolescents in our society who enjoy robust physical health. When the strain of illness and treatment is experienced during these crucial years, the patient may not be able to adapt and compensate. In long-term follow-up on patients treated for end-stage renal disease (ESRD) the most failures in adaptation and the least satisfactory rehabilitation have been observed in patients whose disease manifested itself in adolescence (Korsch et al., 1973). Unfortunately ESRD frequently declares itself during the growth spurt of the adolescent period, which makes these considerations especially relevant to the discussion of ESRD in young patients.

Family function is another basic consideration in assessing the outcome of physical illness in childhood. Related to family function are the personality attributes of the child/patient which will influence adaptation to illness and treatment. There are many observations (Travis, 1976) that a child with high self-esteem who has experienced affection and respect in the early years from family members and others and who does not have an unusually vulnerable temperament may withstand even catastrophic illness and traumatic prolonged treatment without personaiity distortion. Looking at the genesis of these resiliant personality profiles, one confronts certain basic temperamental attributes and also becomes aware that family function, including availability of supportive parents and siblings and others, is most important. Good communication within the family generally and about the illness is one attribute of family function that has been found helpful to the child's response to illness and handicap (Korsch et al., 1973; Pless and Pinkerton, 1973).

Not all determinants of child and family response to illness are in the psychologic sphere. Certain reality factors, such as financial and other resources within the family, distance from the treatment facility, availability of transportation, ethnic, cultural, religious, and educational background, and community resources and support, all play important parts in structuring the illness experience for child and family. Single-parent families, disorganized families, and dislocated and isolated families are least likely to be able to muster the needed support for the sick child, although there are exceptions.

In considering noncategorical, nondisease specific features of chronic illness, another important determinant may be the contribution of the treatment team. It is generally accepted that support, sensitivity, continuity, and a comprehensive family-centered approach will make for better outcome than fragmented, technical care. These assumptions have face validity, but the only evidence derives from studies by Pless indicating that a community worker by supporting families can contribute to the sick child's adaptation (Haggerty et al., 1975; Pless and Satterwhite, 1973). It is difficult to assess how much impact the health professional's contribution, beyond technical competence and appropriate interventions, has on child and family adaptation to illness and on the ultimate level of function. Yet there is a host of clinical anecdotal, and humanitarian information which justifies attempts at ameliorating the illness experience for child and family from day to day even when ultimate outcome has not been documented to be altered.

Illness-Specific Problems

Now if we have accepted the principle that stress exaggerates problems specific to a particular developmental stage, individual child, or family group, we must then also look for illness-specific determinants of functional outcome in chronic illness, including

perception of seriousness

cosmetic, social stigmata

movement restriction

diet, pain

treatment modality

isolation and separation

Isolation because of infectious disease, movement restriction, dietary restriction (especially in a family where food and eating is valued in the mind of the family), and cosmetic effects in another young person are the kinds of specific limitations that can be anticipated to be traumatic, especially if one is attuned to the attributes of the particular child and family.

There are uniquely traumatic experiences involved in a number of disease processes that we see often in children and young people. For example, in the juvenile diabetic, between the emphasis on food restriction and the repeated preoccupation with testing urine and checking chemistries, there are a number of reasons why these children, even though physically normal in appearance, and often not suffering acutely from any symptoms or signs, feel themselves severely different from others and suffer from this isolation. Disease conditions such as diabetes, rheumatic fever, and others, where there is no clearly visible stigma, may be in some ways more unsettling to young people than those that have a clearly identifiable lesion or abnormality.

Another example is asthma in which the fear and discomfort associated with breathing difficulties, the anxious reaction of family and other caretakers or the school, the restrictions in the environment that may be necessary (restrictive diets, removal of favorite toys and soft furnishings, or worst of all having to abandon the favorite pet) all contribute to make asthma in childhood especially painful for the young person.

The psychosocial impact of physical illnesses in children and young adults does not necessarily mirror the severity of the illness or the threat of the illness as we physicians think of it. Some of the conditions that seem relatively mild may have far-reaching psychologic implications and some more clear-cut gross defects can be less traumatic. It has always been hard for me to accept that deafness causes more psychological impact than does blindness. Similarly, Richardson et al. (1961) demonstrated that children shun an obese child more than someone who is in a wheelchair. Thus the meaning of illness to a child, family, and society bears thinking about, rather than assuming that there will be congruence between the medical profession's view and that of the patient.

Other interesting speculations about chronic illness relate to the interaction between the chronically ill child or young adult and society. There is a strong move afoot on the part of the chronically ill not to be classified as "handicapped" and constantly compared to the "normal." This group is militantly demanding that they be looked at for their own needs and the characteristics of their own growth and development, and that an effort be made to make possible for them a life that is normal for them, not normal by our standards. Gliedman and Roth, in their book *The Unexpected Minority* (1977), compare the chronically ill to other minorities such as blacks or other ethnic groups. They point out that these individuals share character attributes and behavior, and that they are uniquely handicapped since they are often raised by parents who do not have an intimate knowledge of the subculture represented by the handicap. Because of this, these parents are less able to teach their children survival skills than a black family would be able to teach a black child.

It has been shown repeatedly that the rehabilitation potential and ultimate level of recovery has more to do with motivation, psychosocial functioning, self-esteem, and psychosocial impact than it does with the degree of physical handicap. Patients can recover or rehabilitate themselves from severe physical assault if they are psychosocially intact, if there is some support, and if there is hope for them. Yet even minor illness, given a vulnerable person from a nonsupportive family, at a difficult stage in their growth and development, can lead to irreversible damage.

Experience with Patients with ESRD

The patients with whom I have had the most intensive experience are children with end stage renal disease. In 1967 at Children's Hospital of Los Angeles I was invited to organize a psychosocial team to document the impact of disease and treatment by conservative means, dialysis, and transplantation on patients and family. The psychosocial team at Children's Hospital of Los Angeles was originally destined to assess the psychosocial impact of illness and treatment on patient and family. Although service needs encroached increasingly on this research effort, it was possible to carry out systematic psychosocial assessment of all patients and families at the time of intake as well as regularly for follow-up.

The aim was to utilize methods of assessment which were easily administered and interpreted by the regular members of the health care team. These did not require the expertise of psychologists and psychiatrists. Simple semistructured interviews to explore family function, communication patterns, sources of support, and family value systems from the point of view of the family and the patient were utilized. Also, a few short pen-and-pencil tests were administered to provide a uniform format for evaluation of individual personality profiles (Korsch et al., 1971, 1973). Questions relating to the patient's activities, self-esteem, and social and personal adjustment appeared to elicit the most helpful information in predicting rehabilitation and in planning appropriate intervention. There is reason to believe that the child's sense of mastery of fate and bodily functions ("internal" vs. "external" controls) also are worth exploring as part of the basic assessment. Instruments for assessing patient rehabilitation are as follows:

child and family interview

California test of personality

Piers-Harris self-esteem scale

draw-a-person test

IQ and developmental testing

STAI; STAIC (self-evaluation questionnaire)

Sarason anxiety scale

health locus of control

The first four are administered to all patients. The results of the tests are suitable for computer processing and are helpful in the provision of comprehensive care. In certain instances a combination of extremely low test results yielded a formula that seemed to be predictive of poor adaptation and noncompliant behavior (Korsch et al., 1973).

Results for Patients and Family

The results of this psychosocial assessment based on follow-up data collected for thirteen years on 238 patients with 322 renal transplants have been published (Korsch et al., 1973). They are not dramatically different from those obtained in other programs for ESRD except for the differences explicable by the higher percentage of cadaveric transplantations and by very eclectic intake criteria for our program.

There was a strong correlation between the number and the extent of biologic complications of dialysis and transplantation and the psychosocial outcome. In this context it can be understood why live related allografts led to better outcomes psychosocially as well as medically. For many children successful renal transplantation made for a better quality of life than did existence with any other type of treatment. For a smaller number, who by choice or for medical reasons remained on dialysis, especially those more recently treated by continuous ambulatory peritoneal dialysis CAPD, acceptable adaptation was achieved without allograft. This was also the case in some who following allograft rejection returned to dialysis.

It was observed that the majority of the children in the sample enjoyed an adequate level of rehabilitation and adaptation one or more years after their renal transplantation. This included essentially normal physical activities, education, or vocational placement, and the assumption of appropriate roles in society, including marriage and procreation (Korsch et al., 1980, 1973). Family life also in most instances returned to preillness equilibrium one or more years after transplantation.

These encouraging conclusions must be tempered by the following consideration: In general the patients' adaptation reflected the preillness personality attributes and functional level but was not necessarily "normal" or desirable. Similarly in many of the more troubled families "return to preillness equilibrium" did not represent a very desirable level of family function. A significant proportion of children and families developed major psychologic or emotional problems at some point in their illness. This was especially true in the adolescent patients. Since there were few comparable populations without renal disease it is difficult to infer to what extent ESRD and its treatment contributed to these problems.

The vulnerability to poor outcome seemed strongly increased for those patients put at risk by the following factors: (1) poor family support, (2) poor family function including family disorganization, (3) vulnerable personality before illness including high anxiety and poor self-esteem, (4) complex medical course, (5) low income and other practical problems such as dislocation and poor community support systems, (6) the experience of renal failure and treatment for ESRD occurring during adolescence.

One form of maladaptation documented in the Children's Hospital program was noncompliance with the immunosuppressive medication following transplantation, leading in some cases to decreased renal function and in some cases to allograft loss (Korsch et al., 1978). The risk factors for noncompliance were essentially the same as those for poor overall adaptation.

Support and intervention in the usual mental health model offered by the team to patients individually and in groups, as well as to families, did not predictably prevent maladaptation, although it was thought to improve the patients' and families' experience with the illness and treatment and made for better cooperation. Limited effectiveness seemed to relate in part to the failure of the most stressed patients and families to participate in psychotherapeutic ventures for practical and psychologic reasons.

In summary then, psychosocial adaptation, functional outcome, and rehabilitation of children with chronic illness is determined by the interaction of a set of complex variables. Prominent among these are nonillness specific determinants, such as child's age and developmental status, personality, and family background. In addition, there are some definable specific effects that can be attributed to the nature of the illness and its treatment.

Optimal planning for comprehensive patient care includes assessment of the biologic problems involved as well as of the child's developmental and emotional needs and of the level of family function. Some of these principles can be illustrated with the model of children and adolescents with ESRD.

References

Gliedman, J., and Roth, W.: *The Unexpected Minority.* New York, Harcourt Brace Jovanovich, 1977.

Haggerty, R.J., Roghmann, K.J., and Pless, I.B.: *Child Health and the Community.* New York, John Wiley and Sons, 1975.

Korsch, B.M., Fine, R.N., Grushkin, C.M., and Negrete, V.F.: Experiences with children and their families during extended hemodialysis and kidney transplantation. *Pediatr. Clin. North Am. 18:*625, 1971.

Korsch, B.M., Fine, R.N., and Negrete, V.F.: Noncompliance in children with renal transplants. *Pediatrics 61:*876, 1978.

Korsch, B.M., Klein, J.D., Negrete, V.F., et al.: Physical and psychological follow-up on offspring of renal allograft recipients. *Pediatrics 65:*275, 1980.

Korsch, B.M., Negrete, V.F., Gardner, J.E., et al.: Kidney transplantation in children: psychosocial follow-up study on children and family. *J. Pediatr. 83:*399, 1973.

Pless, I.B., and Pinkerton, P.: *Chronic Childhood Disorders: Promoting Patterns of Adjustment.* London, Henry Kimpton, 1975.

Pless, I.B., and Satterwhite, B.: A measure of family functioning and its application. *Soc. Sci. Med. 7:*613, 1973.

Pless, I.B., and Satterwhite, B.: Chronic illness in childhood: selection, activities and evaluation of non-professional family counselors. *Clin. Pediatr. 11:*403, 1972.

Richardson, S.A., Boodman, N., Hastorf, A.H., Dornbush, S.M.: Cultural uniformity in reaction to physical disabilities. *Am. Sociol. Rev. 26:*241, 1961.

Stein, R.E.K., Jessop, D.J.: A noncategorical approach to chronic illness. *PH Rep. 97:*354, 1982.

Travis, G.: *Chronic Illness in Children: Its Impact on Child and Family.* Stanford, Stanford University Press, 1976.

14

Health Hazards Associated with Coming of Age in the 1980s

Charles E. Lewis

During the 1950s and 1960s, I spent my time worrying about adult illness behavior, and doing the sort of things internists do, trying to affect patient compliance and deal with denial and overutilization. My colleague, Mary Ann Lewis, kept saying, "You're worrying too late; it begins in childhood." In 1970, when we moved to Los Angeles—where everything is possible—we began to look at the origins of health and illness behavior in childhood. Each of the projects I'm going to describe began with a research question, concerned primarily with the child, but as the projects unfolded they always led back to the family.

Child-Initiated Care

In 1970, the first problem to be solved was how we could look at children's illness behavior with all the adults out of the system. Children's utilization of health services is really adults' utilization of health services in behalf of children. Children are taken to doctors and to nurses; they do not go themselves.

But if children could go on their own for health care in a school environment, what would their patterns of utilization look like? Also, if you allow children to participate actively in decision making about what happens to them, would it affect their attitudes or behaviors?

The University Elementary School (UES), run by UCLA's School of Education, served as our first laboratory. The faculty agreed to let us put care cards in boxes on the premises—on the playground and in classrooms. Teachers agreed that whenever a child felt the need to go to a nurse (the first one was Dr. Mary Ann Lewis), he or she would take one of these cards, tear off the top of it, leave it with the teacher, and go directly to the nurse. There the child would be engaged in a process that involved history taking, an appropriate physical examination, and provision of the database back to the child. Then we asked "What do you think we ought to do about it?" The child was asked to formulate options for care and chose one of those options. (Children got their choices unless they were

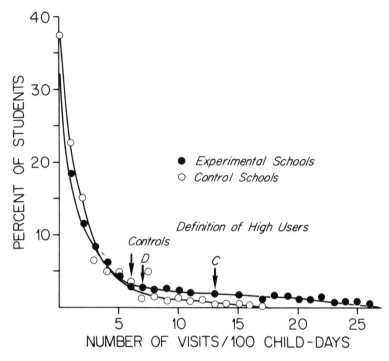

Figure 14–1. **Frequency Distributions of Number Visits by Students, Spring 1977**

absurd or placed them at risk.) We interviewed over 300 children annually for three years. Figure 14–1 shows their patterns of use.

These data are from a replication study in the real world, because when we finished this work, everybody said, "Of course, but that's a laboratory school." We went to the real world of Pomona, California, and redid the study. The UES and Pomona data showed that, just like adults, in an average year, 30–40 percent of kids never went to the nurse (Avnett, 1967; Frogatt and Merritt, 1969). As a matter of fact, if one looks at the data over three years, the same 30 percent never went. Even when they fell down and got bloody, they did not go. Most of these nonusers are boys. On the other hand, there was a worried well-child population representing 10–15 percent of the school who accounted for 50–60 percent of the visits made to the school nurse. Most of them were girls.

We asked the children, "Have you ever been sick and not gone for help?" and if they said yes, the question was, "When you didn't go, what happened?" As shown in table 14–1, boys always got better, and girls tended to not do as well. Looking at patterns of use retrospectively over the year, high users always

Table 14–1
Responses to Question: Have You Ever Been Sick and Not Gone to
the Nurse?

Sex and Use	Got Better	Got worse	Same	No Prognosis
Boys[a]	19.0	0	0	71.5
Girls[a]	4.5	31.8	4.5	50.0
Regular use[b]	17.9	10.7	3.6	57.1
High use[b]	0	26.7	0	66.1

[a]$X^2 = 10.4, p < 0.05.$
[b]$X^2 = 4.60,$ not significant.

got worse. Thus, there is differential perception of the value of care present in this
population of five to twelve year olds.

When we looked at the pediatric records (and most of the mothers used pediatricians), we found a significant association between going to the nurse in the
school setting on one's own and being taken to the pediatrician by one's mother.

The picture of a high-use child is one who has a lot of health knowledge.
They have role models available. They pretend more and are reinforced. We
asked a question I'd always wanted to ask adult patients, "Have you ever pre-
tended to be sick?" and many children, being absolutely honest, said yes. And
when we asked why, they looked at us as they would most adults who are not
really with it and said, "To get out of something." High users are the kids who
pretend more and are reinforced for it. They also have perceived higher benefits
of care; they perceive themselves to be more vulnerable; they are more dependent
and they have lower self-esteem (Lewis et al., 1977).

Nurses could, by taking a history of what's going on in class and what's
going on at home, and asking "Have you ever had this before?" get kids to come
in and say, spontaneously, "Mrs. Lewis, I have a math headache." The attribution
of causality was made by them; they weren't told they had a math headache.
They made the association. This leads to an interesting dilemma: How does one
treat math headaches in a society that only legitimizes medical complaints? We
suggested to this rather free-wheeling educational institution that we create a circle on the playground and allow children to take their chairs out there instead of
going to the nurse. Much to our surprise, they said, "I'm sorry; that's not possible." So we never got to treat math headaches with a time-out break.

Feeling Bad

High users are kids who are troubled; they are not the children with asthma,
cystic fibrosis, or congenital heart disease. They were kids who seemed dis-

tressed, and thus it occurred to us we ought to examine the sources of distress in childhood. We went to the literature, and after going through the voluminous material on adult stress, we found only a few articles relating to stress in childhood. All had a typical adult-dominated perspective, that is, adults decided what was probably stressful to kids and tested them with it. One thing we've learned over fourteen years is the importance of talking to children—and more importantly, listening to what they say. So we went back to the source, and we asked, "What are the things that make you feel bad, get upset, or worried?" And they generated a list of items, shown in table 14–2.

These items fall into three clusters: (1) a group that represent parental conflict (parents arguing in front of the child, parents separating); (2) a peer-related group; and (3) a group related to dislocation (moving and changing schools). When we used this list in a national population of about 2,500 fifth graders, we were able to demonstrate significant associations between the frequency of feel bad items and mental health status items like feeling sad a lot, liking oneself, worrying and even a psychosomatic complaint called "being tired" (Lewis, Seigel, and Lewis, 1984).

There were a couple of items on this list that were enlightening to us—one of the worst items was, "Not spending enough time with my parents." We also found kids felt bad when they were "pressured to do something" they didn't want to do. It occurred to us that perhaps this had some relevance for children's risk-taking behaviors.

Dares

Once more we went back to the source (but a different group) and began talking to children in grades 5–7, asking them, "Have you ever been dared to do something?" Almost every child said he or she had, so we asked, "What have you been dared to do?" After we collected several hundred answers, we inductively derived classifications. Table 14–3 shows what kids say they were dared to do by other kids. Violent behavior includes fighting other kids and knocking down old ladies. Personal risk may involve jumping out of trees or running across the freeway. Sex begins early—kissing first, intercourse later. Stealing, swearing, cheating—most need no interpretation. Pranks may be "throwing water on somebody." House rules are parent-established rules.

The next question we asked was, "How did they try to get you to do it?" We classified what children said into one of the ten categories. Some children said, "I *dare* you to do it." Others said, "*Why* don't you . . . ?" Others used name calling, "You're a chicken if you don't"; still others used threats, "I'll beat you up." Others used peer exclusion, "You won't be one of the gang." Some deemphasized risks, "Come on, it won't hurt you," or engaged in blackmail, "I'll tell if you don't," or bribes, "I'll give you money."

Table 14–2
Responses to Question: What Things Make You Feel Bad?

Parents	Peers	Dislocation
Parents arguing	Feeling sick	Moving
Not spending enough time with mom/dad	Not good at sports	Changing schools
Parents separate	Not enough money	
Fight with parents over house rules	Not able to dress the way I want	
Homework not done on time	Nothing to do	
Pressured for grades	Being late for school	
	Being smaller	
	Being bigger/overweight	
	Not getting along with teacher	
	Left out of group	
	Body changing	
	Pressured to try something new	

Table 14–3
Types of Dares: What Did They Try to Get You to Do?

Category	Examples
Violence	Vandalism to property or cars Violence toward adults Fight another child
Personal risk	Jump out of tree Run across freeway
Substance abuse	Smoke cigarettes or pot Drink alcohol Take drugs
Sexual act	Hug, kiss, flirt Have intercourse
Steal	Take money, property
Truancy	Ditch school Skip class
Swear	Call — a —
Break house rules	Stay out late Sneak out after bedtime
Cheat	Copy from another on test
Prank	Throw water on someone Ring doorbells

Next, we asked, "So what did you say and do in response?" Some of them just said no. (Unfortunately, not enough.) Some of them said, "No, because I'll get sick, or I'll get in trouble." Others said, "I'm sorry, I have to go to the bathroom" (excuse). Others just went to the bathroom (avoidance). Some of them made very sophisticated remarks, "If I have to do that to be your friend, I'm not sure I want to be your friend." Counter-threats and counter-name-calling also were evident.

Table 14–4 shows the prevalence of techniques used. Just asking people to do something seems to be sufficient in junior high. Name calling falls off among older kids. (Apparently that isn't cool any longer.)

Table 14–5 illustrates data from school children in grades 5–8, showing the prevalence of these dares. There were more than 700 children in the study (Lewis and Lewis, 1984). Violence-related dares account for about 20 percent across the four age groups. Dares placing someone at personal risk are more common in elementary school and less frequent among junior high students. On the other hand, sexual activities are the subject of dares more often in eighth grade. More young girls than boys are dared to engage in sexual activities by groups or by other individuals. We asked the kids about the social context in which challenges took place. (Who was involved?) One individual of the same sex was the challenger for almost half the group. "Gang daring" was much more common among boys than girls. However, girls reported being subject to pressure by mixed groups (both boys and girls) rather than single-sex gangs.

ACT for Kids

About the same time we were involved in studying dares and developing the feel bad scale, we were approached by the Center for Interdisciplinary Research in Immunologic Diseases at UCLA. We were asked if we would be interested in developing a curriculum for asthmatic children to teach them self-management of their illness. We agreed, and it took four years to make good on the promise. We decided to use an approach that involved teaching the same content to parents and children *separately* for about an hour, and then merge them to allow sharing of experiences.

To aid learning, we used a simplifying paradigm involving the traffic light colors red, yellow, and green. The analogy involves learning to drive carefully, of being "in the driver's seat." Session 1 focuses on what asthma is, the earliest symptoms (warning symptoms) and patterns of symptom progression. Session 2 is called roadblocks. We teach aggravators or challenges in the environment and how some can be avoided. Session 3 is what to do (taking medicines) and when to do it (tune-ups). This is the only session that involves a physician.

The curriculum was designed to be almost doctor-proof. Our experiences suggest that doctors, in general, have too much information to be good health

Table 14–4
How Did They Try to Get You to Do It?

Technique	Examples
Dare	I dare you to . . .
Ask/urge	Come on, let's . . . why don't you . . .?
Name calling	You're a chicken if you don't.
Physical force	I'll beat you up if you don't.
Group membership	Everyone is doing it; You have to do it if you want to belong.
Minimize risk	It won't hurt you; we won't get caught.
Make appealing	It'll be a blast; you'll feel good.
Bribe	I'll give you $5 if you . . .
Blackmail	I'll tell your mom that you did it, even if you don't.

Table 14–5
Prevalence of Dares by Grade
(*Percent*)

	Grade				
Dare	*5* *N = 174*	*6* *N = 168*	*7* *N = 278*	*8* *N = 151*	*All* *N = 771*
Physical risk					
Violence	20.5	16.7	21.9	25.5[a]	21.9
Personal risk	21.8[a]	23.2	6.7	6.5	11.9
Substance abuse	8.3	5.0	8.6	6.2	6.8
Sexual act	7.7	7.9	7.9	16.4[b]	10.4
Social risk					
Steal	8.3	11.6	8.5	10.7	10.1
Ditch school	0	1.4	10.1	3.1	4.9
Swear	3.8	0.7	3.4	2.3	2.7
Break house rules	1.9	8.6	1.5	3.8	3.4
Cheat	0	1.4	5.2	0	2.2
Miscellaneous					
Prank	8.9	5.8	5.8	9.5	7.5
Not a dare	5.1	14.4	7.6	12.2	9.6
Unclassified	13.7	3.3	11.5	3.8	8.6

Differential sex reporting ($p < 0.01$).

[a]Males > females.

[b]Females > males.

educators. When you ask them to talk to kids about asthma, you get a grand rounds lecture. It's difficult for them to know how much is enough. This curriculum was designed to be taught by an elementary school teacher, who runs the children's groups. If she has a child with asthma and insight into the problem, that's a bonus, but she doesn't have to, because the content is there. If she is a good teacher, she can teach all the material without being an expert. The parent's group is run by a nurse. We chose a nurse, one who has dealt with pulmonary disease or asthma, because parents have lots of medical questions. The parents' group serves as an educational forum as well as a group whose orientations are shifted from "good parents give their children the medicine," to a view that children can responsibly take medicines on their own. In most groups, there is at least one parent in the crowd who says, "Oh, we do that all the time; that's nothing new." One begins to see a shift in normative values among parents who begin to think, "Maybe my child would be okay if I allowed him to take the medicine on his own.

Decision making is the focus of lesson 4. Teaching decision-making skills (Janis and Mann, 1977) to children *is* possible and important. How to balance my wants and needs (lesson 5, maintenance and service) is the only session concerned with health in the broader sense.

We developed a conceptual framework for this program, and I am pleased to report that social science does work in action. The outcomes we wanted to affect were emergency room use and hospitalization. Both required improved compliance with an adequate medical regimen, the use of relaxation techniques (which kids learn rapidly), and a reduction in panic associated with episodes. To achieve these goals, one has to have changes in the home environment, including changes in the child's access to and use of medicines. The medicines have to go to the kids' room or a place they can get them when they need them. And this is mediated by family dynamics. Our experiences suggest that if you don't get both parents in, you're in for a tough time.

We conducted a randomized controlled trial at the Southern California Permanente (Kaiser) group in Los Angeles, involving children with asthma severe enough to require medication 25 percent of the days of a week. These kids, who had averaged two to three days of hospitalization in the previous year, were randomized into control and experimental groups. They were a mixed crowd with equal numbers of whites, Hispanics, and blacks. These children had had asthma for seven or eight years. After following both groups for one year, we found emergency room visits were significantly decreased in the experimental group. The data, however, document the importance of parental involvement. Three-fourths (sixteen of twenty-four) of children who had both parents present at the lessons had significant reduction in emergency room visits versus about a third of those accompanied by only one parent (Lewis et al., in press).

It was serendipitous that members of the Board of the Asthma and Allergy Foundation of America (AAFA) saw a slide-tape we made to teach teachers how to teach ACT (asthma care training). Because Dr. Gary Rachelefsky, a pediatric allergist who was the subject-matter expert of our team, takes care of one of the children of the producer of *Hill Street Blues,* we had access to some of the cast of that television program. Their presence made for a polished product. AAFA approached us in February 1984, saying it would like to buy the ACT curriculum. The regents of the University of California wouldn't sell, but granted the foundation an exclusive license. In May 1984, we began training teaching teams from the chapters and other groups who will distribute the program nationally.

Circle of Care

Circle of Care resulted from our being approached by a foundation in San Francisco, indicating interest in our development of a health education curriculum for Mexican-American children along the U.S.-Mexican border. Dr. Faustina Solis, provost of the Third College at the University of California at San Diego, had worked with Cesar Chavez and was well known to this foundation. Working with her in this project, we went to San Ysidro, on the border opposite Tijuana, to begin to create what I perceived would be an Anglo version of David Morley's Child to Child program. That is, we were going to teach children how to take care of themselves while their parents were working in the fields.

I refer to this as the "grapes of wrath" curriculum, because that's the illusion we had at the beginning. We interviewed a few families; we talked to school personnel; we found the schools wanted us to do something to improve communication between schools and the families. The families wanted us to do something about safety. What became clear was the problem was a lot more complex than we first thought.

We decided to move two UCLA doctoral students in anthropology to San Ysidro for a year, and they provided us a picture of a complex community made up of fourth-generation families who had lived along the border for decades, as well as recent immigrants. The question was how to meet the needs of the schools and the families at the same item. How could we deal with a process parents viewed as beneficial, but which is potentially destructive to family ties? Schools are the ubiquitous social escalators by which their children can become better competitors in the quest for the good life. But in the process, schools socialize children from another culture away from their families. Children become rapidly acculturated into American society,—an English-speaking society,—as a by-product of the process designed to make them better competitors in the world to come.

By this time, we had had experiences in dealing with the ACT parents, but in the case of San Ysidro, we did not have the rallying focus of a sick child. It's easy to talk to parents whose children are wheezing and are going to emergency rooms. Their attention comes easily. But in San Ysidro, parents have a lot of other things on their minds. How could we (the schools) begin to communicate with them?

As we looked at the communication pattern in the schools, it was apparent that the principals and the teachers talked together, and the teachers talked to the child, but the only time the teacher talked to the parents was when the child had problems. There was no dialogue among child, parent, and teacher, and the question was how to create such an interaction. We finally decided one way to do it was to go back to our favorite "stickers and games" approach, and to design curriculum modules with a lesson at the beginning of each module which required homework, to which *only the parents had the right answer.*

The first unit is called "El Arbor de Los Zapatos" ("The Tree of Shoes"). There are stickers of shoes, belonging to mother and father, brother, etc. A large drawing of a tree is used to represent the family. Its branches correspond to the functions of the family—companionship, support, food preparation, and so on. Children put the appropriate shoes on branches illustrating who does what in the family. The usual conclusion is that almost everybody does every role in the family, and the stereotypic roles people think about do not exist.

This is followed by a family tree homework assignment which kids had to bring back. This tree, when completed, showed where parents and grandparents were born. Obviously, only the parents can help complete this tree.

There is a safety module with eight or nine safety "maps" or cartoon drawings which the kids take home, and *with their parents* go through the house and the yard, looking for existing hazards, circling them, and seeing if they can do anything about them (Sometimes, this is difficult).

Homework from the nutrition module features favorite family recipes. We discovered in one of our earlier adventures in schools that one of the biggest problems in school health education is the adults' (teachers') personal beliefs or values. For our first-aid lessons, we decided to bypass the teachers. We designed posters for school bulletin boards, demonstrating the right way and the wrong way to do things—stop a nosebleed, care for a cut, and so on—so kids get some information while they are standing in line for lunch.

Summary

What have we learned from all this? First, children are enormously competent; they are so competent that some adults are threatened and insulate themselves from this reality by devaluating children's abilities. It is disturbing to some adults to see how competent children are, and how little they need us for some things we want to do (as well as how much they need us for other things that we don't want to do.)

Second, adults are part of the problem/solution and cannot be ignored. We naively started our research, hoping we could work only with children. In each case, with the exception of the dare program for adolescents (looking at risk-taking behaviors), we have unraveled each knotty problem back to the family. Conclusion: one must work with the family.

How do you work with a family? You engage them in active, discovery learning, and you grab them in their values. One has to go beyond the information transfer/cognitive sphere, and deal with their feelings. When there are sick children, parents are "engageable," if you have something to offer because they have a problem. On the other hand, what do you do when you have children and parents for whom health is not salient? We learned how abstract the term *health* is for children, how casually we use it, but how really hurt-oriented they are. Few children are interested in that abstract future-oriented admonition, "Live a good life today, so you'll live longer tomorrow." Engaging parents can be done, but it requires ingenuity.

Parents play a significant role in shaping a child's health-related beliefs and behaviors. Those who take care of families, or who look at the family unit, can see the origins of the next generation's health behaviors. Conflicts with parents are significant sources of "feeling bad." Children identify as sources of feeling bad the daily hassles in their lives. Chronic strains—being too short, being left out, not having enough money, and above all, not having anything to do—are major sources of distress to children. Our impression is that there is far more subclinical depression in childhood than we have recognized to date.

Dares are a normal part of growing up, as Erikson notes (1950). But dares, we believe, also contribute to the development of risk-taking behaviors. However, kids can be inoculated; we already have programs teaching kids via kids their same age how to say no to pressures to smoke cigarettes. We are beginning to do this in drug abuse. The extent to which children can be taught to say no to avoid things that put them at personal risk of violence is yet to be explored.

Finally, management of chronic illness in childhood depends on opening channels of communication between parent and child and transfer of real responsibility to the child. One of the touching aspects of the ACT program is listening to interview tapes of families, particularly fathers, talking about the sessions. One father said, "I used to believe my kid was a creep, just somebody who was trying to get out of something. Since we have been coming to this class, I've listened and I understand that he has a problem. And I am part of the problem."

Solutions to the problems I have described depend upon interpersonal skills. Fortunately, that's something we can teach if the learner is receptive. Practice of the new pediatrics will depend more on listening than doing and, above all, on recognition of the basic competence of children.

References

Avnett, H.H.: *Physician Service Patterns and Illness Rates.* New York, New York Group Health Insurance Co., 1967.

Erikson, H.: *Childhood and Society.* New York, Norton, 1950.

Frogatt, P., and Merritt, J.D. Consultation in general practice: analysis of individuals' frequencies. *Br. J. Prev. Soc. Med.23*:1–9, 1969.

Janis, I.L., and Mann, L.: *Decision Making: A Psychological Analysis of Conflict, Choice and Commitment.* New York, The Free Press, 1977.

Lewis, C.E., and Lewis, M.A.: Peer-pressure and risk-taking behaviors in children. *AJPH* 74:580–584, 1984.

Lewis, C.E., Lewis, M.A., Lorimer, A.A., and Palmer, B.B.: Child-initiated care: the use of school nursing services in an adult-free system. *Pediatrics 1977:60:499–507.*

Lewis, C.E., Rachelefsky, G.S., Lewis, M.A., de la Sota, A., and Kaplan, M.S.: A randomized trial of A.C.T. (asthma care training) for kids. *Pediatrics* (in press).

Lewis, C.E., Siegel, J.M., and Lewis, M.A.: Feeling bad: exploring sources of distress among pre-adolescent children. *AJPH* 74:117–122, 1984.

15

Fathers, Families, and Children: New Perspectives

Ross D. Parke

Fathers are increasingly recognized as important contributors to the development of infants and children. To understand the role of fathers, a systems perspective is helpful. According to this viewpoint, it is important to recognize the interdependence among the roles and functions of all family members. Families are best viewed as social systems; in order to understand one member of the system, such as fathers, the complementary behaviors of other members need to be recognized and assessed.

The father influences interaction in the family directly as well as indirectly. He directly influences his wife and children in his relationship with them; he can also indirectly affect them by influencing the nature of the mother-child relationship, that is, through changes in the way in which his wife treats their offspring. In turn, women affect their children indirectly through their husbands by modifying both the quantity and quality of father-child interaction.

To complement a family systems view, fathers and families are also considered from an ecological perspective. Specifically, the embededness of fathers and families within a variety of other social systems, including both formal and informal support networks, merits recognition. Therefore, the role of these systems in modifying fathers' role in the family is examined.

The Father's Role in Infancy

To illustrate some of the ways in which fathers contribute to early development in the family context, let us consider the father's role in early infancy. A number of questions are relevant here: (1) Do fathers play an active role in early infancy? (2) Do they show similar or different patterns of behavior than mothers? (3) Do mothers and fathers play distinctive roles?

In a series of observational studies of fathers and mothers interacting with their newborn infants and infants over the first year of life, my colleagues and I have found a number of encouraging findings—encouraging in view of the increasing pressures on fathers for participation in the care and nurturance of infants and children (Parke, 1979, 1981). First, in our observations of mothers, fathers, and their newborn infants in the hospital setting, we find that fathers—when given the opportunity—are interested and active participants. They are just as likely to hold their infants, and the behaviors that they direct to their newborns are very similar to those of mothers. Fathers engage in a wide variety of behaviors that we generally view as "nurturant." The similarities in quality of maternal and paternal behavior are more striking than are the differences. These patterns are not restricted to American parents; Parke, Grossman, and Tinsley (1981) found similar patterns in a sample of West German fathers and mothers with their newborn infants.

A striking feature that fathers as well as mothers exhibit is a marked change in speech patterns when addressing their young infants. According to Phillips and Parke (1981), who observed fathers and mothers during both feeding and play sessions, parents of either sex spoke in shorter phrases when talking to infants than when speaking to each other. Second, fathers as well as mothers repeated phrases more frequently when talking to infants. Fathers and mothers were both sensitive to contextual cues as well. During feeding, the rate of speech of both parents was slower and the pauses longer than during play. Alternatively, parents repeated phrases more during play than during feeding and used a conversational style of speech (for example, questions and attention-getting tactics) more during play than feeding sesions. These contextual differences suggest that these parental speech adjustments serve to elicit and maintain infant attention. In turn, by focusing the infant's attention more closely on the parents' faces, the infant's learning of the characteristics of the parents' voice and face may be facilitated. Therefore, modifications in parental speech may serve to help familiarize the infant with the caregivers and, in turn, promote closer parent-infant relationships.

Our argument is not to suggest father as a substitute for mother, but to emphasize the importance of studying both fathers and mothers in the context of the family unit. In our studies, comparisons of mothers alone with their infants and fathers alone with their infants in contrast to mother-father and infant together in the family triad suggests that mothers and fathers provide support and stimulation for each other that alters the behavior of each toward the baby. For example, parents smile at their babies and examine them more in the triad context than when each is alone with the infant (Parke and O'Leary, 1976). Parental affect and interest is enhanced by the presence of the spouse. In turn, these observations suggest that our understanding of fathers (and mothers) will be increased by considering the family triad as opposed to the heretofore more common research strategy of considering the mother-child and father-child dyads separately.

Role Differentiation in Infancy

In spite of the interest and involvement of fathers, role differentiation begins early. In our studies of relatively traditional families (Parke, 1979), we have consistently found that mothers feed and caretake more than fathers—both in the hospital and at home. Even when adjustments are made for the amount of time available for caregiving activities of mothers and fathers, the same pattern of greater mother participation is evident (Parke, 1981; Parke and Tinsley, 1981). This pattern is present not only in U.S. samples (Kotelchuck, 1976), but in other countries, such as Great Britain (Richards, Dunn, and Antonis, 1977), Australia (Russell, 1983), and France and Belgium (Szalai, 1972). There are, however, wide individual differences across families in the level of father participation.

Fathers, however, are not necessarily less competent than mothers to care for young infants. In our studies (Parke and Sawin, 1975, 1980), we have found that fathers are sensitive to infant signals during feeding—an important skill to maintain food intake successfully during a feeding session. In addition, infant milk consumption is similar whether mother or father feeds the baby. Fathers do have the capability to execute caregiving activities competently even though they generally contribute less time to this type of activity than mothers do.

Play: The Distinctive Roles of Mother and Father

Although mothers contribute to caregiving more than fathers, fathers are not uninvolved with their infants. Both mothers and fathers are active playmates for their infants and children; however, fathers devote a higher proportion of their time with their children to play than mothers. For example, in one study of middle-class families, Kotelchuck (1976) found that fathers devote nearly 40 percent of their time with their infants to play, while mothers spend about 25 percent of their time in play. Further evidence comes from Lamb (1977) who observed interactions among mother, father, and infant in their homes at seven to eight months and again at twelve to thirteen months. Lamb found marked differences in the reasons that fathers and mothers pick up their infants: fathers were more likely to hold the babies to play with them and mothers were more likely to hold them for caretaking purposes.

Fathers and mothers differ not only in quantity but also in the style of play. Fathers' play is more likely to be physical and arousing, while mothers' play is more verbal, didactic, and toy-mediated (see Parke, 1979; Parke and Tinsley, 1981; Power and Parke, 1981).

To illustrate these stylistic differences, Power and Parke (1981) videotaped mothers and fathers while playing with their firstborn, eight-month-old infants in a laboratory playroom. Fathers played more bouncing and lifting games than mothers. In contrast, mothers played more watching games in which a toy is presented and made salient by moving or shaking it. The mother-father difference in lifting games was qualified by sex of the infant; the game was played primarily by fathers of boys.

Recent observations of father- and mother-infant interaction in unstructured home contexts with older infants indicates similar mother-father differences in style of play. Lamb (1977), in an observational study of infants at seven and eight months and again at twelve to thirteen months in their home, found that fathers engage in more physical, rough-and-tumble, and unusual play activities than mothers. Power and Parke (1981) found that fathers engaged in more physical play than mothers in home observations of infants seven and a half and ten and a half months old. Most recently, MacDonald and Parke (1984a), in a study of the play interaction patterns between mothers and fathers and their three and four year olds, found that fathers engaged in more physical play with their children than mothers, while mothers engaged in more object-mediated play with their children than fathers. According to a recent survey of 390 families, fathers' distinctive role in a physical play partner changes with their age, that is, as they become older, there is a decreased likelihood that they will engage their children physically (MacDonald and Parke, 1984b).

What are the implications of those stylistic differences between mothers' and fathers' play styles? In a recent study, MacDonald and Parke (1984a) examined the relationship between father-toddler play and peer-peer interaction. Specifically, fathers and their three-year-old boys and girls were observed in twenty minutes of structured play in their homes. In addition, teachers ranked these children in terms of their popularity among their preschool classmates. For both boys and girls, fathers who were rated as exhibiting high levels of physical play with their children and elicited high levels of positive affect in their children during the play sessions had children who received the highest peer popularity ratings. For boys, however, this pattern was qualified by the fathers' level of directiveness. Boys whose fathers were both highly physical and low in directiveness received the highest popularity ratings, while the boys whose fathers were highly directive received lower popularity scores. Possibly, children who interact with a physically playful father and, at the same time, have an opportunity to regulate the pace and tempo of the interaction, a characteristic of low-directive fathers, learn how to recognize and send emotional signals during social interactions. "Through physically playful interaction with their parents, especially fathers, children may be learning the social communicative value of their own affective displays as well as how to use these signals to regulate the social behavior of others. In turn, they may learn to decode accurately the social and affective signals of other social partners" (MacDonald and Parke, 1984a). This issue clearly merits more attention by researchers.

The Modifiability of Father's Role in the Family

A variety of factors may affect the extent to which the traditional role allocations of father as playmate and mother as caregiver are in fact valid. Changes in type of childbirth and birth status (for example, prematurity, perinatal trauma) and work status of women are all modifiers of both mothers' and fathers' level of participation in caregiving as well as the amounts of play exhibited by fathers and mothers. More importantly, these shifts illustrate the capacity of both mothers and fathers to change their traditional patterns of behavior in response to new conditions and demands.

Recent research suggests that certain medical practices, such as caesarean childbirth, can alter the fathers' level of participation in routine caretaking activities. In a recent study, Pedersen et al. (1980b) found that fathers of caesarean-delivered infants engaged in significantly more caregiving at five months than fathers in a comparison group whose infants were vaginally delivered. While the fathers of the caesarean-delivered infants were more likely to share caregiving responsibilities in several different areas on an equal basis with the mothers, fathers in the comparison sample tended to "help out" with the mothers still doing the major proportion of caregiving. Others confirm this general finding (Grossman, Eichler, and Winickoff, 1980; Vietze et al., 1980). These data suggest that mothers, as a result of the surgery, are unable to assume a fully active role in caregiving during the early postpartum weeks. Fathers, as a result of their increased involvement in early care, continue this caregiving activity even after the time that mother is able to resume a more active role.

Another situation that may increase father's role in early caregiving is the premature birth of a baby. Investigators in both England and the United States have recently found that fathers of premature infants are more active in feeding, diapering, and bathing their infants than fathers of full-term babies, both in the hospital and at home (Hawthorne, Richards, and Callon, 1978; Yogman, 1980). The fathers' more active participation in caregiving is particularly helpful because premature infants usually need to be fed more often than full-term infants, and they experience more feeding disturbances. Premature infants also can be less satisfying to feed and to interact with because they are often less responsive to parental stimulation than full-term infants. By sharing more than usual in caregiving, the father of a premature infant relieves the mother of some of this responsibility, giving the mother some time to rest, but also indirectly influencing the baby by positively affecting the relationship between mother and baby. The father's support is important in other ways as well. Often a premature infant is kept in the hospital for a period of time, and the father can play an important role by visiting and becoming acquainted with the baby during this period. Furthermore, recent research by Minde et al. (1978) has shown that mothers who have supportive husbands tend to visit their premature babies in the hospital more often, and that mothers who visit more have fewer later parenting problems than mothers who visit less frequently. Again, we see that fathers can influence their infants indirectly by affecting the mother-infant relationship. Understanding the father's role in infant development clearly requires that the father's behavior be viewed in the context of his role within the family.

Changes in women's employment status are also resulting in shifts in the level of father participation in child care. In a recent national sample, Pleck (1979) found that husbands of women who were employed outside the home devoted significantly more hours per week to child care. These changes toward father assumption of a larger share of child-care tasks may not only improve his relationship with his children, but may also alter the mother-child relationship by relieving mother of some of the routine child care.

The increases in maternal employment outside the home, however, may affect play patterns as well. In contrast to the usual finding that fathers play more than mothers, Pedersen et al. (1980a) found that mothers played more with their five-month-old infants if the mothers held a job outside the home. Since the observations took place in the evenings after both parents came home from their jobs, Pedersen and colleagues suggest that the mother played more as a way of reestablishing contact with her baby after being away from home for the day. One result was that fathers in these two-income families had less play time with their infants. Family work organization can clearly affect father's status as primary playmate. Whether these mothers continue to be active play partners as the baby grows older remains unanswered. In summary, neither caregiving or play patterns usually associated with mother and father roles are fixed and unalterable; rather in response to changing circumstances family roles are open to modification.

Increasing Support for Fathers: An Ecological Analysis

In the light of the social and economic changes that are promoting increased father involvement in the caregiving of infants, it is important to provide cultural supports for fathering activities. First, there needs to be an increase in opportunities for learning fathering skills. These supports can assume a variety of forms such as the provision of both prepartum and postpartum training classes for fathers to learn and practice caretaking skills and to learn about normal infant development. Parenthood training, however, need not wait until pregnancy or childbirth. As many have advocated (Levine, Pleck, and Lamb, 1983), such training, including information about infant development and infant care, as well as the economic realities of child rearing, should be provided in high school or even at an earlier age in light of the increasing number of teenage pregnancies.

Second, there needs to be increased opportunities to practice and implement these skills. To provide the opportunity to share in the early caretaking of the infant, paternity leaves should be given wider support. These leaves could be usefully extended to the pregnancy period to permit the father to attend classes and to share in obstetric visits with the mother. Other shifts in societal arrangements, such as shorter work weeks, flexible working hours, and split jobs, whereby a man and woman share the same position, are all changes that will increase the potential participation of men in fathering (Russell and Radin, 1983; Parke and Tinsley, 1984).

Another positive change involves modification of maternity ward visiting arrangements to permit fathers to have more extended contact with the newborn infants. To date, father-infant interaction in the newborn period is largely under institutional control. As a result, it is frequently hospital policy rather than father interest that determines the degree of father-newborn involvement. In the United States, there is an increasing trend toward greater father participation in both labor and delivery, and the opportunities for contact between father and infant during the early postpartum period are increasing.

However, providing the opportunity for contact is only a first step and may be insufficient to significantly modify either mother or father involvement with their infants (Goldberg, 1983; Lamb and Hwang, 1982). In addition, supportive intervention that may aid fathers in learning caretaking and social interactive skills can be provided during this early postpartum period as well. Recent evidence of the impact of hospital-centered intervention for fathers comes from several recent investigations.

Intervention can assume a variety of forms. Recent work has shown that exposure to a demonstration of Brazelton Neonatal Assessment Scale (BNAS) can have positive effects on the quality of father-infant interaction. Beal (1984) exposed first-time fathers to a Brazelton demonstration on their two-to three-day-old infant. A control group of fathers received no intervention. To assess the impact of this brief interventon, father-infant interaction was assessed at eight weeks postpartum. During the paternal-infant interaction session, the interaction patterns among the intervention group were characterized by a higher degree of father-infant mutuality. In addition, fathers who received the BNAS demonstration perceived their infants as less difficult than fathers in the control group. These findings suggest that both father-infant interaction patterns as well as paternal perceptions can be modified by this type of intervention. Since all the fathers also attended prenatal classes and both labor and delivery, it would be interesting to assess whether this type of demonstration would be effective for less interested and involved fathers.

Another approach involves direct teaching through the use of a videotaped intervention. In this study (Parke et al., 1980), fathers viewed a videotape that portrayed other males engaged in play, feeding, and diapering. All fathers received the intervention in the hospital in the postpartum period. In contrast to a control group who saw no videotape, the fathers exposed to this fifteen-minute presentation were more knowledgeable about infant perceptual capacities, were more responsive to their infants during feeding and play and fed and diapered their babies more often at three months in the home. However, the effect held only for fathers of boys; fathers of girls were unaffected by the intervention. The same sex effect is similar to other reports of greater father involvement with sons than daughters (see Parke, 1979, for a review of this research).

Further evidence of the effectiveness of a film intervention during the postpartum period comes from a recent study by Arbuckle (1983). In this project, Arbuckle used a film intervention developed by Parke et al. (1980). Entitled *Becoming a Family*, the film demonstrated the same behavior, such as feeding and diapering, playing, and infant capabilities as were included in the Parke et al. (1980) film intervention. In contrast to the earlier film, this film depicted both mothers and fathers actively engaged in caregiving and game playing. Assessment of the impact of the film four to six weeks later indicated that first-time fathers who saw the film in comparison to a no-film control group of fathers had greater knowledge of infant sensory and cognitive capabilities and were higher in their perception of the importance of providing infant affection and stimulation. Moreover, the experimental fathers reported higher levels of involvement in the daily caregiving of their babies four to six weeks after the intervention. No infant sex differences were reported. In spite of the limitation of this study by the reliance on self-report measures, the similarity of the findings across these two film intervention studies underscores the potential value of this approach for modifying paternal behavior. Further work is clearly justified; particularly important would be studies that isolate the effective components of these film intervention programs. Finally, comparison of film interventions with other types of interventions, such as medical staff instruction, discussion groups, or information booklets, would be helpful. By addressing the relative effectiveness of different approaches, the most optimal and most cost-effective procedures for different groups will become evident.

Another set of studies illustrates the potential of health care providers, such as pediatricians, to play a supportive role for parents of young children. Although these studies have focused on mothers, these types of interventions could provide a useful strategy for promoting father parenting competence as well. In a study by Chamberlin (1979), mothers who participated in an educational program concerning child development during pediatric well-baby visits increased their knowledge of child development and their perceptions of being supported in the caregiving role. A related study (Whitt and Casey, 1982) suggests that mothers who were provided with an office-based pediatric intervention program emphasizing physical and preventive child care, developmental norms, and information on infant communication abilities during well-baby exams demonstrated a more positive relationship with their infants. The potential of this type of intervention for fathers will depend, in part, on changes in the flexibility of work schedules, which would permit fathers to participate more regularly in visits to the pediatrician.

Although the full potential of hospital and other health care facilities as settings for providing support for fathers is not yet realized, these studies illustrate their value for modifying the parenting behavior of fathers as well as mothers.

Conclusions

It is clear that fathers play an active and important role in infancy and early childhood. Fathers and mothers each contribute in unique and different ways. Finally, it is important to provide support for fathers if their potential contribution to family development is to be fully realized. By supporting fathers, all members of the family system will be enhanced—fathers, mothers, and their children.

References

Arbuckle, M.B.: The effects of educational intervention on fathers' relationships with their infants. Doctoral dissertation, University of North Carolina at Greensboro, 1983.

Beal, J.A.: The effect of demonstration of the Brazelton Neonatal Assessment Scale on the father-infant relationship. Paper presented at the International Conference of Infant Studies, New York, April 1984.

Chamberlin, R.W.: Effects of educating mothers about child development in physicians' offices on mother and child functioning over time. Paper presented at the American Psychological Association, New York, 1979.

Goldberg, S.: Parent-infant bonding: another look. *Child Dev.* 54:1355–1382, 1983.

Grossman, F.K., Eichler, L.S., and Winickoff, S.A.: *Pregnancy, Birth and Parenthood.* San Francisco, Jossey-Bass, 1980.

Hawthorne, J.T., Richards, M.P.M., and Callon, M.: A study of parental visiting of babies in a special care unit. In Brimble-Combe, F.S.W., Richards, M.P.M., and Roberton, N.R.C. (eds.): *Early Separation and Special Care Nurseries.* London, Simp/Heinemann Medical Books.

Hoffman, L.W.: Increased fathering: effects on the mother. In Lamb, M.E., and Sagi, A. (eds.): *Fatherhood and Family Policy.* Hillsdale, N.J., Erlbaum.

Kotelchuck, M. The infant's relationship to the father. In Lamb, M.E. (ed.): *The Role of the Father in Child Development.* New York, Wiley, 1976.

Lamb, M.E.: Father-infant and mother-infant interaction in the first year of life. *Child Dev.* 48:167–181, 1977.

Lamb, M.E., and Hwang, C.: Maternal attachment and mother-infant bonding: a critical review. In Lamb, M.E., and Brown, A.L. (eds.): *Advances in Developmental Psychology,* Vol. 2. Hillsdale, N.J., Erlbaum, 1982.

Levine, J.A.: *Who Will Raise the Children? New Options for Fathers and Mothers.* New York, Lippincott, 1976.

Levine, J.A., Pleck, J.H., and Lamb, M.E.: In Lamb, M.E. and Sagi, A. (eds.): *Fatherhood and Family Policy.* Hillsdale, N.J., Erlbaum, 1983.

MacDonald, K., and Parke, R.D.: Bridging the gap: parent-child play interaction and peer interactive competence. *Child Dev.,* 1984a (in press).

MacDonald, K., and Parke, R.D.: A survey of parent-child physical play: sex and age differences. Unpublished manuscript, University of Illinois, 1984b.

Minde, K., Trehub, S., Corter, C., Boukydis, C., Celhoffer, B., and Marton, P.: Mother-child relationships in the premature nursery: an observational study. *Pediatrics* 61:373–379, 1978.

Parke, R.D.: Perspectives on father-infant interaction. In J. Osofsky (ed.): *The Handbook of Infant Development*. New York, Wiley, 1979.

Parke, R.D.: *Fathers*. Cambridge: Harvard University Press, 1981.

Parke, R.D., Grossmann, K., and Tinsley, B.R.: Father-mother-infant interaction in the newborn period: a German-American comparison. In Field, T. (ed.): *Culture and Early Interactions*. Hillsdale, N.J., Erlbaum, 1981.

Parke, R.D., Hymel, S., Power, T.G., and Tinsley, B.R.: Fathers and risk: a hospital based model of intervention. In Sawin, D.B., Hawkins, R.D., Walker, L.O., and Penticuff, J.H. (eds.): *Pyschosocial Risks in Infant-Environment Transactions*. New York, Bruner/Mazel, 1980.

Parke, R.D., and O'Leary, S.E.: Father-mother-infant interaction in the newborn period: some findings, some observations and some unresolved issues. In Riegel, K., and Meacham, J. (eds.): *The Developing Individual in a Changing World*. Vol. 2, *Social and Environmental Issues*. The Hauge, Mouton, 1976.

Parke, R.D., and Sawin, D.B.: Infant characteristics and behavior as elicitors of maternal and paternal responsibility in the newborn period. Paper presented at the biennial meeting of the Society for Research in Child Development, Denver, April 1975.

Parke, R.D., and Sawin, D.B. The family in early infancy: social interactional and attitudinal analyses. In Pedersen, F. (ed.): *The Father-Infant Relationship: Observational Studies in a Family Context*. New York, Praeger, 1980.

Parke, R.D., and Tinsley, B.R.: The father's role in infancy: determinants of involvement in caregiving and play. In Lamb, M. (ed.): *The Role of the Father in Child Development* (2nd ed.). New York, Wiley, 1981.

Pedersen, F.A., Cain, R., Zaslow, M., and Anderson, B.: Variation in infant experience associated with alternative family organization. Paper presented at the International Conference on Infant Studies, New Haven, April 1980a.

Pedersen, F.A., Zaslow, M.T., Cain, R.L., and Anderson, B.J.: Caesarean birth: the importance of a family perspective. Paper presented at the International Conference on Infant Studies, New Haven, April 1980b.

Phillips, D., and Parke, R.D.: Father and mother speech to prelinguistic infants. Unpublished manuscript, University of Illinois, 1981.

Pleck, J.H.: Men's family work: three perspectives and some new data. *Family Coordinator* 28:481–488, 1979.

Power, T.G., and Parke, R.D.: Play as a context for early learning: lab and home analyses. In Sigel, I.E., and Laosa, L.M. (eds.): *The Family as a Learning Environment*. New York, Plenum, 1981.

Richards, M.P.M., Dunn, J.F., and Antonis, B.: Caretaking in the first year of life: the role of fathers and mothers' social isolation. *Child Care Health Dev.* 3:23–26, 1977.

Russell, G.: *The Changing Role of Fathers*. St. Lucia, University of Queensland Press, 1983.

Russell, G., and Radin, N.: Increased paternal participation: the fathers' perspective. In

Lamb, M.E., and Sagi, A. (eds.): *Fatherhood and Family Policy.* Hillsdale, N.J., Erlbaum, 1983.

Sawin, D.B., and Parke, R.D.: Adolescent fathers: some implications from recent research on parental roles. *Ed. Horiz. 55:*38–43, 1976.

Szalai, A. (ed.): *The Use of Time: Daily Activities of Urban and Suburban Populations in Twelve Countries.* The Hague: Mouton, 1972.

Vietze, P.M., McTurk, R.H., McCarthy, M.E., Klein, R.P., and Yarrow, L.J.: Impact of mode of delivery on father- and mother-infant interaction at 6 and 12 months. Paper presented at the International Conference on Infant Studies, New Haven, April 1980.

Whitt, J.K., and Casey, P.H.: The mother-infant relationship and infant development: the effect of pediatric intervention. *Child Dev. 53:*948–956, 1982.

Yogman, M.W.: Development of the father-infant relationship. In Fitzgerald, H., Lester, B., and Yogman, M.W. (eds.): *Theory and Research in Behavioral Pediatrics,* Vol. 1. New York, Plenum Press, 1982.

16
Hypnotherapy with Children: Its Past and Its Potential

Karen N. Olness

E xperience with child hypnotherapy offers the practicing physician unique insights into biobehavioral or psychosomatic issues. Not only is hypnosis an effective therapeutic tool when appropriately used but it also provides communication skills to the physician and a base for psychophysiologic research.

Hypnosis per se has an unfortunate mystique and is both over- and underrated. The primary misconception concerning its use is that someone with magical powers, that is, the hypnotist, imposes behaviors onto a subject who is unaware of what is going on and is not in control. This misconception probably derives from egocentricity on the part of some therapists who would like to be powerful, and wishful thinking on the part of some patients who would like instantaneous cures that involve no effort on their parts.

In fact, all hypnosis is self-hypnosis, although the assistance of a teacher or coach is helpful initially, and is called heterohypnosis. Attainment of therapeutic goals requires effort and practice on the part of patients. For example, the self-hypnosis exercises taught to Olympic contenders in Sweden required nine weeks of daily practice of at least thirty minutes. Many adults do not stay with practice long enough to succeed. Fortunately, children seem to learn more quickly and require less practice and, from a clinical point of view, do better than adults.

A useful clinical definition of hypnosis is "an altered state of awareness in which the person is able to accept suggestions which allow him or her to use his or her mental and physical skills in optimal fashion." This definition does not support the idea that a person untrained and unskilled in guitar playing or figure skating can perform optimally; it does allow for improved performance in the person who has trained in a specific area, and it allows persons to become aware of certain autonomic processes and develop voluntary control of them.

History

Hypnotherapy with children was first applied formally by Franz Mesmer in the late eighteenth century. The Franklin Commission, which evaluated Mesmer's work, studied two children in its remarkable experiments. The commission concluded that the therapeutic successes related, not to magnetic rods, but rather to application of the imagination. Although Mesmer was discredited in France, physicians in England and in other European countries studied and applied his work. Dr. John Elliotson, a well-known English physician, wrote of treating several children with mesmerism and included descriptions of surgery completed while children were in a "mesmeric trance."

James Braid (1795–1880), an English surgeon, coined the word *hypnosis*. His theories were subsequently adopted by Broca, Charcot, Liebault, and Bernheim. He recognized that successful application of imagery skills was central to effective hypnosis. In his writings he noted that he began investigating mesmerism as a complete skeptic but ultimately recognized the hypnotic process to be a valuable addition to available treatments. He wrote, "It appears to me quite certain, that the imagination has never been so much under our control, or capable or being made to act in the same beneficial and uniform manner, by any other mode of management hitherto known."

Dr. Hippolyte Bernheim, a professor at the School of Nancy, founded by Dr. Liebault, published a book in 1884 which represented the first effort to compare hypnotizability from one state to another. He noted a high proportion of somnambulists in children. His emphasis on eye closure and somnambulism in children is very different from our criteria for judging hypnotic responsivity today. Dr. August Forel, Professor of Psychiatry in Zurich, also wrote in the late nineteenth century concerning the treatment of children with hypnotherapy for various habit disorders. Of interest is the fact that Charcot stated that children could not be hypnotized; in fact he had not worked with any children in application of hypnosis and relied on his graduate students for his erroneous information.

Dr. J. Milne Bramwell from England began using hypnotherapy in 1889 and reported many children responsive to his authoritative methods of hypnotic induction. In 1959 Weitzenhoffer published a bibliography of available references on hypnosis in children which spanned the years 1886–1959. It included eighty-seven references of which only thirteen were American. Between 1900 and 1949 there were no articles published on hypnotherapy with children in the American literature. In 1946 an article was published on the use of hypnotherapy in treatment of stuttering. In 1958, in the first issue of the *American Journal of Clinical Hypnosis,* Erickson wrote an article on children and hypnosis. He stressed the ease with which children can experience hypnosis. Wright wrote similarly concerning the natural imagery skills of children and the requirement for naturalistic approaches in teaching hypnotic techniques to them.

However, training in child hypnotherapy in the United States was not formally available until the 1970s. Formal hypnosis workshops were taught in the United States throughout the 1950s and 1960s; however, children were mentioned only briefly and there was insufficient recognition of their innate skills in self-hypnosis and of the potential for therapeutic application in pediatrics. In

1976, the Society for Clinical and Experimental Hypnosis offered a full three-day workshop on hypnosis with children taught by Olness and Gardner, in addition to its workshops on hypnosis in psychotherapy, medicine, and dentistry, as part of its annual meeting program. The American Society of Clinical Hypnosis also began offering separate seminars or workshops on children in connection with its annual meeting as well as its regional workshops.

In 1980, Gardner published a bibliography on available references concerning hypnosis with children published between 1955 and 1978. Dr. Gardner noted that the majority of these papers were clinical in nature and that only a few reflected research, particularly those concerning norms of hypnotizability. Altogether Gardner found 114 references in her search.

The five years from 1979 to 1983 produced more than ninety articles on hypnotherapy with children referenced in *Index Medicus*. Many reflect the beginnings of research studies to explain clinical phenomena previously recorded in publications. Of note is the work in hypnotherapy and pain control reported by Hilgard, Morgan, Varni, Zeltzer and LeBarron. Articles are now being published by conventional pediatric journals, and one can anticipate a geometric increase in this fascinating area which relates to much of pediatric diagnosis and treatment.

Normative studies on hypnotizability in children were published by London and Cooper in 1969, and Morgan and Hilgard in 1973. These studies represent laboratory assessments. They do not correlate well with clinical outcomes, and it seems likely that an important focus of future research will be development of psychological and physiologic predictors of hypnotic responsiveness in children. A difficulty with present hypnotic susceptibility scales is that children tend to score high. They therefore lack sensitivity in predicting which child will be clinically most responsive. There is a need for valid and efficient predictors of clinical responsivity.

Uses

Clinical experience recorded over the past two centuries has documented that hypnotherapeutic interventions can be helpful in acute as well as in chronic or long-term situations. Knowledge of hypnotherapeutic communication techniques is especially useful in emergency situations and can be used not only to increase the comfort level of the injured child but also to program more positive responses for future emergencies that the child may encounter. Hypnotherapy has been used successfully in a wide variety of habit disorders including thumb sucking, nail biting, sleep walking, tics, fears, enuresis, drooling, and others. Self-regulation of pain can be learned through hypnotherapeutic techniques in conditions such as juvenile migraine, malignancies, juvenile rheumatoid arthritis, hemophilia, and sickle cell disease. In such conditions, while training in self-hypnosis is regarded as adjunctive, it does provide a coping method under control of the child which seems to enhance the sense of mastery in chronically ill children.

Hypnotherapeutic techniques are often taught to children for reduction of performance anxiety. This general area, largely ignored in the United States until recently, has been a well-recognized application of hypnosis in Russia, Eastern European countries, and in Sweden for many years. For example, Olympic contenders are well trained in self-hypnosis techniques to reduce performance anxiety and maximize performance. In the 1984 Winter Olympics, television reports noted that such techniques are very useful to participants in the biathalon. The biathalon athlete needs to slow down rapidly after cross-country skiing in order to be able to aim with steady hands. Through self-hypnosis techniques, the athletes learn to reduce their cardiac rates much more rapidly than would normally occur in the course of the race. Popular books such as *The Inner Game of Tennis* and *The Inner Game of Skiing* describe techniques identical to those used for induction of hypnosis.

The popularization of some of these techniques may be likened to the popularization of books on a variety of regimens for weight reduction. The method recommended may be unsuited to the hopeful learner who has purchased the book. Furthermore, if by chance the method is suitable, the necessity for long-term practice must not be underestimated. The prospective learner who does not find immediate results is likely to become discouraged. The effective and appropriate use of hypnotherapeutic techniques, like other therapies, requires careful analysis of the problem and the patient. In particular, there is a need to focus on the patient's learning abilities and styles and to tailor reinforcement through self-hypnosis in ways which are acceptable and understandable. Techniques for children vary according to their developmental stages. A single technique does not exist. Presently, there is a plethora of hypnosis tapes available which purport to solve all life's problems. They are not individually tailored and hence not recommended.

There is already general agreement that children learn and use hypnotherapeutic techniques more readily than adults. There is evidence that children move in and out of altered states of awareness frequently in the process of playing, drawing, singing, watching movies, and television. A concern about altered states of consciousness induced by television is that the child may accept suggestions made in television ads or programs and may develop undesirable behaviors on the basis of such indirect suggestions. There is also evidence that children are adept at developing voluntary control of some autonomic processes and that such control can be facilitated by self-hypnosis practice. Biofeedback protocols usually include "relaxation exercises" prior to biofeedback; these are often identical to hypnotic inductions. Controlled studies have noted the ability of children to self-regulate peripheral temperature, audioevoked potentials, bronchial dilatation, transcutaneous oxygen flux, cardiac rate, and anorectal sphincter responses. Thus far, clinical applications of such skills have included anorectal biofeedback for control of fecal soiling in children, treatment of asthma, treatment of Raynaud's disease, hyperhidrosis, and migraine. Skills in self-regulation of autonomic processes in children need to be studied intensively, and more understanding of such skills may have important implications for pediatric diagnosis and treatment. For example, if children can increase warmth of their hands and if this change is effected through blood flow changes, is it possible that children can self-regulate blood flow in other body areas? Could they learn to move chemotherapeutic agents into selected areas? Could children with a genetic predisposition to hypertension learn self-regulation of blood pressure at an early age and reduce the likelihood of requiring antihypertensive drugs later in life?

Of particular interest with respect to self-regulation controls in children is documentation of the ability of children to control warts through self-hypnosis exercises. This coincidence, also reported to occur in adults, raises the question concerning possibilities for self regulation of neuroimmunologic processes, particularly in terms of malignant diseases. Early work by Black and Good documented the ability of adults to suppress delayed cutaneous hypersensitivity responses. More recent work by Hall has noted that young adults can effect lymphocyte changes through self-hypnosis. We have done pilot studies in children and found them to produce changes in granulocyte functions in association with brief periods of hypnosis. The significance of this is not yet apparent. Limited existing data does encourage further research in this area of potential self-regulation.

Study of hypnosis leads to a recognition of the extraordinary responsivity of children to suggestions, particularly when they are afraid or stressed as when in the hospital setting. There is evidence that both adults and children move into an altered state of awareness in emergency situations. This may also be true for health care professionals. In such situations "negative hypnotherapy" may occur inadvertently. The apparently oblivious or inattentive child may accept positive or negative suggestions given when he or she is in an emergency situation. The suggestions may be nonverbal as well as verbal. The child may regress to a time when most information was perceived from nonverbal messages. For example, the frightened child with acute asthma will gradually follow the breathing pattern of an alert physician who makes an effort to initially synchronize his or her breathing with the child's pattern, and who makes indirect positive remarks ("I wonder if you will find your breathing easier in one minute or in two minutes?") as breathing is slowed and the child's breathing pattern is entrained to this slower pattern.

The Future

Our recent review of the literature in child psychophysiologic studies confirms that data neither exist to document physiologic responses to stress in children nor to confirm what the more vulnerable developmental stages are in terms of negative physiologic responses to stress. Common sense tells us that well-known adult physiologic responses to stress must develop earlier in life. It is well documented that some of these responses can be extinguished through self-hypnosis training; a reasonable hope is that they could be avoided altogether if recognized at the beginning.

One can conceive of an eight-year-old girl who has been out of school for a few days with gastroenteritis. Although she has some residual nausea she returns to school. Her teacher asks her to do a multiplication problem on the chalkboard. Having been absent, she does not know how to complete the problem and makes a mistake. Her classmates laugh. In her mind, nausea and public appearances have been linked. Twenty years later, when asked to give a speech she refuses because she knows she will be nauseated as soon as she reaches the podium.

In animals the conditioning of immunosuppression is well documented. Is it farfetched to think of such conditioning in humans? One can think of a seven-year-old boy who develops a severe case of chickenpox with unrecognized but nonetheless concomitant immunosuppression. During this period of chickenpox and immunosuppression, his mother tempts his appetite in vain. Finally, the boy takes pistachio ice cream in large quantities and his mother feels more comfortable. Later on, with the chickenpox long gone, will pistachio ice cream trigger immunosuppression in this boy? If so, it may be relatively minor and of no consequence unless a particular infectious agent invaded his system at the same time.

Review of data involving both clinical and research hypnotherapy confirms that hypnosis not only can be used to determine the event that conditioned a repetitive negative physiologic response, but that the undesirable response can be eliminated via suggestion reinforced through self-hypnosis.

As the behavioral pediatric medicine research model seeks to understand disease as behavioral factors that contribute to or cause it, or to relate compliance to treatment, it would seem that hypnotherapeutic techniques provide excellent research tools. They can be used to document and explain what biologic processes can be directly modified, to what degree self-regulation is possible and predictable, what knowledge is state specific and whether certain therapeutic regimens must be state specific, how learning abilities and styles as well as genetics relate to self-regulatory abilities, whether circadian rhythms affect states of consciousness and ability to self-regulate physiologic processes, and whether the state of awareness of the therapist affects patient responses.

The dairy industry uses a number of biochemical measures to help determine which cows should be culled for inefficient use of nutrients and poor productivity. Successful dairy farmers are aware that laboratory studies will be invalid if the cows are anxious during the venipunctures. Therefore, efforts are made to relax the animals prior to testing. With respect to children, we do not know precisely how anxiety may affect laboratory studies, and no one has developed a systematic relaxation system for children prior to venipunctures. This would seem to be a practical area for application of techniques of hypnotherapy.

Hypnotherapy and related therapy modes, with increased understanding of mechanisms, may be used with increased precision in a number of areas:

1. Self-regulation of physiologic responses such as rate and volume of blood flow, blood pressure, absorption of nutrients, intestinal motility, release of neurotransmitters, or peripheral temperature. This may relate to medication requirements, timing of medications, or side effects.
2. Reduction of fear, anxiety, and pain in diagnostic and treatment settings.
3. Precise methods of preventing persistence of harmful repetitive habits in autonomic functions which may develop early in life.
4. Improved, efficient, maximum task performance in areas ranging from figure skating to college entrance exams.
5. Ability to adapt communication methods to learning styles of children.
6. Development of state-specific therapy and teaching for improved therapeutic understanding and efficiency.
7. Stress reduction for health care professionals.

Physicians wishing to pursue this area should take basic workshops in hypnotic techniques provided by the American Society of Clinical Hypnosis and the Society for Clinical and Experimental Hypnosis. These workshops emphasize initial practice in acquiring personal skills in self-hypnosis before applying these techniques to patients. The American Board of Medical Hypnosis, formed in 1958, administers examinations to certify physicians who can demonstrate knowledge and clinical skills in application of hypnotherapy within their own specialty areas.

References

Gardner, G.G.: Hypnosis with children: selected readings. *Int. J. Clin. Exp. Hypn.* 28:289, 1980.

Gardner, G., and Olness, K.: *Hypnosis and Hypnotherapy with Children.* New York, Grune and Stratton, 1981.

Kohen, D., Olness, K., Colwell, S., and Heimel, A.: Self-hypnosis in management of 500 pediatric behavioral problems. *J. Dev. Behav. Ped.* 5:21–25, 1984.

Olness, K.: Hypnosis in pediatric practice. *Curr. Prob. Pediatr.* 12:1–47, 1981.

Olness, K., and Gardner, G.G.: Some guidelines for uses of hypnotherapy in pediatrics. *Pediatrics* 62:228, 1978.

Zeltzer, L., and LeBaron, S.: Hypnosis and non-hypnotic techniques for reduction of pain and anxiety during painful procedures in children and adolescents with cancer. *J. Pediatr.* 101:1032–1035, 1982.

17
Caring for High-Risk Infants and Their Families

Kathryn E. Barnard
Mary Hammond
Sandra K. Mitchell
Cathryn L. Booth
Anita Spietz
Charlene Snyder
Teresa Elsas

T he purpose of this chapter is to discuss caring for high-risk infants and their families. We will draw on our work from the past fifteen years to define the infant and family who are vulnerable, to describe the nursing interventions we are testing with these high-risk infants and their families, and to suggest some conclusions we have come to that guide both our further thinking and practice.

Defining High Risk

Since 1971 we have been involved with studies attempting to identify early risk factors that increase the probability of poor developmental outcomes. The main project was called the Nursing Child Assessment Project (NCAP). In this study a group of approximately 200 families was studied from the mothers' pregnancy to the child's entry into second grade (Barnard and Eyres, 1979; Eyres, Barnard, and Gray, 1979; Hammond, Bee, Barnard, and Eyres, 1983). All families were enrolled in a prepaid health maintenance organization in Seattle, Group Health Cooperative of Puget Sound. The cases were selected specifically to represent a sample stratified on maternal education (high and low) and complications of pregnancy (high and low). This stratification was to allow later analysis of the respective predictive power of maternal education and pregnancy complications which in 1970 were identified as the best predictors of later developmental problems. We wanted to know what else predicted later child outcomes. What about the infant's behavior? What about the infant's environment? What about the parents' perceptions? And what about the parents' life change? Since 1971, we intensively studied the NCAP sample, providing no specific intervention. The period of investigation included pregnancy, the birth period, the first year of life at

Table 17–1

Descriptive Statistics for Measures of Family Status and History, Based on Interviews with the Mothers when the Children Were in Second Grade[a]

Measure	M	SD	N
Number of other children in the home	1.11	.72	151
Number of adults in the child's home	1.87	.50	151
Number of child moves in the past year	.28	.57	151
Years child spent with both natural parents	6.53	2.52	151
Years child spent with only one parent	1.26	2.36	151
Years at least one parent was at home full time	4.76	3.05	151
Child's age in months when mother began work	22.6	23.6	114[b]
Number of different care arrangements made for child since birth (other than parental care)	2.83	2.71	151
Mother's years of education at second-grade interview	14.8	2.4	151
Father's[c] years of education at second-grade interview	15.8	2.9	134
Social Status (Hollingshead Four Factor Index)	48.0	12.3	151
Life Change (Schedule of Recent Events)	162.5	128.5	148
Median income range at second grade (1981–82)	$25,000–29,000 (N = 150)		

[a]Taken from eight-year follow-up report. Hammond, M.A., Bee, H.L., Barnard, K.E., & Eyres, U.J. (1983). Child Health Assessment, Part 4: Follow-Up at Second Grade.
[b]Thirty-seven mothers had not been employed at any time in the child's first eight years.
[c]The "father" is, as required for the Hollingshead Index, the male figure living in the home. In some cases (10) this is a step-father rather than the natural father.

one, four, eight, and 12 months, and at two, four, and eight years. NCAP was a methodological study; the families and children had good preventive obstetric and pediatric care at the Group Health Cooperative of Puget Sound. The total socioeconomic spectrum of Seattle was represented in the sample. There were, in fact, welfare clients in this Health Cooperative, because Medicare coupons were available and accepted. The ethnic distribution was also representative of Seattle: 85 percent of the families were Caucasian.

The results when the children were four years of age have been reported in Bee, Barnard, Eyres, Gray, Hammond, Spietz, Snyder, and Clark (1982). These results indicated the importance of family and parent-child interaction measures in predicting four-year outcomes.

At eight years we assessed 151 out of the 193 original subjects (table 17–1 presents selected demographics). Maternal education averaged 14.8 years, and paternal education 15 years. The child's average age when the mother resumed work was 22.6 months. The average number of years living with only one parent, for our sample, was 1.26 years. The median family income was $25,000–29,000. Data in table 17–2 describes selected child outcomes at age 8. On the

Table 17–2
Descriptive Statistics for Assessments of Child Functioning at Second Grade[a]

Source	Variable	M	SD	N
Peabody Individual Achievement	Mathematics	111.3	10.8	141
Test (PIAT)	Reading recognition	118.8	11.2	141
	Reading comprehension	113.4	8.7	139
	Spelling	111.3	10.0	141
	General information	113.3	9.0	141
	Total test	116.2	9.3	141
Wechsler Intelligence Scale	Verbal IQ	112.9	14.8	150
for Children (WISC-R)	Performance IQ	113.1	13.9	150
	Full scale IQ	114.2	13.6	150
McDaniel-Piers Young Children's	Feeling self	72.7	17.1	142
Self Concept Scale	School self	86.1	15.3	142
(in percent positive responses)	Behaving self	84.6	16.8	142
	Total self concept score	80.1	12.5	142
Myklebust Pupil Rating Scale	Verbal score	31.9	5.5	135
(PRS)	Nonverbal score	53.0	8.6	135
	Total score	85.0	13.0	135
Teacher Questionnaire Ratings	Reading performance	2.82	0.74	136
(in grade equivalents)	Mathematics performance	2.61	0.48	135
	Spelling performance	2.64	0.69	133
	Oral skills	2.82	0.64	132
	Written skills	2.59	0.58	130
	Handwriting skills	2.51	0.48	132
Parent Interview	Child's self help age (in mos.)	101.9	8.6	146
	Medically attended accidents in past year	0.64	0.80	151
	Illnesses, past year	2.76	4.64	151
	Medically attended illnesses	0.85	1.12	151

		N	%	
Examiner assessment	Height/weight ratio			
	0–24th percentile	16	8.8	
	25th–50th percentile	37	27.2	
	51st–75th percentile	43	31.6	
	76th–90th percentile	31	32.8	

Table 17–2 continued

		N	%
	91st–95th percentile	4	2.9
	96th percentile and above	5	3.7
Mother's report	Children with behavior problems	27	17.9
Teacher's report	Children with behavior problems	15	10.9
	Children in remedial classes	10	7.2
	Children in advanced/gifted classes	14	10.2
	Children in learning disability classes	3	2.2
	Mentally retarded/special class	1	0.7

[a]Taken from eight-year follow-up report. Hammond, M.A., Bee, H.L., Barnard, K.E., and Eyres, S.J. (1983). Child Health Assessment, Part 4: Follow-Up at Second Grade.

WISC-R the mean was 114.2, the McDaniel-Piers Self Concept Scale mean was 80 percent, and the Myklebust Pupil-Rating Scale mean was 85.

We also used categorical definitions of child status in relation to school performance. There were 15 children who were judged by their teachers to have behavior problems, representing 11 percent of the sample. The behavior problems were aggression, temper tantrums, stealing—mainly conduct disorder types. Ten (7 percent) of the children were in remedial classes; 14 (10 percent) of the children were in classes for the gifted; three (2 percent) had what the school called learning disability; and one child was mentally retarded.

We wanted to ask predictive questions about the outcomes clinicians deal with in their practice (Mitchell, Bee, Hammond, and Barnard, in press). What discriminated children having a learning problem or a behavior problem from those who did not? The definition of a learning problem was based on both teacher report and the scoring of the Peabody Individual Achievement Test (PIAT) with the child being at least three-quarters of a year behind the expected grade level. The statistical technique we used to determine which predictors maximally differentiated those children with and without learning problems, was discriminant function analysis (table 17–3 presents the analysis). This analysis indicated that the sex of the child discriminated those with and without learning problems. Boys were more often identified as having learning problems than girls. Low birth weight was also a discriminating variable. This was the only perinatal variable in our sample associated with later performance function.

Children with learning problems in second grade also had less optimal scores on a mother-infant interaction measure during feeding at 12 months; at 24 months they had poorer expressive language and higher motor development

Table 17–3
Overall Discriminant Analyses (across Clusters) for Learning Problems versus No Learning Problems

Step/Variables	Standard Discriminant Function Coefficients
1 Sex	.39
Birth weight	−.25
2 IQ (48 mos.)	−.23
Motor development (36 mos.)	.22
Expressive language (24 mos.)	−.23
Medically attended accidents (48 mos.)	.30
3 Years with only one parent	.30
4 Infant feeding (12 mos.)	−.43
HOME Inventory (48 mos.)	−.37
Canonical correlation = .64	

Note: Group controls: learning problems, 1.89; no learning problem, −0.36.

scores; at 48 months they had more medically attended accidents and lower IQ scores. The 48-month Caldwell HOME Inventory scores were also lower in the families of children with learning problems and these children had also spent more years with only one parent. The canonical correlation from this set of variables was .64. Because discriminant function analysis results are highly dependent on the sample used, these results can only provide tentative clues for further testing.

The same analysis was repeated using behavior problem as the outcome variable. This was defined totally by teacher report. There were no perinatal variables that qualified to enter in the discriminant function analysis. The variables that maximally discriminated those children with and without behavior problems were language, IQ, psychomotor development, medically attended accidents, years with only one parent, and the social support the mother reported prenatally. Again the canonical correlation was .70, accounting for almost half of the variance (See table 17–4).

We also performed simple correlational analyses between second-grade outcome variables (such as the WISC-R full scale, the Pupil Rating Scale, and the PIAT) and measures of the family environment and parent perception. Variables such as maternal education, the family's social status, including income and occupation, and the total amount of social support for the mother, were positively related to the child's scores on the WISC-R, PIAT, and Pupil Rating Scale. We found that maternal report of life change measured from the perinatal period was

Table 17–4
Overall Discriminant Analyses (across Clusters) for Behavior Problems versus No Behavior Problems

Step/Variables	Standard Discriminant Function Coefficients
1 (No perinatal status variables entered)	
2 Expressive language (12 mos.)	.47
IQ (48 mos.)	−.26
Receptive language (12 mos.)	.27
Psychomotor development (12 mos.)	−.36
Medically attended accidents (48 mos.)	.29
3 Years with only one parent	.50
Social support (prenatal)	−.33
Life change (24 mos.)	−.20
4 Mother feeding (12 mos.)	−.52
Infant feeding (4 mo.)	.35
Canonical correlation = .70	

Note: Group controls: behavior problems, 2.79; no behavior problems, −0.34.

negatively correlated with these outcomes. In fact, we found that the information collected around the birth period seemed to be particularly potent predictors in terms of identifying children at risk. In other words, for the variable of life change, measures taken at birth but relating to the two years prior to pregnancy were better predictors of later childhood outcomes than were measures of life change that the family experienced during the child's early years.

We feel these studies offer information relative to the screening process. The perinatal period is important for data collection: identification of the child at high risk can come from information about the child's birth status, that is, birth weight, the amount of support available to the family, and the amount of life change. Low birth weight, low social status, and/or high life change are all factors that warrant further monitoring in health-care systems. We should make every effort to both monitor these factors and provide a supportive environment for the child and the family.

Early Intervention

In the remainder of the chapter we will discuss experiences our research and clinical team have had over the past five years studying intervention with children identified before or at birth as being vulnerable for greater developmental problems. The first project was called the Models of Newborn Nursing Intervention (Barnard, Booth, Mitchell, and Telzrow, 1983). This project was based on our thinking in the late 1970s that the most vulnerable infants were those whose mothers had complications of pregnancy and whose families showed evidence of vulnerability, in terms of a lack of education or money, or numerous family problems. In the Models of Newborn Nursing Intervention we worked with the Seattle–King County Public Health Department in identifying those families who were in a special departmental maternal and child health program, in which prenatal care was provided by the health department and all infants were delivered at the University of Hospital in Seattle.

In the Models of Newborn Nursing Intervention project we compared several types of nursing care. There were three models. Nursing, Parent and Child and Environments (NPACE) was the model in which the nurses assessed the environment and the needs of the child and the family and then, based on these assessments, designed an individual intervention program for each family. The care involved providing support to the family, information, referrals, guidance, and counseling—whatever the family needed. There was no restriction on the number of visits. The second model, NSIBB (Nursing Support, Infant Bio-Behavioral) was based on the assumption that despite the differing needs of each family, an important need that they all shared was to relate to and care for a newly born infant. To be a successful parent of a newborn, it is helpful to understand certain behavioral changes in early infancy. These include sleeping patterns, crying patterns, nonverbal behavior cues, and judging the infant's need for stimulation. We designed a curriculum in which the nurse visited the family at one week, three weeks, five weeks, eight weeks, and 12 weeks postpartum. During these visits the nurse taught the mother to observe and assess her baby, to know her baby, to help her adapt, and to support the mother-infant interaction. In addition, standard physical assessment of the mother and newborn was provided. The third model, NSTAC (Nursing Standard Approach to Care), was the traditional public health model with an emphasis on physical health and well-being and centering on the client's stated problem. (Appendix 17A gives details of each model.)

The intervention occurred the first three months postpartum. We had hypothesized that providing intervention while the families were organizing and adapting to the new infant would be the most effective. We evaluated mother and infant outcomes at three, 10, and 24 months. There were 169 cases at the newborn period, 153 at three months, 118 at 10 months, and 58 at 24 months. The 24-month follow-up yielded lower rates because (due to funding problems) we started the follow-up after a number of subjects had already passed their second birthday.

We found no differences in either mother or infant outcomes at any time point as a function of the type of nursing intervention. In other words, all intervention approaches worked equally well. We continued to analyze child out-

Table 17–5
Comparison of NCAP Low-Education and Models Samples on Lester Clusters

Variable	Sample	n	Mean (sd)	t
Habituation	NCAP	73	5.90 (1.40)	2.64[a]
	Models	110	6.45 (1.33)	
Orientation	NCAP	81	6.00 (1.50)	−2.60[a]
	Models	156	5.45 (1.60)	
Motor	NCAP	84	4.80 (0.90)	3.29[b]
	Models	161	5.18 (0.76)	
Range of State	NCAP	84	3.90 (0.90)	−1.04
	Models	158	3.77 (0.95)	
Regulation of State	NCAP	84	6.20 (1.40)	−4.23[b]
	Models	148	5.41 (1.29)	
Autonomic Stability	NCAP	84	4.80 (1.20)	9.89[b]
	Models	160	6.32 (1.00)	
Reflexes	NCAP	84	2.40 (2.30)	−1.43
	Models	157	1.97 (2.04)	

Note: Low education = 12 years or less.
[a]$p \le .01$
[b]$p \le .001$

comes to determine how mother, infant, or family characteristics influenced the development course. The variables demonstrating important relationships were newborn behavior and type of family problem.

From the newborn period we found on that the models sample was different from the previously described low-risk NCAP sample on the Brazelton Neonatal Behavioral Assessment Scale (See table 17–5 for the assessment exam scores for two samples at 2 days of age). In this comparison with the infants of low education mothers we found that the models babies habituated a little better, oriented less well, had slightly higher scores on the motor cluster, lower scores for regulation of state, and more autonomic stability. There were no differences in reflexive behavior. Therefore, these high-risk infants whose families we had selected because of pregnancy complications and social vulnerability were less capable of regulating their state and less responsive to the caregiver. Yet they came with better habituation skills and slightly superior motor performance. We speculate that the better habituation of these infants had related to their need, even prenatally, to adapt to a noisier, more chaotic environment. Already in infancy they learned to cut out environmental overload by state lowering. They were less interactive with the environment, which may be critical to the establishment of optimal parenting.

After the three months of intervention, the nurses who were carrying the cases said that these families, although they were high-risk and met the selection

Table 17–6
Incidence of Family Problems in Newborn Models Subjects
(N = 183)

	Percent
Lacks information	44
Financial	42
Baby's health	41
No supportive partner	32
Mother's health	29
No problems	28
Inadequate support	25
Mother lacks skills	24
Depressed or emotionally upset	21
Multiproblems	20
Childrearing (abuse/neglect)	20
Cesarean birth	19
Mother-infant interaction	18
High mobility	11
Adolescent	10
Cultural differences	10
Alcohol or drug abuse	10
Mother without transportation	10
Abused mother	7
Premature infant	7
Death or grief	6
Intellectually slow mother	4

criteria, were quite varied. To capture these differences we developed a problem checklist that the nurses, using their clinical judgment, filled out at the end of the intervention program (see table 17–6 for a list and frequency of problems). There were 23 designated problem areas, ranging from lacking general information (44 percent), no-other-problem (28 percent), to heavy use of drugs or alcohol (10 percent).

This family problem list has prompted us to focus on the balance of vulnerabilities in terms of the infant's vulnerability and the family's vulnerability and how the two risks interact with our attempts for intervention. The remainder of the outcome data we are reporting considers how the intervention interacted with family problems. For this analysis we used all the families judged by the nurses as having multiple problems compared with the families where the nurse identified no family problems. Our definition of multiproblem families was the family who lived in a disorganized environment, was in constant crisis, and/or experiencing high life change.

To examine how the intervention was influenced by characteristics of the families, we analyzed the cases identified by the nurses as multiproblem and compared them with families with none of the problems listed in table 17–6 from the newborn nursing sample.

Table 17–7 lists the characteristics of these cases. The no-other-problem families had a significantly higher social status. The Bayley Mental Development Index (MDI) was consistently above average for the no-problem group and at two years was higher than the MDI for the multiproblem group. In examining the parent-child interaction scores during the first two years the mothers' scores for the multiproblem families were lower for both the Feeding and Teaching scale both at three months and at the end of the intervention. By 10 months the feeding interaction still showed a group difference, but the teaching interaction scores did not. Both no-problem and multiple-problem dyads had lower mean scores on the feeding and teaching interaction scales during the first year when compared to a middle-class sample (Barnard et al., 1983). For the HOME Inventory, again the multiproblem family scores were lower than those of the nonproblem families at three, but not at 10, or 24 months. We hypothesize that this lower competency on the part of the mothers had a long-term influence on the child's mental performance for the multiproblem families.

We know that the multiproblem families were all faced with difficult life circumstances. It may have been asking too much to expect that the mother improve her mothering while facing many problems. How to manage these demanding situations is a challenge in early intervention. From our experience we speculate that with the multiple problem family the nurse needs to be quite directive regarding the improvement of parent-child relationships and caregiving. This means giving actual prescriptions "to smile at the baby when he smiles," "to respond to his verbalizations or sounds," or giving a series of games and exercises to do with the baby on a daily basis. Another strategy may be to engage other members of the family in interaction, that is, involve siblings in play and stimulation with the baby. In some situations the best alternative may be therapeutic daycare. Our evidence suggests that the parents from multiple problem families did not improve in parenting enough during the first year even though they did improve by two years. At two years we saw a decline in mental development in the children of multiproblem families, typical of that demonstrated in disadvantaged populations. This suggests a challenge to meet the problems of the parents in the multiproblem family and at the same time provide the ideal environment for the child.

Intervention—Phase II

A second project currently underway, Clinical Nursing Models (Grant No. MH 36894-03), is based on the results of the preceding project. This work has been funded by the National Institute of Mental Health, Prevention Branch. This project uses a nursing framework to look comparatively at the use of a mental health model and an information resource model in a sample of mothers who have low social competency as identified by low social support. Again, collaborating with the Seattle–King County Public Health Department, we have identified the women as early as possible during pregnancy. We hypothesized that it would be important to start the intervention before the baby's arrival, since we have learned that change is a long-time proposition. From our Models of Newborn Nursing Project we learned that the newborn period was a difficult time in which to establish a relationship with the mother and therefore a poor choice of time to begin intervention with a socially at-risk parent. The pregnant women showed evidence by history or current situation of poor support systems. Typically they did not have friends, or had problematic relationships. We are testing the value of the two intervention strategies. The mental health model focuses on developing social competencies and relationship building. The nurse uses herself in a therapeutic relationship with the mother to help her eventually establish a relationship with others, and to build her support network. We hypothesize that relationship building and the establishment of social competencies in the mother will put the new mother in a better position for parenting and mother-infant interaction and stimulation.

The second model is called the information/resource intervention. This is a typical public health model in which we are trying to advocate for the health of the individual. The specific goals of this model relate to providing the women with access to information about pregnancy and childrearing, such as appropriate nutrition, importance of prenatal care, and care of the infant.

In working with high-risk families we have found that a paradigm developed by Dr. Larry Brammer in his book, *The Helping Process,* is very useful. Brammer lists the several stages in the helping process—entry, clarification of why you are there, setting up a structure for what is going to happen, dealing with give-and-take in the relationship, getting to exploration and mutual problem solving, consolidating the plan, planning how to proceed, and then terminating. We have found, doing early intervention with mothers who have little support from others, that the first four steps in the helping process can be very time-consuming. It may take many contacts with the parent before she is ready to work with the nurse. At that time we find it important to deal with both the resistance and acceptance. It is tempting to move on to the task of attempting to improve the parenting. Learning how to both accept where the parent is and also promote a better environment for the infant is the dilemma the professional dealing with

Table 17–7
Comparison of Medical/Social Risk Families with and without Multiple Problems

Background Factors	High Risk/No Problems (N = 35)		High Risk/Multiple Problems (N = 35)		
	$\overline{X}$	S.D.	$\overline{X}$	S.D.	P
Mother's age	23.6	4.8	22.4	5.0	N.S.
Father's age	28.3	6.4	24.7	4.8	.03
Mother's years schooling	12.1	2.5	11.4	1.6	N.S.
Social status (Hollingshead)	32.0	12.2	23.4	7.8	.001
Medical risk (1–10)	1.9	1.2	2.3	1.8	N.S.
Social risk (1–10)	1.6	1.4	2.4	1.7	.01
Bayley Infant Development Score					
MDI 3 months	109.7	12.3	107.5	14.3	N.S.
10 months	109.9	12.0	106.9	13.0	N.S.
24 months	109.4	9.5	91.2	9.9	.001
NCAFS					
Mother score 3 months	39.5	6.4	33.3	8.6	.02
10 months	36.4	8.1	31.1	6.8	.06
Infant score 3 months	18.2	5.4	16.2	4.6	N.S.
10 months	19.3	4.4	17.3	4.5	N.S.

NCATS

Mother score	3 months	35.6	8.0	31.0	6.6	.03
	10 months	31.8	8.7	30.4	8.0	N.S.
	24 months	39.1	7.9	37.9	8.0	N.S.
Infant Score	3 months	12.0	4.0	11.1	4.4	N.S.
	10 months	13.7	4.2	13.0	5.1	N.S.
	24 months	16.5	3.9	16.4	3.0	N.S.

HOME

3 months	29.0	5.5	25.2	6.2	.004
10 months	33.9	7.0	30.7	6.4	N.S.
24 months	35.9	6.2	32.7	5.6	N.S.

Notes: 1. *Italics* indicate that differences remain with social status controlaled for in analysis of covariance.
2. Numbers at various time points:
   3 months: High risk/No problems = 31; High risk/Multiproblem = 27
   10 months: High risk/No problems = 17; High risk/Multiproblem = 18
   24 months: High risk/No problems = 11; High risk/Multiproblem = 13

early intervention faces. We have concluded that the work proceeds best when there is an intervention plan. The plan can be modified, but the problems of the family are likely to overwhelm intervention based entirely on the family's needs.

On the other hand we have recognized that the problems in relationships have been developing for 10, 15, 20, or 25 years. These problems will not disappear immediately, but we are convinced that improving the social skills of the mother and helping her to build a supportive relationship with the nurse are the first steps in the right direction. This is an important process and one which we have found to be psychologically complex for the intervenor. We have found that it is exceedingly important for our nurses to have access to a clinical psychologist while relationship building with these clients. This clinical guidance to the nurses encourages a constructive therapeutic relationship with the parent without forcing unfunctional dependency.

The finding that infants in the Newborn Models Project were less responsive and more likely to have health problems, has caused us to consider the infant's contribution to the early parenting deficit. We need to access the health needs and seek whatever remedy possible. Special emphasis needs to be placed on teaching the parent how to assist the baby in getting in the right state for being responsive. This involves teaching the parents appropriate modes of stimulating the baby, such as talking to the baby, changing the baby's position, dressing or undressing the baby, providing an object that makes noise or that can be visually followed.

Any time a parent is dealing with other problems, such as an unsupportive or absent partner, a lack of intimate relationships, a lot of financial problems, and drug or alcohol abuse, the intervention must involve not only helping that parent grow but fostering the best parenting possible for the infant who is growing so rapidly. When parents are psychologically unavailable to the child, alternative caregivers need to provide support for the infant, who may need especially sensitive and responsive care. This fits into our model for child health assessment and intervention, in which the child, the parent, and the environment are all crucial elements. We view the dyadic relationship as a window where the work of both assessment and intervention center. We aim to help the parent be sensitive to the cues and the developmental issues of the child, to increase their ability to alleviate the distress of the child, to promote growth, and to help them when the child's cues are either unclear or the child is not responsive.

References

Barnard, K.E., and Eyres, S.J. (eds.): *Child Health Assessment, Part 2: The First Year of Life.* DHEW Pub. No. (HRA) 79-25, Stock No. 017-041-00131-9. Washington, D.C., U.S. Government Printing Office, 1979.

Barnard, K.C., Booth, C.L., Mitchell, S.K., and Telzrow, R.W.: *Newborn Nursing Models Project Final Report*, Grant No. R01-NU-00719. Washington, D.C., prepared for the Division of Nursing, Bureau of Health Manpower, Health Resources Administration, Department of Health and Human Services, 1983.

Bee, H.L., Barnard, K.E., Eyres, S.J., Gray, C.A., Hammond, M.A., Spietz, A.L., Snyder, C., and Clark, B.: Prediction of IQ and language skill from perinatal status, child performance, family characteristics, and mother-infant interaction. *Child Development 53*:1134–1156, 1982.

Clinical Nursing Models Project, Grant No. MH 36894-03, National Institute of Mental Health.

Brammer, L.M.: *The Helping Relationship Process and Skills.* Englewood Cliffs, N.J., Prentice-Hall, 1973.

Eyres, S.J., Barnard, K.E., and Gray, C.A.: *Child Health Assessment, Part 3: 2–4 years.*Final report of project supported by Grant No. R02-NU-00559, Division of Nursing Bureau of Health Manpower, Health Resources Administration, Department of Health & Human Services, 1979.

Hammond, M.A., Bee, H.L., Barnard, K.E., and Eyres, S.J.: *Child Health Assessment, Part 4: Follow-Up at Second Grade.* Final report of project supported by Grant No. R01-NU-00816, Division of Nursing, Bureau of Health Professions, Health Resources and Services Administration, U.S. Public Health Service, 1983.

Mitchell, S.K., Bee, H.L., Hammond, M.A., and Barnard, K.E. (in press). Prediction of school and behavior problems in children followed from birth to age eight. In W.K. Frankenburg, R.N. Emde, and J. Sullivan (Eds.), *Early identification of children at risk: An international perspective.* New York: Plenum.

Appendix 17A
Details of Nursing, Parent, Child, and Environment Models

NPACE Program Goals

Although the goals were the same for both the NSIBB and NPACE programs, the basic difference was in how the goals were achieved. The goals were divided into one broad goal of the program, and several specific goals which assisted in attaining the broad goal. The specific goals included infant, parent, and parent-infant goals. There were three infant goals, three parent goals, and two parent-infant goals. The following examples illustrate the ways in which the NPACE nurses attempted to meet each goal.

Broad Goal: To increase the levels of adaptive behaviors shown by the child and the parents.

Specific Goals: Child

1. *To increase the rhythmicity and predictability of the infant's daily sleep/wakefulness cycle.* This goal was best accomplished by having the mother keep a record of her infant's sleep/wake cycle (NCASA). The record increased the mother's awareness of the frequency of feedings, length of alert periods, and fussy times, as well as duration of day and night sleep. As a result of this increased awareness the mothers tuned into their infant's "schedule" and were able to provide more consistency or regularity to the day's events. This record was also a springboard for discussion about changes in sleep/wake activity that could be expected during the three month period.

2. *To improve the mental and motor development of the infant.* The assessments that best helped the nurses attain this goal were those that assessed the mother's developmental expectations of her infant and the father's level of involvement (Barnard and Eyres, 1977). From these assessments the nurses could identify areas that would help the mother to tune into the overall development of her child. Interventions included providing the mother with developmental

guidelines that gave her specific ways of interacting with her infant in regard to gross and fine motor development, and social and language development.

3. *To increase the infant's clarity of behavioral cues and responsiveness to parent.* Often this goal was attained through observation of a feeding or a teaching interaction or through the interpretation of a sleep/wake record. Once the infant's positive areas were identified and communicated to the mother, ways in which the mothers could elicit or read behavioral cues were discussed. Clarifying hunger and satiation cues or teaching the mothers how to elicit behaviors such as smiling, or clarifying misconceptions about her child's behavior often helped increase the infant's adaptive behavior.

Specific Goals: Parent

1. *To increase the level of stimulation found in the home environment.* This goal was most often met through discussion of age-appropriate play materials, encouraging parents to talk to their infants, engaging them in play activities with their infant as well as demonstrating ways to make the most of caregiving times.

2. *To make the parent's perceptions about her infant more positive.* This goal was often accomplished by listening to a parent's concerns and validating her perceptions about her infant, but most often this goal was achieved by demonstrating the infant's unique abilities and behaviors, such as seeing, hearing, and self-consoling capabilities.

3. *To increase the parent's adaptive behaviors as shown by her response to distress, and cognitive, and social-emotional growth fostering activities.* Assessment of the parent's behavior during feeding, teaching, and general caregiving activities gave the nurses insight into strengths and weaknesses that could be included in short-term goals for improvement in these areas. By providing the parents with information regarding life change and coping and its influence on one's ability to adapt helped achieve this goal.

Specific Goals: Parent-Child

1. *To increase the amount of time the parent and infant spend together.* One way this was carried out in the NPACE program was to assign specific activities for the parents to engage in with their infants on a weekly basis. For example, a mother of a one-month-old might be asked to try to elicit a smile from her infant or to get her infant to reach for a rattle over the course of the week.

2. *To increase the synchrony and improve the quality of parent-infant interaction.* Using the observational tools, such as the feeding and teaching scales and providing feedback to the parents regarding specifics of their own and their infant's behavior, was directly helpful in improving the quality and the synchrony of the interaction.

NSIBB Program Goals

The NSIBB program (Nursing *Support* for *Infant Bio-Behavior*) was a structured educational curriculum designed to facilitate the mutual adaptation process between the caregiver and the infant. The program was developed with an agenda so that the content presentation during the program would follow a specific protocol. Although the content and the goals remain the same for each client, the specific details were individualized to the personality and style of each mother and infant. The NISBB program was developed from the knowledge of common concerns and problems of parents during their child's first three months of life. The NSIBB program's content and activities were developed or selected from the known bio-behavioral changes that occur in all infants during their first three months of life. These bio-behavioral changes are listed below.

Week 1: The primary task of the parents during this period is to acquaint themselves with their baby and to understand their baby's unique characteristics. They begin to identify who their baby is and develop ways of meeting the baby's needs. At this time the parents may express frustration about their infant's sleep-wake schedule, which will gradually increase in predictability.

Week 3: During this period babies may be quite fussy, since the infant's peak amount of crying begins at approximately two weeks. These crying periods are extremely frustrating and overwhelming for parents. Crying may interfere with pleasurable periods between parent and infant and may hinder any kind of positive communication they may have established.

Week 5: This is a transitional time for parents and infants. Parents are often more at ease with their role and feel more confident in caring for the baby. The infant's feeding and sleeping patterns may be more predictable. The parents begin to observe the infant smiling and establishing eye contact. On the other hand, the infant may still be fussy and his or her parents may be losing their patience with the baby.

Week 8: During this period infants consolidate their behaviors and give clearer cues. Parents observe sociable behaviors in their babies such as smiling, visual tracking, ceasing to cry when they have been picked up, and differentiating the parents from other people. These behaviors make the parents feel that the infant recognizes them as specific individuals.

Week 12: At this time many parents have established routines in caring for their baby. The parent and infant usually have learned to read each other's cues and to respond appropriately. When the parent and infant are together they exhibit a "give and take" rhythm. This rhythm is usually evident in most interaction periods.

The NSIBB visits were focused on the facilitation of the mother-infant adaptation and attachment processes. Each visit's precise goals were clear to the mothers and determined the visit's content. New information was presented in a clear and systematic way in order to reach the program goals. Each visit was structured and goal-directed.

The structure of the home visits was consistent from visit to visit. The visits began with a brief *introduction,* or a setting of the stage for new learning and sharing. During this time the mothers often mentioned new abilities demonstrated by their infants, concerns they had about the infant or themselves, or some information such as the infant's latest weight from their most recent well-baby checkup. After the mother's immediate concerns or questions were answered, the content from the previous home visit was reviewed. The mother's observation records and sleep-wake records (NCASA record) were discussed and interpreted in light of previous visit content. Mothers often noted how the infants had changed since the time they had completed the records. Their growing awareness of their infant's development was encouraged and validated during these discussions with the nurse.

During this period of *content review,* the mothers would do their return demonstration of the infant activity they had learned during the previous visit. Following the content review, the visit would move to the *new content* to be covered. Various teaching methods were utilized to convey new content and to make it easily understandable. As the NSIBB program is an educational, information-based intervention program, there were many teaching methods used during the home visits. Following the content presentation, the new information was summarized. This summary further clarified the information for the mother and provided her a chance to ask questions. Before ending the visit, *anticipatory guidance* was given as to what she might expect to occur with her infant in the weeks before the next visit. For example, during the second visit, when the infant was three weeks old, the mother was prepared for the possibility of her infant's increased fussiness and was given suggestions on how to cope with it. The visits were ended with an *assignment* to the mother. For example, she might be asked to complete an NCASA record or an observation record before the nurse's next visit. The visit was *terminated* with the scheduling of the next visit and the nurse preparing the mother as to its content.

This format provided structure for the NSIBB families during a period of family disorganization and disequilibrium. In addition, the nurses' and the mothers' roles were well defined, thus decreasing possible ambiguity. Clearly defined role expectations helped to lessen possible ambiguity. Clearly defined role expectations helped to lessen the mothers' need to mobilize additional energy for the nurses' visits.

NSTAC Program Goals

The Nursing Standard Approach to Care (NSTAC) program was a nonstructured general support program for mothers and new infants. The NSTAC program was part of the overall Seattle Public Health Nursing Department and was an informal assessment-planning format designed to "start where the mother is, meeting her needs and offering reassurance and advice." Specifically, the mother is assisted with problem-solving to set both short- and long-term goals for herself and her infant. Attention was given to the mother's health and recovery from pregnancy. In addition, the mother was taught aspects of infant behavior, stimulation, physical care, immunization, nutrition, and growth and development.

A large part of the NSTAC program involved informal, flexible assessment and monitoring of the mother-infant system as it involved the mother, the infant, other family members, and any social or emotional needs and problems that might arise. To meet these needs, referrals to other helping agencies or persons who could give support and keep in contact with the families were made. Referrals might involve follow-up in the various health clinics (family planning, OB/GYN, child health, etc.), WIC support for those in financial need, or mother-infant group involvement as a means to help these families cope with the task of parenting.

Program

Normally families seen by the nurses in the public health department may be the result of: (1) previous or current contact with the public health department, that is, prenatal care in the clinics or birth of previous child; (2) family request; or (3) from referrals for a high-risk situation, for example, premature infant, mother's health, social or educational factors such as an adolescent or a single mother. Only those families identified as high-risk (high-risk involving physical, social, and emotional criteria, defined by referring agency or public health department) or those currently being seen in the clinics are visited at home. Those families who seem most in need (financial, physical, or social) receive a home visit. Only those families screened by the models program were assigned to and participated in the NSTAC program.

The following framework submitted by the NSTAC Models nurses summarized the procedures used by them in planning and providing care for families with new babies:

I. Phone contact: To assess the need for a home visit
    A. Family request
    B. High risk situation: premature infant, or social, or educational factors
    C. Systematic interviewing, history taking, and anticipatory guidance

    D. Assignment to mother: 24-hour record of infant's sleep, waking, wetting, and bm; write down questions for nurse.

II. Home contact

    A. Mother assessment
1. Establish rapport with flexibility to meet family needs first
2. Physical exam: examine breasts, nipples, palpate fundus, examine perineal area, and check for signs of problems of circulation in legs

    B. Newborn assessment
1. Physical exam of unclothed baby, to help establish the normalcy of this particular newborn
2. Detect possible anomalies

    C. Assessment of physical and emotional needs
1. Building on inner strengths of all persons involved in postpartum and newborn care
   a. bonding
   b. sharing responsibilities with significant other
   c. nurse interprets findings and helps families to recognize newborn's needs and to respond appropriately
2. Long-term planning
   a. medical supervision—OB/gynecology, pediatric
   b. birth control and family planning
   c. immunizations
   d. activity levels (postpartum exercise and activity)
   e. establish need for WIC program if appropriate
   f. mother-infant-toddler group involvement
   g. care plan with family, telephone call or home visit.

Performance anxiety, 240
Perinatal period, 15, 113, 250
Phenylketonuria, 120
Physical asymmetry of brain, 116–17
PL 94-142, 109, 129–30, 133
Placement, school, 132–33
Plasticity, 7
Play, roles of mother and father in, 227–28
Polyhalogenated biphenyls, 119
Polyhalogenated hydrocarbons, 119
POSSLQ, 79
Postencephalitic syndrome, 98
Predictors of high-risk, 248–50
Pregnancy, ambivalence in, 54–56
Premature birth, 229
Prenatal/Early Infancy Project, 38, 39–40
Prenatal maternal substance abuse, 2
Prenatal variables, 15
Prenatal visit, 54–58, 71–72, 73
Preoperational stage, 66
Preschool experiences, 110
Pressures, cultural, 53
Prevalence of psychosocial problems, 70–71; eating disorders, 158–59; school-age development dysfunction, 104–7
Prevention, primary, defining, 84–85
Preventive intervention, 30–48; biopsychosocial model to, 145, 147, 148; CIDP model program, 40–47; comprehensive clinical approach to, 14–16; efficacy studies of, 32–39; for high-risk youth, 197; multiple lines of development and, 13–14; programs, 30–40; promotion in pediatrics of, 8–9; psychosomatic medicine and, 148
Primal scene, 187
Problem schools, 109–10
Psychobiology: developmental model in, 196; disorders of, 2; of health and disease, 4–8; implications for pediatrics, 8–10
Psychogenic symptoms, 150–55
Psychoimmunology, 5
Psychoneuropharmacology, 8
Psychopathology: common childhood, 67–68; developmental basis for, 18–23
"Psychosocial biopsy," 197, 199, 202–3
Psychosocial problems, prevalence of, 70–71
Psychosocial sequelae, 2
Psychosomatic medicine, 146–49
Puberty: eating disorders and, 160–61; onset of, biologic basis of, 173–74; preparation for, 178; secondary sex characteristics of, 189; society's response to, 177–78
Public policy for children, 270–72
"Pure" hyperactivity, 99
Purging behaviors, 159. *See also* Eating disorders
Pyloric stenosis, malnutrition from, 113

Rapid retrieval difficulties, 122, 125
Reading/learning problems, 106
Receptive language disorders, 122, 124
Recovery, capacity for, 59
Recurrent abdominal pain, 151
Referrals, 76
Regularity dimension in therapeutic relationship, 42–43
Rehabilitation from ESRD, 209–11
Relationships: capacities for, 16; with clients, building, 258; parent-child, 56–57, 59–60, 262; therapeutic, 40–44, 46
Representational capacity, 21, 22–23, 26–27
Research, opportunities for collaboration, 8–10
Reserve, 7. *See also* Mastery
Resiliency, 7, 109
Retardation. *See* Mental retardation
Reye syndrome, 115
Right from the Start (film), 81
Right-left disorientation, 115
Risk factors: in adolescence, 195–203; in infancy and early childhood, 24–30; multiplicity of, 112; in rehabilitation from ESRD, 211
Risk profile, 197–203
Risk-taking behaviors, 216–18
Risk variables, 28
Role differentiation in infancy, 226–27

Salicilates, 120
School-age child, developmental dysfunction in, 103–43; associations with, 108–12; clinical phenomenology of, 121–28; community response to, 106, 128–33; etiology of, 112–20; prevalence of, 104–7
Schools: adolescence, preparation for, 182; as agents of change, 129–30; placement, 132; problem, 109–10
Screening process for high-risk infants, 250
Seattle Public Health Nursing Department, 251, 265
Secondary gains, 151, 152, 154–55
Self-hypnosis, 237, 240–41
Self-image in adolescence, 175, 176, 189–90. *See also* Identity
Self-sufficiency, defining, 81
Sensorimotor stage, 66
Serotonin metabolism, 119
Services. *See* Support services
Sex roles, adopting adult, 180
Sex symbol, 158
Sexual activity, dares concerning, 218–20
Sexual information, processing of, 187–88
Sexual intercourse, children witnessing parent's, 187
Sexuality: adolescent, 185–93; discussion of, 178; eating disorders and, 161; mid-

Contributors

Kathryn E. Barnard, R.N., Ph.D. Professor of Nursing, Department of Parent and Child Nursing, University of Washington. Affiliate, Child Development and Mental Retardation Center.

Cathryn L. Booth, Ph.D. Research Associate Professor in Nursing, Department of Parent and Child Nursing, University of Washington. Affiliate, Child Development and Mental Retardation Center.

T. Berry Brazelton, M.D. Associate Professor of Pediatrics; Chief, Child Development Unit, Harvard Medical School

George D. Comerci, M.D. Professor of Pediatrics and Family and Community Medicine; Head, Adolescent and Young Adult Medicine Section, University of Arizona, Department of Pediatrics, Tucson

Teresa Elsas, R.N., M.N. Staff R.N., Overlake Hospital, Bellevue, Washington. Childbirth educator for Childbirth Education Association, Seattle.

Stanford B. Friedman, M.D. Professor of Psychiatry and Human Development and Professor of Pediatrics; Director, Division of Child and Adolescent Psychiatry, University of Maryland School of Medicine, Baltimore

Richard H. Granger, M.D. Professor of Pediatrics, Child Study Center, Yale University

Stanley I. Greenspan, M.D. Chief, Clinical Infant Research Unit, Intramural Research Program, NIMH, Mental Health Study Center, Adelphi, Maryland

Mary Hammond, Ph.D. Research Associate Professor in Nursing, Department of Parent and Child Nursing, University of Washington. Affiliate, Child Development and Mental Retardation Center.

Barbara M. Korsch, M.D. Professor of Pediatrics; USC School of Medicine, Division of General Pediatrics, Children's Hospital of Los Angeles

Charles E. Lewis, M.D. Professor of Medicine; Chief, Division of General Internal Medicine and Health Services Research, UCLA Department of Medicine, UCLA Medical Center

Iris F. Litt, M.D. Associate Professor of Pediatrics; Director of Adolescent Medicine, Stanford University Medical Center

Richard G. MacKenzie, M.D. Assistant Professor of Pediatrics and Medicine, USC School of Medicine; Children's Hospital of Los Angeles

Sandra K. Mitchell, Ph.D. Associate Professor in Nursing, Department of Parent and Child Nursing; Adjunct Associate Professor in Psychology, Department of Psychology; and Affiliate, Child Development and Mental Retardation Center, University of Washington.

Robert A. Nover, M.D.   Research Psychiatrist, Clinical Infant–Child Development Research Center, Division of Maternal and Child Health—HRSA and NIMH, and Clinical Associate Professor of Psychiatry and Behavioral Sciences and of Child Health and Human Development, George Washington University School of Medicine

Karen N. Olness, M.D.   Director of Research and Behavioral Pediatrics, Minneapolis Children's Health Center, University of Minnesota Medical School, Minneapolis

Donald P. Orr, M.D.   Associate Professor of Pediatrics; Director, Section of Adolescent Medicine, Indiana University School of Medicine, Indianapolis

Judith S. Palfrey, M.D.   Associate Director, Community Services Program, The Children's Hospital Medical Center, Boston

Ross D. Parke, Ph.D.   Professor of Psychology. Department of Psychology, University of Illnois at Urbana-Champaign

Julius B. Richmond, M.D.   Professor of Health Policy, Harvard University Medical School, Boston

Charlene Snyder, R.N., M.N.   Research Assistant Professor in Nursing, Department of Parent and Child Nursing, University of Washington.

Anita Spietz, R.N., M.N.   Research Assistant Professor in Nursing, Department of Parent and Child Nursing, University of Washington.

Esther H. Wender, M.D.   Associate Professor of Pediatrics; Director, Division of Behavioral Pediatrics, Montefiore Hospital and Medical Center, Bronx

Bernice Weissbourd   President, Family Focus, Inc., Evanston, Illinois

Serena Wieder, Ph.D.   Co-Director, Regional Center for Infants and Young Children, Silver Spring, Maryland

Barry G. Zallen, M.D.   Fellow in Development Pediatrics, Director Young Adult Team, The Children's Hospital, Boston

About the Editor

Morris Green, M.D., is the Perry W. Lesh Professor and Chairman, Department of Pediatrics, Indiana University School of Medicine and Physician-in-Chief of the James Whitcomb Riley Hospital for Children in Indianapolis. Dr. Green is a 1944 graduate of the Indiana University School of Medicine. Before his return to Indiana University in 1957, he was on the faculty at the Yale University School of Medicine. Dr. Green has made major contributions in the delivery of health services to children, for example, the advancement of ambulatory care and general pediatrics; the introduction of the concept of a parent care pavilion in a children's hospital; the implementation of a PEP (parent education and participation) unit for the early involvement of parents of infants with long-term handicaps; and planning of an Infant Nurture Intensive Care Center. In recognition of these achievements, Dr. Green was awarded the George Armstrong Award of the Ambulatory Pediatric Society and the C. Anderson Aldrich Award of the American Academy of Pediatrics. Dr. Green is coeditor with Dr. Robert J. Haggerty of *Ambulatory Pediatrics,* now in its third edition, and the author of *Pediatric Diagnosis,* published in its third edition. Dr. Green is a frequent contributor to the pediatric literature and is a member of several editorial boards. He was chairman of the Health Forums for the 1970 White House Conference on Children. Dr. Green is chairman of the Study Group on Pediatric Education, a member of the Residency Review Committee for Pediatrics, past chairman of the Section on Child Development, chairman of the Committee on the Psychosocial Aspects of Child and Family Health of the American Academy of Pediatrics, and a member of the Institute of Medicine, the National Academy of Sciences.